The Middle Passage

Herbert S. Klein

THE MIDDLE PASSAGE

Comparative Studies in the Atlantic Slave Trade

PRINCETON UNIVERSITY PRESS
PRINCETON, NEW JERSEY

TO THE MEMORY OF

JULES ELLIOTT RUDOLPH

Table of Contents

List of Tables and Graphs

List of Tables and Graphs

LIST OF GRAPHS

Introduction

The massive forced migration of Africans as a result of the Atlantic slave trade is one of the central phenomena of both modern African and American historical developments. Its impact is still felt today within the African areas that experienced the forced migration and in the New World, where the descendants of African slaves form an important element within the national societies. Yet for all its importance, the Atlantic slave trade remained until recently one of the least explored aspects of modern economic and social history. Although a large body of literature now exists on the subject, the majority of it is based on unsystematic analysis or represents the experience of only a small number of vessels.

While the imagination of many writers from the time of the trade to our own period have been deeply stirred by the inhumanity of the "Middle Passage," it was not until the third decade of the 20th century that the first serious efforts were begun to reconstruct and analyze that experience. With the work by Rinchon and Gaston-Martin on the French slave trade, and most especially that of the port of Nantes in the 18th century, scholars finally began to explore metropolitan and colonial archives to obtain the most basic information on the nature of the trade, the numbers involved, and the processes by which this massive migration was financed.[1] To the pioneering efforts of the French scholars was added the equally innovative work of Elizabeth Donnan as she gathered together the extant materials available on the British slave trade to North America. Yet despite this important early research, for another four decades writers contin-

---

[1] Dieudonné Rinchon, *La traite et l'esclavage des congolais par les européens* (Bruxelles, 1929); and *Le trafic négrier, l'organisation commerciale de la traite des noirs* (Bruxelles, Nantes, Paris, 1938), are Rinchon's basic works on the numbers and ships involved. He has also written several later volumes on the economics of the trade which include the following: *Les armaments négriers au xviiie siècle* (Bruxelles: Memoire de la Académie des Sciences Coloniales, 1955), and *Pierre Ignace Liévin van Alstein, Capitaine négrier* (Dakar: Memoires of IFAN, no. 71, 1964). The most fundamental of Gaston-Martin's studies in this area is his famous *Nantes au xviiie siècle, l'ère des négriers (1714-1774)* (Paris, 1931) and his summary volume, *Négriers et bois d'ébène* (Grenoble, 1934).

ued to treat the trade from the perspective of the traditional literature.[2]

It was in the context of the broader concern with the Afro-American experience as well as of the development of the new sub-discipline of African history, that interest again focused on the Atlantic slave trade. As the history of black culture and the process of acculturation became a major concern to Americans, both the history of slavery and the nature of the Atlantic slave trade became important subjects of enquiry. Equally, it was perceived that the African experience with Europeans in the pre-colonial and colonial periods was intimately related to the history of the trade. From these two perspectives, a whole new set of studies developed that have systematically begun to reconstruct the Atlantic slave trade experience. These studies have ranged from detailed histories of the early monopoly trading companies,[3] through the imaginative recreation by Pierre Verger of the mutual flow of persons, ideas, and cultures between West Africa and Bahia,[4] to Philip Curtin's major effort to provide the basic framework for the analysis of the trade in terms of numbers, participation, and direction.[5]

From this perspective began my own research on the Atlantic slave trade. Turning to the study of the black experience and

[2] Elizabeth Donnan, *Documents Illustrative of the History of the Slave Trade to America* (Washington, D.C., 1930), 4 vols.

[3] The two major studies of this kind, are K. G. Davies, *The Royal African Company* (London, 1957); and Abdoulaye Ly, *La Compagnie du Senegal* (Paris, 1958).

[4] Pierre Verger, *Flux et reflux de la traite des négriers entre le golfe de Benin et Bahia de todos os Santos du dix-septième au dix-neuvième siècle* (Paris, 1958).

[5] Philip Curtin, *The Atlantic Slave Trade, A Census* (Madison, Wisconsin, 1969), and his updating article, "Measuring the Atlantic Slave Trade" in Stanley Engerman and Eugene Genovese, eds., *Race and Slavery in the Western Hemisphere: Quantitative Studies* (Princeton, 1975), pp. 107-128, and his "Measuring the Atlantic Slave Trade Once again: A Comment," *Journal of African History*, xvii, no. 4 (1976). For recent re-analyses of these figures, see Roger Anstey, "The Volume and Profitability of the British Slave Trade, 1761-1807," Engerman and Genovese, *Race and Slavery*, pp. 3-31; *The Atlantic Slave Trade and British Abolition 1760-1810* (London, 1975), pp. 38-39; "The Volume of the North American Slave-Carrying Trade from Africa 1761-1810," *Revue française d'histoire d'Outre-Mer*, LXII, nos. 226-227 (1975), pp. 47-66; "The Slave Trade of the Continental Powers, 1760-1810," *Economic History Review*, forthcoming; and J. E. Inikori "Measuring the Atlantic Slave Trade: An Assessment of Curtin and Anstey," *Journal of African History*, xvii, no. 2 (1976), pp. 197-223.

slavery in Brazil, I was confronted with the problems created by the paucity of sources. The destruction of a vast body of quantitative materials, and the crucial lack of censuses in the first half of the 19th century, led me into one of the few areas of extant records, that of the slave trade. Initially using these records within the larger context of the study of Brazilian slavery, I found myself more and more intrigued by the study of the Atlantic slave trade itself. From the initial port registers for Rio de Janeiro in 1795 I found myself searching through the Lisbon archives to study the Angolan trade from which the bulk of the Rio de Janeiro slaves had come. Studying the mortality in the South Atlantic trade led me to question its incidence and cause in the North Atlantic trade. Before long, I found myself returning to my original studies on Cuba and Virginia in the quest to place my Brazilian trade findings in their broader perspective. The re-sults of this ever-widening circle of interests finally led me to summarize and synthesize this research in this book.

My aim has been to analyze both the basic demographic features of the trans-Atlantic slave trade, and the special part of that trade dealing with the experiences of what contemporaries called the "Middle Passage," or the trans-oceanic crossing. The Middle Passage has been the best known and most controversial aspect of the entire trade. Yet what the "typical" voyage might have been in any trade or during any period is virtually unknown. Moreover, the age, sex, and mortality experience of the departing Africans and the manner in which they were transported is only partially understood. To begin a systematic analysis of these issues in an effort to determine the basic characteristics of the Middle Passage experience, I have concentrated in these several parallel studies on the Africans, the ships, the sailors, and the European traders. I attempt to assess the manner of carrying slaves, their mortality experience, and the American and African factors that influenced the routes, the timing, volume, and demographic characteristics of the forced African migration. The re-sulting study covers a century and a half of European slaving activity and an area from Senegal to Mozambique, and from the Chesapeake to Guanabara Bay. How and when these slaves were moved trans-Atlantically and which European merchants controlled this vast migration enterprise are also examined from this same spatial and temporal dimension.

Because of my interest in the quantitative aspects of the trade, this study is limited primarily to the period from 1700 to the mid-19th century. As yet, the European and colonial archives have not yielded quantitative sources on a major scale for the pre-1700 period, except for the unique case of the Dutch West India Company. Equally, almost all scholars now agree that the 18th and early 19th centuries were the period of dominance for the Atlantic slave trade, even within the context of African history. It was only in the 18th century that the trade in slaves became the single most valuable export from Africa.[6] At the same time, the period from 1700-1860 accounted for some 80 percent of the estimated 9.5 million Africans transported to America.[7] This same period also marks the end of the dominance of the monopoly company traders and the rise of free trading open to all European competition along most of the routes of the Atlantic trade. Thus, in terms of the quality of the available materials, of the numbers transported, of the importance of the trade, and of its commercial organization, the period since 1700 forms a coherent whole.

Along with the limitations in time, I have also been selective in my analysis of the several trades. Due to the efforts of other scholars, I have not dealt with the smaller Danish or Dutch trades, but have incorporated the findings on these trades wherever possible. Equally, because of problems with sources, I have not treated all the various routes even within the Portuguese, English, French, or Spanish trades that I do study. The quality of the available data has varied greatly, not only between nations, but also by individual routes. Nevertheless, even within the limitations that have been imposed, my data are a representative sample of the entire Atlantic slave trade, and I feel confident that the broader aspects and individual variations of the trade are revealed in these 18th- and 19th century collections of slave voyages.

The Atlantic slave trade, of course, was more than just the Middle Passage. The capture, transportation to the coast, sale to the Europeans, and subsequent sale and delivery to the inland American slave owners are all relevant to this experience. But given the limited work done on these subjects and the nature of

---

[6] Richard Bean, "A Note on the Relative Importance of Slaves and Gold in West African Exports," *Journal of African History*, xv, No. 3 (1974), pp. 354-355.

[7] Curtin, *The Atlantic Slave Trade*, p. 265.

my own concerns, I have treated these aspects only insofar as they have a direct bearing on the trans-Atlantic experience. I think it worth stressing as well that I am not attempting in any major way to re-evaluate the numbers generated by Curtin on the volume of the African migration itself. Curtin's work was primarily based on available published materials and attempted to estimate total volumes and trends. My data are primarily unpublished archival sources that are samples of the entire trade. I am therefore concerned with determining the demographic and shipping patterns revealed by these direct sources and do not make a serious effort to attempt to generalize total volume from these data.

In the face of these qualifying statements, readers still may be concerned over the relevance of doing yet another volume on the Atlantic slave trade. What is the masochistic urge to revel in one of the worst crimes of modern Western imperialism? Why treat this horrible period with seemingly scientific detachment and concern ourselves with its minutiae of ships, ports, and persons? The most obvious immediate answer is because the trade had a permanent and lasting impact upon both the African societies from which the slaves came and the American societies to which they arrived. It determined the living and dying patterns of the black communities that developed in the New World, and it helped to shape their ultimate cultural adaptation to the new American environment. The trade equally is probably the best documented aspect of pre-colonial African economic history and provides a fundamental insight into the African response to the international economy developing under Western imperialism. It also closely paralleled the rise of the Industrial Revolution in Europe and was linked to its development. Finally, the trade was the medium for the movement of crops and diseases between Africa, America, and even Europe itself. Thus the more detailed and secure the reconstruction of the history of the trade, the more insight is gained into both African and Afro-American historical development, as well as into the process of European expansion into the Atlantic world.

I have organized the study into several broad divisions based on geographic, chronological, and organizational considerations. After attempting to assess the demand factors in America that brought the Africans to the New World and that determined the outlines of the Atlantic slave trade, I delineate the history of the South Atlantic slave trade to Brazil in the 18th and 19th centuries, and the migration of Afro-Brazilian slaves after the end of the trade. These three chapters on the South Atlantic trade develop in detail both the history of the longest and one of the largest trade routes, and the major concerns for which all the later trades will be analyzed. The numbers of Africans shipped from Africa, the mortality they experienced, the types of tonnage and crew size of vessels employed, their specialization, the response of shipping and mortality to seasonal conditions, commercial organization and the opening up of new African sources—all are analyzed from the point of view of defining the limits of the trade as seen from the South Atlantic. This section ends with a study of Brazil's internal slave trade that evaluates the broader questions of the long-term impact of the original Atlantic slave trade settlement pattern on the redistribution of the resident slave population through the development of a post abolition internal trade.

In the next sections, the English trade to Virginia and Jamaica in the early and later 18th century, the contemporaneous French slave trade to the West Indies, and finally the largely 19th-century Spanish slave trade to Cuba are treated in a comparative framework to determine both their common and unique characteristics. Each of the trades and routes selected represents alternative patterns. In the case of Virginia, there is the development of a relatively minor international trade that nevertheless accounted for about a third of the African arrivals to British North America. Moreover, its early mixture of local and long-distance slave trades anticipates arrangements found in the early period of the trades to Cuba and the British and French West Indies. The data for the British West Indies in the last decades of the 18th century show probably the most intensive trade at its height, and they also permit an evaluation of the attempts by government to regulate the trade for humanitarian reasons. Finally, the Cuban trade is unique for both its early years of open competition and also the data it provides on the changing age and sex of the arriving African slaves in the perspective of almost a half century of activity. It also provides, along with the Rio de Janeiro materials of the 1820s, the only detailed data available on the crucial changes that occurred in the trade in the 19th century.

In the concluding chapter, I attempt to summarize the common features that all the trades exhibited in the 18th and 19th centuries, as well as the problems in analysis that still remain. Also, a brief attempt is made to view some of the more general influences of the trade on the Atlantic world in this period.

This quantitative analysis has been made as highly comparable as possible, and certain minimum standards have been enforced for the analysis of all data. I have not tried to use estimated slave figures for any trade when analyzing the experience of individual ships. Only those ships with complete data on the number of slaves purchased and/or the number of slaves delivered are used. Equally, I have eliminated all ships that did not complete the voyage, either because of slave revolts, capture, or shipwreck. Finally, only those ships which indicate slave mortality were included in the various discussions of mortality, since I assumed that zero mortality was simply a missing category. Finally, in no two trades were all variables identical, and thus fully comparative analysis was not always achieved on all issues. In some cases tonnage figures were missing from the naval recordings; in others the times of departure and arrivals were not complete. When such variables were available, however, attempts have been made to be as comparative as possible, so as to place each trade in perspective with the others.

From the very beginning of this study, I have had the invaluable support of friends who guided me in the field of quantitative analysis and who helped me to understand the problems involved in the analysis of the trade. Jonathan Kelley, Donald Treiman, Michael Edelstein, Peter Decker, and Phillip Schmitter helped me to develop the skills needed to utilize the vast body of quantitative data I had been gathering. Philip Curtin constantly offered his invaluable encouragement and criticisms, from my earliest efforts to the final manuscript. As a friend, co-author, and mentor, Stanley Engerman was instrumental in assisting me in all phases of the study. He and I also worked intensively together on the basic questions involved in analyzing slave mortality, which resulted in several joint papers that provide the background to this discussion throughout the book. I would also like to thank Harriet E. M. Klein, Richard Wortman, David Eltis, Joseph Miller, Charles Garland, and Ralph Austen for reading the manuscript for me. Daniel Charles Klein supplied useful research support.

The archivists and directors of the several European and American archives cited in this work were extremely helpful, and I am grateful to the staff of the Arquivo Nacional of Brazil for special permission to use their collections. I am equally indebted to both friends and fellow researchers, who generously shared their unpublished data with me and allowed me to use them in this book. These materials came from the late Jean Mettas, Philip Curtin, Roger Anstey, Robert Stein, Nancy Naro, David Eltis, Stuart Schwartz, Serge Daget, Walter Minchinton, and David Syrett. I am also indebted for financial assistance during the research phase of this project to the universities of Chicago and Columbia, the Social Science Research Council, and the American Council of Learned Societies. Free computer time was provided by the university computer centers of Columbia, Toronto, and Oxford. All the data used in this book have been deposited in machine-readable form, along with the relevant codebooks, with the Data and Program Library Service of the University of Wisconsin. These materials are available to the public and may be obtained at cost.

Abbreviations

A&P	Great Britain, House of Commons, Parliamentary Papers, *Accounts and Papers*
ADLA	Archives Départemental de la Loire Atlantique, Nantes
ANRJ	Arquivo Nacional, Rio de Janeiro
AHU	Arquivo Historico Ultramarino, Lisbon
ANTT	Arquivo Nacional, Torre de Tombo, Lisbon
AGI	Archivo General de Indias, Seville
AGM	Arquivo Geral da Marinha, Lisbon
AHN	Archivo Historico Nacional, Madrid
BM	British Museum, London
BNRJ	Bibiloteca Nacional, Rio de Janeiro
BNL	Biblioteca Nacional, Lisbon
CRHFA	Centre de Recherches sur l'Histoire de la France Atlantique, Nantes
HLRO	House of Lords, Record Office, London
IHGB	Instituto de Historia e Geografia Brasileira, Rio de Janeiro
PRO	Public Record Office, London

The Middle Passage

Chapter One

The American Demand for Slaves and the Afro-American Patterns of Settlement

The forced migration of the peoples of sub-Saharan Africa to the New World was the direct outgrowth of a seemingly inexhaustible demand for labor on the part of the European colonizing powers. Though the Western Hemisphere contained between eighty and one hundred million Indians at the time of its discovery, this population was incapable of surviving both the initial conquest and the introduction to the continent of a whole range of new European diseases. By the end of the first century of European colonization, no more than ten million Indians were left in the New World.[1] This demographic decimation seems merely to have intensified the demand for labor in the Americas, for the production of precious metals was constantly on the increase during this period of population decline. At the same time, new colonizing empires were moving into areas so far uninhabited by the Spanish and Portuguese pioneers.

Though this movement into previously unsettled areas of the New World attracted many European settlers, they did not come in sufficient numbers to guarantee mineral and commercial-agricultural production. To the 140,000 or so Portuguese and Spanish who inhabited the hemisphere by the last third of the sixteenth century, the English, French, and Dutch added several hundred thousand more, so that by 1650 there were over 800,000 white colonists in the Americas.[2] Still, these white colonists formed a largely exploitive elite in relation to the dwindling Indian population, and the demand for labor from other sources persisted.

[1] Henry F. Dobyns, "Estimating Aboriginal American Population . . . ," *Current Anthropology* 7 (October 1966), 395-416; and Nicolás Sánchez-Albornoz, *The Population of Latin America: A History* (Berkeley, 1974), Chapter II.

[2] Unless otherwise indicated, these and all subsequent New World population figures are taken from Angel Rosenblat, *La población indígena y el mestizaje en America,* vol. 1 (Buenos Aires, 1954).

Since the European laborers (except those from northern Europe) proved unwilling to migrate in large numbers, and since the costs of transportation and settlement of those who did migrate were so great for the creole, or native-born, elite, all the colonizing regimes turned toward slave labor on a massive scale. Though only the Iberians actively practiced slavery in western Europe at this time, slavery in the Old World was an ancient institution. In the fifteenth century, Jews, Moors, Berbers, Arabs, and Eastern Europeans were all part of the slave labor force of the Mediterranean world. These traditionally enslaved peoples, however, were rapidly being replaced by the relatively unexploited African peoples. In the early part of the century, new caravan routes between North Africa and the Sudan were developed, and after the 1440s the Portuguese were able to bring African slaves to the Continent via direct Atlantic sea routes. Slavs, Muslims, and even Canary Islanders still formed large slave populations in the Old World during the last half of the century, but the sub-Saharan black population had by that time become the predominant group in the western Mediterranean slave labor force.[3] Thus, when the New World looked to the Old for a new supply of labor, it turned to sub-Saharan Africa, the closest source of large numbers of slaves to be obtained readily and cheaply. The result was the mass forced migration of Africans to the New World.

For the first half-century of the Atlantic slave trade, from the 1440s to 1500 approximately, Europe itself was the market for African slaves. Large numbers of slaves were brought to Portugal and Spain, where they assumed many of the social roles they would eventually play in the New World. From the beginning, Africans were employed in both rural and urban occupations, performing both domestic and gang labor.[4] But the European slave

[3] A summary of slavery in the Mediterranean in the 14th and 15th centuries is presented in Charles Verlinden, *Les origines de la civilisation atlantique* (Paris, 1966), pp. 174-175. On the North African trade, see Ralph Austen, "A Census of the Transsaharan Slave Trade: A Tentative Census," MSSB Conference Paper, Waterville, Maine, 1975.

[4] It has been estimated that the Portuguese exported something like 140,000 slaves from Africa, primarily to Europe, between 1450 and 1505 (Vitorino Magalhães Godinho, *A Economia dos descobrimentos henriquinos* [Lisbon, 1962], p. 209). In the port of Valencia on the Spanish Mediterranean coast, to give just one example of the African impact on the peninsula, about two-thirds of the slaves imported from 1489 to 1516 were Afri-

labor market had developed in response to labor shortages during an age of major economic expansion, and it was not without limits. As European populations themselves began to expand late in the 15th and 16th centuries, the need for slave labor on the Continent declined.[5]

The European experience with African slave labor and the high level of commercial organization achieved by the early Atlantic slave trade were crucial factors in the almost immediate introduction of African slave labor to the New World at the end of the 15th and the beginning of the 16th century. African slaves participated in the initial conquest of the West Indian islands and, later, in the conquest of the mainland regions.[6] Within half a century, African and creole slaves were often as numerous as the white conquistadors in the newly won lands.[7]

Since the conquered Indians were still the largest single group in the labor force of the New World, the settlement and occupational patterns of the incoming African slaves tended to be influenced by those of the American Indian population. In the highlands of Mexico and Peru, where Indians had survived the demographic upheaval and the several epidemics that accompanied the arrival of the Europeans, the Negro slaves were employed almost exclusively as skilled and semi-skilled urban artisans or domestic servants. Where large bodies of Amerindians

---

can, and an average of about 250 Africans were imported annually (Vicenta Cortes, *La esclavitud en Valencia durante el reinado de los reyes católicos (1479-1516)* [Valencia, 1964], pp. 57-60). By the 16th century, such central areas as Portugal and Andalusia already had large slave populations. By 1551 some 9,950 slaves were counted in Lisbon, out of a total population of 100,000, and by 1573 the whole of Portugal was said to contain over 40,000 slaves, a large number of whom were sub-Saharan African Negroes (Federic Mauro, *Le Portugal et l'atlantique au xviie siècle* [Paris, 1960], p. 147; Charles Verlinden, *L'esclavage dans l'Europe médiévale*, vol. 1 [Bruges, 1955], p. 837). Philip Curtin, *The Atlantic Slave Trade, A Census* (Madison, 1969), pp. 17-21.

[5] On the population expansion of 16th-century Europe, see Marcel R. Reinhard and Andre Armengaud, *Histoire générale de la population mondiale* (Paris, 1961), pp. 84ff.

[6] José Antonio Saco, *História de la esclavitud de la raza africana en el nuevo mundo . . .* (Barcelona, 1879), pp. 71ff.

[7] Rosenblat estimates that the population of Spanish America in 1570 consisted of 118,000 whites and 230,000 Negroes, mulattoes, and mestizos. Though mestizos and mulattoes are lumped together with Negroes in this estimate, it seems likely that between one-half and two-thirds of the total colored population were Negro at this early date.

had not survived—primarily in the lowland and coastal regions and on the West Indian islands—the Europeans turned almost exclusively to African labor, and slaves were employed in all types of occupations, rural as well as urban.

During the first two centuries of American colonization, Negro slaves could be found in all parts of the New World. From the beginning, they made up half or more of the conquering armies, and they intermingled quite freely to form a new intermediate social grouping of *castas*, or people of mixed Indian, white, and Negro ancestry. As early as 1570 the Viceroyalty of New Spain, as Mexico was then called, had a Negro slave population of about 20,000, more than the Spanish and creole white populations combined. Of these 20,000, it was estimated that at least 2,000 had already become fugitives. In addition, there was a free colored population of about 2,435 in Mexico. The Negro slave population there grew slowly, and a half-century later, in 1646, it was estimated at about 35,000; the maximum level reached seems to have been under 50,000. In contrast, the free mulatto and Indian-Negro populations increased enormously during this period, numbering about 116,000 combined in 1646. Because of the Africans' greater resistance to European diseases, and because of their close contact with the Indians, it appears that mixed Indian-Negro and Afro-mestizo (African and Spanish-Indian) populations grew rapidly, passing 600,000 combined by 1810 and thus representing 10 percent of the total Mexican population and around 25 percent of the total *castas*.[8] In Peru, too, Africans quickly came to form a substantial part of the population. It was estimated that by the 1580s there were about 4,000 Negro slaves in Peru, roughly the same as the number of whites.[9]

After the first century of rapid expansion, however, the Spanish

[8] Gonzalo Aguirre Beltran, *La población negra de Mexico, 1519-1810* (Mexico, 1946), pp. 208-213, 221, 237. It has been recently estimated that 224,205 African slaves were introduced into the Spanish Indies between 1521-1639, of which just half (110,525) went to Mexico. Colin Palmer, *Slaves of the White God. Blacks in Mexico, 1570-1650* (Cambridge, Mass., 1976), p. 28.

[9] James Lockhart, *Spanish Peru, 1532-1560: A Colonial Society* (Madison: University of Wisconsin Press, 1968), p. 230. By 1600 blacks and mulattoes represented 46 percent of the 14,262 population of Lima, and by 1636 their number in the city had grown to 11,619 or 43 percent of the total population. Frederick P. Bowser, *The African Slave in Colonial Peru, 1524-1650* (Stanford, 1974), pp. 339-340.

colonies on the American continent tended to absorb fewer Africans, and their slave populations tended to stabilize at relatively low numbers—less than 50,000 in Mexico and less than 100,000 in Peru. By 1650, there were probably no more than 345,000 Negro slaves in all of Spanish America, in addition to some 135,000 mulattoes.[10]

In 17th-century Spanish America, the African slaves and freedmen played a crucial role in the developing creole society. Particularly in the areas of heavy Indian population, they tended to identify with white culture and were considered part of the dominant society. As far as the Indians were concerned, they were one with the conquerors, and they were treated in much royal legislation as a distinct element of the Western cultural elite. They spoke Spanish, learned European skills and crafts, and sometimes exploited the Indians as mercilessly as did the whites.[11]

This type of slavery within the context of an Indian peasant economy was largely urban-oriented, slaves being used primarily in skilled and unskilled urban occupations, local truck farming, and, in the rare case of Nueva Granada, in placer gold mining as well.[12] The classic type of plantation slavery was slow to develop in Spanish America, where it was not to make its major appearance until the second half of the 18th century, after certain basic economic changes had taken place. The early lack of importance of plantation agriculture in the Spanish empire was largely due to the fact that the Spaniards concentrated on ex-

[10] These figures are derived from Rosenblat's estimates in *La población indigena.* From his total figure of 857,000 Negroes in the New World, I have subtracted 122,000, the estimated number of North American and Brazilian blacks in the population, as well as 390,000 for the black population of the Dutch, English, and French West Indies. This leaves 345,000 for the population of the Spanish empire, about 10,000 of whom probably inhabited the Spanish islands. I have estimated the mulatto population at 130,000 for continental Spanish America, plus 5,000 for the Spanish Antilles. Given the fact that the majority of the mulattoes were listed as freedmen in almost all available census records, it would seem reasonable to suppose that there was a free colored population of at least 67,500 in Spanish America by 1650.

[11] See 16th-century complaints of black and mulatto interventions in Indian communities in Richard Konetzke, ed., *Colección de documentos para la historia de la formación social de Hispanoamérica, 1493-1810,* Vol. 1 (Madrid, 1953-1962), pp. 213-321.

[12] William F. Sharp, "The Profitability of Slavery in the Colombian Chocó, 1680-1810," *Hispanic American Historical Review,* Vol. 55, No. 3 (August 1975).

ploiting the great mineral wealth of the New World along with the free labor of the Indian masses. They therefore tended to settle in urban centers, and primarily in the major areas already inhabited by the Amerindians, leaving the future plantation areas for the most part to subsistence agriculture.[13]

In contrast, when the other European colonizing powers arrived in the New World, they found these two vital sources of immediate wealth closed to them. The Spanish had preempted almost all the easily accessible mining areas and almost all Indian populations native to these regions. The Indians who remained, those who made their homes outside the Central American and Peruvian centers, were not peasant village agriculturalists but semi-nomadic peoples or simple village agriculturalists, accustomed to a subsistence economy and unaccustomed to a stratified multi-community state. Hence they found it impossible to adapt to life as slave laborers, or even dependent rural laborers, and thus to integrate themselves into colonial society. Indeed, they were unable even to survive the initial encounter with the Europeans, and were decimated by the onslaught of new communicable diseases. When the colonizing powers, finding themselves with neither mines nor a dependent peasantry, sought to develop commercial agricultural products for European consumption and began experimenting with Indian labor, disease and the lack of technological and social development drove the Indians to virtual extinction.

The Europeans, left without a labor base for their society, since they themselves were too few in number to develop large-scale plantation economies, turned to Africa for a new supply of slaves. Whereas the Africans brought into the central areas of Spanish America had been drawn into the cultural elite of the plural societies developing there, those brought into the new colonies, as well as into the marginal areas of Spanish America, found themselves in the bottom half of a two-part, racially segmented regime. Here there were no Indians to fill the bottom positions of unskilled labor or to make possible the emergence of a third major social group such as the *castas* of Peru and Mexico. Pre-

[13] Many of the ideas in this and the following paragraphs grew out of insights presented in two major works: Silvio A. Zavala, "Relaciones históricas entre indios y negros en Iberoamérica," *Revista de las Indias*, 28 (1946), 55-65; and Charles Gibson, *Spain in America* (New York, 1966).

8

cisely because of the large Indian population in these older regimes, especially in Mexico, the Afro-American had found it far easier to enter into colonial society, transforming it into a multiracial creole society in which the Afro-mestizo population was virtually indistinguishable from the mestizo population. There, too, where the Indians made up the exploited element of the society, the colonial patterns of prejudice and oppression would have a much milder effect on the blacks and mulattoes than in societies where they alone made up the agricultural and urban masses. Though the creole societies that formed in the newer colonies in the Americas would eventually contain tripartite color groupings of blacks, mulattoes, and whites (in all areas except continental North America), the Africans in these societies would take the place of the exploited Indians, and the process of lower-class integration into a multi-racial community would be considerably slower.

Whereas the slaves of 16th- and 17th-century Spanish America were primarily miners, truck gardeners, and urban and domestic laborers, the slaves brought into the colonies of the new imperial powers were almost exclusively employed in plantation agriculture. Though a host of crops—including cotton, indigo, tobacco, and rice—would eventually become important colonial agricultural products, the primary export crop of New World expansion was sugar. A product that was fast becoming a European staple, sugar had been developed as a plantation crop in the eastern Mediterranean by the 12th century and had then spread to Cyprus and Sicily in the 13th century and to the southern Iberian peninsula by the 14th. Finally, in the middle of the 15th century, it reached the Madeira islands. When these Atlantic islands became the center of European sugar production, it was inevitable that the Spanish and Portuguese should transport the crop to the New World.[14]

Thus sugar came to be grown throughout the Spanish Caribbean area, though it remained a relatively minor crop. The Portuguese, however, made it a major crop in the second half of the 16th century, when they decided to exploit their Brazilian holdings to the fullest. In this they had the support of a key group

[14] Charles Verlinden, *Precedents médiévaux de la colonie en Amérique* (Mexico, 1954), pp. 45-52; and Noel Deerr, *A History of Sugar* (2 vols., London, 1949-1950).

of merchants, the Flemish and Dutch traders. The production of sugar was one of the most capital-intensive industries then known to European agriculture and industry. Aside from the large sums of money needed to purchase slave labor, the producer had to invest in expensive processing machinery and in mills to extract the sugar, in even its crudest form, from the cane. The Flemish and Dutch merchants had the required capital, and it was they who provided everything from the slaves and the boilers needed to get production underway to the ships used for transporting the finished product to market. In fact, the very first *engenhos*, or sugar mills, established in Brazil early in the 16th century were built with the assistance of Flemish and Dutch capital.

At the beginning of the 16th century, when Spain first began to issue *asientos*—monopoly grants to merchants for supplying slaves to the Spanish Indies—the Flemish and Dutch merchants came away with the prime contracts and subcontracts. By the end of the 16th century, the Dutch merchant marine had become the largest in Europe and was already actively engaged in the trans-Atlantic carrying trade, bringing slaves from Africa to the Americas and carrying American products to Europe.[15] While the Spanish Indies were reasonably well served in these early years by a national merchant marine and so were able to retain control of their own commerce, the Portuguese, with their overextended Asian empire, had few resources left for supplying the New World. They therefore adopted a policy of semi-free trade as far as Brazil was concerned, and this permitted the Dutch to make major inroads in the New World. Antwerp and later Amsterdam became the principal importing ports for Brazilian sugar.[16]

Sugar production in Brazil was concentrated in the northeastern region of Bahia and Pernambuco, with a minor center in the south at Rio de Janeiro. By 1580 production had reached such dimensions that Brazil had replaced the Madeira islands as Eu-

[15] C. R. Boxer, *The Dutch Seaborne Empire: 1600-1800* (New York, 1965), pp. 20ff. Though Dutch merchants were thus involved in the slave trade from the beginning, the Dutch did not dominate the trade until the last part of the 17th century. (See Chapter 2 of Rolando Mellafe, *La esclavitud en Hispanoamérica* [Buenos Aires, 1964].)

[16] Sergio Buarque de Holanda, ed., *Historia geral da civilização brasileira*, 8 vols. to date (São Paulo, 1963-), Tomo 1, vol. 1, 235-236, Tomo 2, vol. 2, 204. Celso Furtado, *Formacion económica del Brasil* (Mexico, 1962), pp. 18-19.

rope's chief source of sugar.[17] With this firm base in sugar, the Portuguese were able to turn Brazil into a prosperous commercial farming or plantation colony, the first exclusively agricultural colony created in the New World. By the end of the 16th century Brazil was the world's largest producer of sugar and already had a slave labor force roughly estimated at between 13,000 and 15,000.[18]

But Brazil's leading role as a sugar producer was eventually to be challenged by a series of external circumstances centering around events in Europe. In 1580 Portugal became subject to Spain, under Philip II. In the same period, the Dutch provinces of the Low Countries united to begin a long rebellion against Spanish domination. Because of their preeminence at sea, the Dutch concentrated on attacking the overseas Iberian empire. In 1594 a Dutch fleet sailed to the East Indies, and in 1589 Philip II retaliated by confiscating all Dutch shipping in the Portuguese empire. However, while the Dutch and the Portuguese were in active competition in East Asia, their interests in Brazil were at this point too closely connected and too profitable for them to cease cooperating. Thus, despite the bans of Philip II, Dutch-Portuguese sugar trade continued and even increased, until by 1609 the Dutch were carrying from half to two-thirds of all Brazilian exports to Europe.

This trade by special agreement could not long survive the conflicts of interest between the two countries in Europe and East Asia, however. In 1621 the Dutch created the West Indies Company for colonization and trade in both the New World and Africa. In 1630, after several abortive attempts, the Dutch finally gained control of large sections of northeastern Brazil, thus acquiring title to Europe's largest source of sugar. From 1630 to 1654 they controlled most of northeastern Brazil, centering around Recife in Pernambuco, and, in Africa, the Costa da Mina, the island of Fernando Po in the Bight of Biafra, and Angola, which they also captured from the Portuguese. Thus they were able to control the major sources of slave labor as well as the major sources of sugar.[19] But the Portuguese, after breaking away from Spanish domination in 1640 and losing a large part of their

[17] Federic Mauro, *Le xvie siècle européen: aspects economiques* (Paris, 1966), p. 151.
[18] Mauro, *Le Portugal et l'atlantique*, p. 179.
[19] Buarque de Holanda, *História geral*, Tomo 1, Vol. 1, 1: 235ff.

East Asian empire in the Dutch wars in the first half of the century, still had more energies to concentrate on retaking Brazil; and since the planters in the northeast had remained Portuguese during the period of Dutch dominion, it was relatively easy to overthrow the Dutch with direct aid from Lisbon. By the middle of the century the Brazilians had succeeded in expelling the Dutch from Brazil.[20]

But the departure of the Dutch was to prove disastrous to Brazil's position as the world's foremost sugar producer. Though Angola and the African islands were recaptured from the Dutch, the crucial link with European markets was now broken. Equally important, the Dutch now took their capital, their technology, and their commercial expertise to the West Indies, becoming the crucial middlemen in the establishment of the sugar empires of the French and English in the New World.[21] From the middle of the 17th century on, the West Indies gained ground in terms of world sugar production, while the Brazilian industry receded into a secondary position.

The first surge of the new development in sugar-plantation agriculture came in the British West Indies. By 1650 the small island of Barbados was producing both tobacco and sugar and was well on its way toward the creation of a large plantation system with over 20,000 slaves.[22] When Jamaica was taken by the British under Cromwell in 1655, this hitherto marginal island was rapidly brought into sugar production and quickly came to challenge the leadership of Barbados. By 1700 Jamaica had some 45,000 slaves and had become the single largest producer of sugar in the world; and by the middle of the 18th century, the British

[20] One of the leading captains in the war against the Dutch was the colored freedman Henrique Dias, who led an army of several hundred ex-slaves and freedmen and was eventually rewarded by the Portuguese Crown with a title of nobility (see José Antonio Gonsalves de Mello, *Henrique Dias, governador dos pretos, crioulos e mulatos do estado do Brasil* [Recife, 1954]).

[21] On the role of the Dutch in introducing sugar cultivation and slaves to the West Indies, see Arthur Percival Newton, *The European Nations in the West Indies, 1493-1688* (London, 1933), pp. 196ff. While Dutch marketing and technology were important in the rapid expansion of the West Indian sugar industry, it has recently been suggested that this new development antedated the collapse of Pernambuco. See Mathew Edel, "The Brazilian Sugar Cycle of the Seventeenth Century and the Rise of West Indian Competition," *Caribbean Studies*, IX, no. 1 (April, 1969).

[22] Newton, *The European Nations*, p. 197.

West Indies islands as a group had become the great center of plantation agriculture.[23]

This position of dominance was very soon challenged by the French. By 1700, the French had imported some 16,000 slaves into the small island of Martinique alone, and they had brought another 20,000 into the just developing Saint Domingue (present-day Haiti). The plantation system on both islands expanded rapidly thereafter, but Saint Domingue far outstripped Martinique and the other French possessions within the next fifty years. By 1750 its slave population had risen to over 230,000, a phenomenal increase, and it was rapidly surpassing Jamaica as the world's leading sugar producer.[24] By the 1780's all the unoccupied islands in the West Indies had been brought into cultivation, and this plantation region had reached the apogee of its production. At that time, the French and British islands together held over a million slaves and some 47,000 freedmen.[25]

Meanwhile, during the 17th century, a new stronghold of slavery was established as the North American continent was settled by British colonists. Here, as in the other English and French colonies, Dutch traders proved to be vital suppliers of both capital and slave labor. The first shipment of African slaves to British North America, arriving in 1619, was carried from the West Indies by a Dutch vessel. Of course, the climate in the continental colonies was more temperate than in the other English colonies, so sugar was not a feasible crop there. Further, the northern colonies were a greater risk for capital investment, and the funds needed to develop a commercial crop economy were not available. As a result, the colonists were initially forced

[23] Frank W. Pitman, *The Development of the British West Indies, 1700-1763* (New Haven, Conn., 1917), p. 373.

[24] Lucien Peytraud, *L'esclavage aux antilles françaises avant 1789* (Paris, 1897), pp. 237-239. *Deerr, History of Sugar,* i, 198, 240; and John James McCusker, Jr., "The Rum Trade and the Balance of Payments of the Thirteen Colonies" (Ph.D. thesis, Department of History, University of Pittsburgh, 1970), pp. 232-256. Saint Domingue alone produced over one-third of all West Indian sugar and was harvesting almost two times as much sugar as Jamaica, its closest rival.

[25] Of these over million slaves, the French held some 673,500 (*ibid.*, p. 139) and the English some 465,276 (Sir William Young, *The West-India Common-Place Book* [London, 1807], p. 3). Of these, Saint Domingue and Jamaica respectively had 452,000 and 256,000 slaves. In addition, there were 36,400 free colored in the French islands and 10,569 in the English possessions.

to develop crops that were not capital-intensive for export to Europe. Fortunately for the inhabitants of Virginia, tobacco proved an ideal crop in both ecological and economic terms. Virginia leaf quickly became an effective competitor to the Cuban tobaccos, which were of better quality but limited in supply, and the capital generated by this export was sufficient to finance the importation of slave labor on a major scale.

Thus, for the first time in the New World, tobacco became a plantation crop worked by slave labor on large estates. Along with tobacco, the southern colonies of continental British America were soon producing rice, some sugar, and finally cotton on plantations worked by slaves. By 1790, when the colonial period ended, British North America held over 757,000 Afro-American slaves and freedmen.[26] Still, this was only about two-thirds the number of Afro-Americans in the French and British West Indian islands. Thus, while the thirteen continental colonies were becoming a major slave and plantation zone by the end of the 18th century, they were still not equal to the sugar-producing areas of the West Indies.

The North American colonies were not the only continental area to develop plantation and slave economies in the 18th century. The Spanish Crown, in the second half of that century, heavily subsidized sugar, indigo, cacao, rice, and cotton plantations in such areas as Guatemala, Colombia, Venezuela, and Ecuador. It also promoted its previously neglected West Indian islands, Cuba and Puerto Rico, and after 1789 replaced the granting of monopoly contracts with free trade in African slaves, thus promoting massive immigration to these islands. The net result was that by the end of the 18th century, Spanish America contained a colored population of about two million, including both slaves and freedmen.

In Brazil, where the first plantation economy had developed, an entirely new pattern of slave labor was to appear in the 18th century with the opening up of the mines in the hinterland. Beginning in the 1690's, when gold was first discovered in Minas Gerais, slaves poured into the Brazilian interior, and a new mining economy based on colored slave labor began to develop.

[26] These and all subsequent figures on United States populations are taken from the Bureau of the Census, *Negro Population, 1790-1915* (Washington, D.C., 1918).

While mining had been practiced with slave labor in Colombia, Mexico, and Peru, the majority of mine workers throughout the Spanish empire were still Indians.[27] In Brazil, however, all mine workers were black and Minas Gerais and Goias became major new centers of black population and of a whole new mining-slave-labor economy.[28]

The basic system of slave labor—plantation, urban, and mining—which had been elaborated by the end of the 18th century was to remain unchanged until well after abolition. There would be major shifts in crops and in the plantation centers during the 19th century as new areas came into sugar production or as such staples as indigo were replaced by other products, but the economic, social, and legal structures that were to prevail in the Americas had all been roughly established by the time the colonial period ended.

Unquestionably the single most important event to affect the post-colonial plantation system occurred late in the 18th century. This was the Haitian revolution of the 1790s—a revolution with a profound impact, for not only did it serve as a terrifying example to slave masters throughout the New World, but it helped to reorder the centers of plantation agriculture in the Caribbean. From the 1750s to the 1790s Haiti—or Saint Domingue, as the French then called it—was the world's leading producer of high-grade, low-cost sugar. The efficiency and the productivity of the French plantations were proverbial, and French West Indian sugar dominated the European market, driving the higher-priced English and Brazilian products out from all but their protected

[27] Alexander Humboldt, *Political Essay on the Kingdom of New Spain* (4 vols.; London, 1811), I, pp. 124-126; III, pp. 246-247. Of the major mining areas, the two largest, Mexico and Peru-Chile, used virtually no colored slave labor. Among the secondary mining regions, Venezuela had a large colored slave force but also a large force of slave and free Indians. Further, Venezuelan mines were exhausted by the 18th century and ceased to employ significant numbers of slaves (Federico Brito Figueroa, *La estructura economica de Venezuela colonial* [Caracas, 1963], pp. 80ff.). Only in Colombian mines were colored slaves used extensively throughout the colonial period, and even there Indian labor was also used. Aquiles Esclalante, *El negro en Colombia* (Bogota, 1964, pp. 121-127); and German Colmenares, *Historia economica y social de Colombia, 1537-1719* (2d. ed.; Medellin, 1975), chap. v.

[28] C. R. Boxer, *The Golden Age of Brazil, 1695-1750: Growing Pains of a Colonial Society* (Berkeley, 1969), and Sergio Buarque de Holanda, *Historia geral*, Tomo 2, vol. 2, are the best available studies of Minas and Goias colonial mining society.

15

metropolitan markets.[29] However, with the uprising led by Toussaint L'Ouverture and the eventual destruction of the Haitian slave regime, there was a mass exodus of planters and capital from the island. Just as the Dutch exodus from Pernambuco over a century earlier was followed by a relocation of the production centers, the Haitian loss of capital and technological and commercial knowledge worked to the gain of other regions in the New World—especially the traditional sugar regions of northeastern Brazil and the island of Cuba, which eventually replaced Haiti as the world's largest producer of cane sugar.[30]

With Haitian capital at its disposal, and with the effective elimination of Haitian competition in sugar production, by the first decades of the new century Cuba was fast becoming a major slave plantation economy. Beginning with a slave population of only about 44,000 in 1774, Cuba by 1861 had a slave population of 399,000 and a total colored population of 613,000.[31] By the middle of the 19th century, it had taken the lead in world sugar production and had over 150,000 slaves engaged in sugar production alone.[32]

An even more important outgrowth of the Haitian revolution was a shift in the centers of coffee production. Until the 1790s Haiti had also been the largest producer of coffee in the New World. When the old regime was brought to an end, many French coffee planters shifted their operations to Cuba, where some 50,000 slaves were employed in coffee production in the 1830s. Cuban coffee interests, however, soon faced mounting competition from growers in Rio de Janeiro.

The exportation of Brazilian coffee on a major scale began in the 1820s, and by the 1830s the coffee boom was on. First growing up in the area around Rio de Janeiro, the coffee plantations spread to the southwest down the Paraiba valley and then, by the middle of the 19th century, into the flat highlands surrounding the city of São Paulo. In the West Paulista plains, as these

[29] Eric Williams, *Capitalism and Slavery* (Chapel Hill, 1944), pp. 113-114, 122-123.

[30] Roland T. Ely, *Cuando reinaba su majestad el azucar* (Buenos Aires, 1963), pp. 77ff.

[31] Herbert S. Klein, *Slavery in the Americas: A Comparative Study of Cuba and Virginia* (Chicago, 1967), Table 2, p. 202.

[32] Jacobo de la Pezuela, *Diccionario geográfico, estadístico, histórico de la isla de Cuba* (4 vols., Madrid, 1863-1866), I, p. 61.

highlands were called, coffee thrived with a vigor unknown, until then, to any crop in Brazil.[33] The São Paulo area thus became a center for coffee production, and the slave population in the area increased rapidly.

Despite these developments, however, the old mining region of Minas Gerais continued throughout the 19th century to have the largest slave population of any state in Brazil. Though the gold mines of this area had been seriously declining since the middle of the 18th century, Minas Gerais was able to develop a thriving, diversified economy built upon cattle raising, sugar and coffee production, and truck gardening—all of which had absorbed some 370,000 slaves by the 1870s. The south-central states of Rio de Janeiro and São Paulo had also developed major slave populations by this time, whereas the slave populations of Pernambuco and particularly Maranhão—both in the old northeast —had dropped considerably. Despite the relative decline of the northeastern states as slave centers, however, the Afro-Brazilian population did not shift as radically as one might suspect over the 19th century, for the rapidly increasing free colored population remained geographically immobile. Thus, by the first census of 1872, taken when slavery still flourished in Brazil, the old northeastern region plus the coastal state of Bahia contained over 2,900,000 colored persons, making up 51 percent of the total Afro-Brazilian population of 5,700,000.[34]

In the United States, the settlement patterns that had evolved by the end of the 18th century were to change slowly as the American population moved inland from the Atlantic seaboard. In 1790, 92 percent of the black population was located in the South Atlantic states—Virginia being the leader, with over 300,000 persons. Following technical innovations in the ginning of cotton in the 1790s and the increasing mechanization of the English textile industry during the same period, cotton production expanded dramatically in the United States, and cotton became far and away the largest slave labor crop on the North American continent. With the Louisiana Purchase and the War

[33] Klein, *Slavery in the Americas*, p. 152. Stanley Stein, *Vassouras: A Brazilian Coffee County, 1850-1900* (Cambridge, Mass., 1957). Affonso de E. Taunay, *Historia do cafe no Brasil* (15 vols., Rio de Janeiro, 1939-1943), especially vols. 3-5.

[34] Herbert S. Klein, "The Colored Freedmen in Brazilian Slave Society," *Journal of Social History*, 3 (Fall 1969): 35-36.

of 1812, the key Gulf Coast states of Alabama, Mississippi, and Louisiana were opened up to cotton, and by the 1820s the cotton kingdom of the South was in full operation. By 1840, the total Afro-American population of the United States was 2,800,000 persons, 92 percent of whom lived in the southern states. Of these, almost half a million inhabited the Alabama-Mississippi region.

In the next two decades, as slavery further expanded into the new southwestern states, the center of the black North American population, which by then stood at 4,400,000 persons, shifted westward. By 1860 the South Atlantic seaboard states held less than half of the total slave labor force in North America, and the eastern south-central states—Arkansas, Louisiana, Oklahoma, and Texas—held just under one-fourth of the total slave population. Thus the shift was from the upper south toward the deep south, and the southwest. Though Virginia was still the largest slave state in 1860, with a population of some 548,000 slaves, the geographical center of the black population was now located in northwestern Georgia, well over four hundred miles to the southwest of its center in Virginia in 1790.

In all of continental America except the United States, however, slavery was on the decline by the 19th century. Late in the 18th century mining went into a serious depression in Peru, Mexico, and the Colombia-Venezuelan regions, thereby eliminating a major market for slave labor. At the same time such thriving plantation crops as indigo, which was the major export crop of Guatemala, began to lose ground in the face of serious competition from artificial dyes in Europe. To the changing resources and changing market conditions was finally added the holocaust of civil war. In Venezuela, to take an extreme example, the plantations, though they suffered because of the decline in the market for indigo, continued to absorb large numbers of slaves until 1810. But the long-drawn-out wars for independence from Spain, which began in 1810 and lasted over a decade, brought the wholesale arming and freeing of slaves as well as the devastation of the plantation areas. As a result, by 1825 there were half as many slaves in the country as there had been just fifteen years earlier, when the struggle for independence had begun.[35] In peripheral

[35] Federico Brito Figueroa, *Ensayos de historia social venezolana* (Cara-

18

slave regions such as Ecuador, Uruguay, and Colombia, the course of events was much the same.[36] Thus by the 1820s, slavery, although it was still legal in most areas of South America, had become virtually obsolete, and the vast majority of the colored population were freedmen.[37] With several forces working against it—the decline of plantation agriculture, the chaos of war, and the fervent liberalism of the independence period in general—slavery became a moribund institution in continental Spanish America by early in the 19th century.

Indeed, by the 1830s, on the eve of British abolition, slavery was a vital institution only in the West Indies, Brazil, and the United States, and it was shortly to expire in the British and French islands. Also by this time, the trans-Atlantic slave trade

---

cas, 1960), pp. 254-55. Whereas there were an estimated 87,000 slaves in Venezuela in 1810, only 49,782 remained after the wars of independence (*ibid.*, p. 238. Federico Brito Figueroa, *La estructura social y demográfica de Venezuela colonial* [Caracas, 1961], p. 58). However, it should be pointed out that a succession of slave rebellions and an extremely serious problem with the *cimarrones*, the runaway slaves, had begun to undermine the Venezuelan slave regime even before independence was declared (see Miguel Acosta Saignes, *La vida de los esclavos negros en Venezuela* [Caracas, 1967], pp. 297ff.). Further, the indigo crisis at the end of the 18th century had disrupted plantation society and contributed to the formation of a very large free colored class—by 1800, there were something like 407,000 free mulattoes and 33,362 free Negroes in Venezuela (Brito, *La estructura social*, p. 58); also see John V. Lombardi, *The Decline and Abolition of Negro Slavery in Venezuela, 1820-1854* (Westport, Conn., 1971).

[36] The crisis of the slave regime in Colombia toward the end of the 18th century is described in Jaime Jaramillo Uribe, "Esclavos y señores en la sociedad colombiana del siglo xviii," *Anuario Colombiano de Historia Social y de la Cultura* 1 (1963): 50-55.

[37] Though data on the free colored population of Spanish America toward the end of the 18th century is scarce, the rapid rise in the number of freedmen is clearly documented for many areas. In Montevideo, Uruguay, in 1778, there were already 594 freedmen in a total colored population of 1,304; by 1781, the number of freedmen had risen to 1,103 (Ildefonso Pereda Valdes, *El negro en el Uruguay, pasado y presente* [Montevideo, 1965], p. 125). In the marginal area of Puerto Rico, the free colored already outnumbered the slaves 16,414 to 13,333 by 1802 (Luiz M. Diaz Solar, *Historia de la esclavitud negra en Puerto Rico, 1493-1890* [Madrid, 1953], p. 110). And in the bishopric of Caracas, Venezeula, in the first decade of the 19th century, there were 163,275 free mulattoes, or *pardos*, and 34,463 free Negroes, compared to 64,462 slaves. The free colored population was in fact the largest single racial grouping in the region, with whites numbering 108,920 and Indians 56,083. John V. Lombardi, *People and Places in Colonial Venezuela* (Bloomington, 1976), p. 132.

had almost ceased to operate in all areas except Cuba and Brazil. To these two areas, however, the slave ships would bring the largest annual number of Africans in their history, until the close of the Brazilian trade in 1850 and the Cuban trade a decade later. Alone among the major slave states in the Western Hemisphere during the 19th century, the United States did not engage in an international slave trade. In 1808 the international trade was effectively terminated, and the result was the full-scale development of an internal slave trade unmatched in any other New World society.[38]

Even in Cuba and Brazil, where slavery flourished long after it had ceased to exist in most parts of the New World, it had begun to lose its foothold by the middle decades of the 19th century. Especially in Cuba, there was a general awareness of the inevitable coming of abolition well before the final decrees of the 1880s. As early as the 1840s Cuban planters began to import alternative groups of laborers, including Yucatecan Indians and Chinese coolies, and by the 1860s over one hundred thousand East Asians had been introduced into the island, not to mention other labor groups. In addition, the planters began to shift from plantation slavery to various forms of sharecropping and other agricultural labor systems, especially after the North American Civil War. By the end of the first Ten Years War (1868-1878), Cuba's first attempt to win independence, slavery was no longer the dominant labor system it had been, and freedmen made up the majority of the Black population.[39]

Although Brazilian sugar and coffee planters refused to experiment with nonslave labor until the late 1870s, even in Brazil slavery was fading by the 1850s. By this time at least 50 percent of the total colored population were freedmen, and when the first national census was taken in 1872, over 70 percent of the colored

[38] On the history of U.S. slave trade legislation, see W.E.B. Du Bois, *The Suppression of the African Slave Trade to the United States of America, 1638-1870* (Cambridge, Mass., 1896). For the development of the internal slave trade, see Frederic Bancroft, *Slave Trading in the Old South* (New York, 1931), while the most complete modern assessment is by Lawrence J. Kotlikoff, "Towards a Quantitative Description of the New Orleans Slave Market" (University of Chicago, Workshop in Economic History, Report #7475-21, 1975).

[39] Klein, *Slavery in the Americas*, Chapters 7, 9; and Franklin Knight, *Slave Society in Cuba During the Nineteenth Century* (Madison, 1970).

population of 5,700,000 were free.[40] The coffee planters were the last to give up their slaves, but they too were finally forced to concede defeat; in the 1880s they turned to massive Italian immigration to solve their labor problems. During the last years of slavery in Brazil, the Brazilian army and the urban population encouraged the mass defection of slaves. The planters could put up no effective resistance to abolition when it finally came in 1888.[41]

Like the Brazilian coffee planters, slave owners in the United States tried to resist the change of their labor force from a slave status to a free status. Southern planters made no attempts to set up sharecropping systems, to employ free labor, or to encourage the immigration of European or Asian contract labor. Here slavery was a profitable enterprise to the end, and since the Cuban and Brazilian slave empires had survived the French and English manumission of slaves in the first half of the century, the Southerners felt no external threat to their slave labor system. It was only with the effective rise of abolitionism within the United States which terminated in the Civil War, that the slave regime was finally destroyed. When North American slavery was terminated in 1865, the end of the regimes in Cuba and Brazil was inevitable.

The demise of these great slave regimes in the last half of the 19th century did not seriously affect the settlement patterns of black Americans anywhere in the New World. In no state did abolition bring the payment of reparations to the former slaves. With neither land nor capital and with no way of acquiring new skills, the ex-slaves were forced into sharecropping or debt-peonage systems and thus remained bound to the old plantation economies. For the most part, the freed black laborers remained on their plantations or in their old plantation regions. "Free" sugar, cotton, and, to a lesser extent, coffee were now produced throughout the New World by the same black workers as before abolition. Thus, until well into the 20th century, the black settle-

[40] Klein, "The Colored Freedmen," p. 36; also see Peter L. Eisenberg, *The Sugar Industry in Pernambuco, 1840-1910* (Berkeley, 1974), chapter VII.

[41] Robert Brent Toplin, *The Abolition of Slavery in Brazil* (New York, 1972); and Robert Conrad, *The Destruction of Brazilian Slavery, 1850-1888* (Berkeley, 1972).

ment patterns that emerged at the height of the slave trade during the 18th and 19th centuries persisted, and major black belts remained in all the old plantation areas. Not surprisingly, it would take revolution, industrialization, and the end of large-scale European immigration finally to break up these pre-abolition concentrations of black population.

Chapter Two

The Portuguese Slave Trade from Angola in the 18th Century

Of all the major Atlantic slave trades, the South Atlantic migration of Africans from the Congo and Angola to Brazil has been the least studied. Until recently only a few attempts were made even to estimate its volume and direction, let alone to study its commercial organization or the demographic structure and mortality experience of the slaves transported. While these latter subjects received only scant attention in the other trades, which have been moderately explored, the literature reveals almost nothing about the Portuguese slave trade. The important monographs of Verger, Carreira, and Birmingham finally opened a broader perspective on the, until then, little understood processes that moved some 3.5 million Africans into Portuguese America. The work by Verger on the Benin-Bahian connection, the detailed study by Carreira of the slave trade carried out in the mid-18th century by the Pombaline Monopoly companies to the Northeast of Brazil and the history of the Portuguese operations in Angola by Birmingham, all provided a firm comparative and analytical base for understanding the dynamics of the South Atlantic Slave Trade. But these studies only partially analyzed the vast quantity of archival material that was available on this subject.

Financial and personal commercial records that allow the trade to be analyzed in a systematic quantitative fashion for the first time may be found in the archives of Brazil and Portugal. Long runs of shipping lists have also been discovered, which include export and import naval lists from Angola and Brazil, and the detailed shipping news in the Rio de Janeiro newspapers of the 19th century. All of these sources have been combined here to provide the information on the Portuguese and Brazilian trades.

This chapter, the first of four on the Africa-Brazil trade, is designed to show the outlines of this trade from a number of perspectives. First of all, it explores archival records to obtain figures for the total volume of the trade by year from the two major ports of Luanda and Benguela in the 18th century. Next, the direction of this Angolan trade is determined from the leading Brazilian ports of entry, with attempts to assess the carrying capacity of the vessels employed in the trade, and to measure the effects of year, month, and season on the flow of persons. The age and sex composition of the transported Africans is then considered, along with the changes in these characteristics that may have occurred over time. Next, the commercial organization of the trade is analyzed on the basis of detailed records of a leading 18th-century Luanda merchant as well as the material drawn from the Pombaline Company archives by Carreira for the study of the commercial arrangements of the Companies. Finally, detailed consideration is given to the nature of the shipping itself, the types of vessels employed and the frequency with which slaving voyages were made.

In the following three chapters (3, 4, and 5), the themes developed in this study of the 18th-century trade from Angola are put into the perspective of the trade coming into Rio de Janeiro in the late 18th and early 19th centuries. Here, two very large samples of ships from different sources (naval lists and newspaper reports) are used to analyze the movement of Africans into Rio de Janeiro—the largest importing port of Brazil—the carrying capacity of the arriving ships, their origins from the different parts of Africa, and the response of the trade to seasonal variations. But even more significantly, the importing records for Rio de Janeiro can be used to examine the process of mortality within the "Middle Passage." Thus the two chapters (3 and 4) concern themselves with analyzing the mortality experience of the Africans arriving in Rio de Janeiro and how it differed by port of origin, time of arrival, and the period in which the trade occurred, as well as by the nature of the commercial organization within Brazil.

These chapters thus concentrate on the basic demographic commercial and organizational structure of the Brazilian slave trade as seen from its two major centers, Angola in Africa and Rio de Janeiro in Brazil. The reason for selecting Angola for study is based on the primacy it achieved as Portugal's chief source of slaves for the Atlantic slave trade. Angola also provides the most complete materials currently available for any region of Portuguese Africa.

From the early decades of the 16th century until the middle of the 19th, Angola produced a steady supply of African slaves. This enormous human migration was unique by slave trade standards both for the long-term stability in numbers and the almost exclusive monopoly maintained over this trade by Portugal. Although the Loango coast remained a free trade area for most of this period, the dominant trade of Angola was under Portuguese control, and a majority of the forced migration went to Brazil. The Dutch, of course, did temporarily seize Angola from the Portuguese in the early 17th century, but, even then, the trade continued to flow into the ports of Brazil.[1]

By the 18th century, the boom in the gold fields of central Brazil brought even further demands for slave labor from African sources and Angola, as well as the traditional sources on the Upper and Lower Guinean coast supplied them. If the estimates reported by Curtin are accepted, then Angola accounted for 70 percent of the Brazilian-bound slaves.[2] Within the Angolan region itself, the primary exporting center until 1800 remained Luanda. From early in the 16th century and until well into the 18th, Luanda overwhelmingly dominated the trade.[3] But Luan-

---

[1] Good surveys of this area and its economic history are Phyllis M. Martin, *The External Trade of the Loango Coast, 1576-1870* (Oxford, 1972), and David Birmingham, *Trade and Conflict in Angola: the Mbundu and their Neighbors under the Influence of the Portuguese, 1483-1790* (Oxford, 1966).

[2] Curtin has used earlier sources to estimate Portuguese slave purchases from the West African coast at 611,000 between 1701 and 1800. Portuguese transport of slaves from Angola during this same period were over double that, or 1,414,500, thus representing 70 percent of the total slaves shipped. As for Angola's relationship to the total volume of the slave trade, its 1.4 million represented 26 percent of total Africans who were forced to migrate by all nations in the 18th century. These estimates are taken from Philip D. Curtin, *The Atlantic Slave Trade, A Census* (Madison: University of Wisconsin Press, 1969), p. 211, table 63.

[3] While the port of Luanda was not colonized by the Portuguese until 1575, slave trading in the region was already a fully developed system in the first half of the century. With effective occupation, and the keeping of more exact records, as well as formal contracts, it would appear that departures for the next century may have gone from 5,000 to 10,000 per annum, though the reliability of these estimates is questionable. Edmundo Correia Lopes, *A escravatura (subsidios para a sua historia)* (Lisbon, 1944), pp. 85-87.

da's supremacy was beginning to be challenged by the end of the period by the previously minor port of Benguela. Benguelan trade had been quite small until the middle decades of the century, when between 1,000 and 2,000 slaves per annum began leaving its shores. After 1760, however, its participation expanded greatly, and by the 1780s accounted for one quarter of the trade, a percentage it would maintain until the end of the century.[4] As for the period from 1741 to 1780 (see table 2.1), Luanda itself accounted for 69 percent of the total Portuguese slave exports from Angola. Cabinda, the third leading slaving zone of Angola, where French, British, and Dutch, as well as Portuguese slavers, traded, was a free trade area until the end of the century.[5]

[4] While port registers for neither city are available for all years in the 1790s (see Appendix Tables A.2 and A.3) a rough idea of slave migrations can be obtained from Rio de Janeiro port registers. Since Rio de Janeiro accounted for over half of the exports in this period, its figures can be considered a reasonable reflection of trade conditions. Thus in the period 1795-1800, Benguela accounted for 38,990 slaves, or 43 percent out of a total of 90,329 shipped from Angola to that port. See Herbert S. Klein, "The Trade in African Slaves to Rio de Janeiro, 1795-1811; estimates of mortality and patterns of voyages," *Journal of African History*, x, No. 4 (1969), p. 545. It would seem that by the first decade of the 19th century, Benguela probably came close to supplying half of the total Africans from the region, since its total share of the trade into Rio de Janeiro from 1795 to 1811 was 50 percent. See below Table 3.2. For further details on the changing roles of the Angolan ports, see Joseph C. Miller, "Legal Portuguese Slaving from Angola: Some Preliminary Indications of Volume and Direction, 1760-1830," *Revue française d'Histoire d'Outre-Mer*, LXII, Nos. 226-227 (1975), pp. 135-163.

[5] The Portuguese tried to settle Cabinda permanently several times, and even succeeded in establishing a fort there in 1783, but it was destroyed by the French a year later. For the details of the Portuguese expedition of the 1780s see the initial exploration report of Antonio Maximo de Souza Marques in *AHU*, Angola, caixa 37, report dated 16 March 1780. On the setting up of the fort, see the letters of the Governor at Luanda to the Crown in 1783 in *AHU*, Angola, cx. 38, letters dated 10 and 11 August 1783. This apparently was not the first such settlement attempt by the Portuguese, according to Grandpré, and the French, when they destroyed the fort built in 1783, did not replace it with one of their own. Luis O'Hier Grandpré, *Voyage à la côte occidentale d'Afrique fait dans les années 1786 et 1787* (2 vols.; Paris, 1801), i, 31-32. By the second decade of the 19th century, however, the Portuguese must have more firmly established themselves at Cabinda, for in both 1814-1815 and 1817-1818 the port registers of Luanda list a sizeable number of vessels that temporarily stopped at Luanda on their way from Brazil to Cabinda. The figure was 9 ships in 1814, 3 in 1815, 4 in 1817, and 11 in 1818. *AHU*, Angola, cx. 62, 31 January 1815; and cx. 64, 31 January 1816; cx. 65, 14 January 1818; cx. 66, n.d. for 1818 report.

Table 2.1
Estimates of African Slave Movements from Angola in the 18th Century[a]

Decades	Luanda	Benguela	Total: Angola	Curtin's Estimates
1701-1710	...	...	...	70,000
1711-1720	58,841	...	...	55,300
1721-1730	73,488	...	...	67,100
1731-1740	98,632	17,035	115,667	109,300
1741-1750	106,575	12,796	119,371	130,100
1751-1760	107,697	23,709	131,406	130,100
1761-1770	82,842	49,465	132,307	123,500
1771-1780	97,533	54,732	152,265	131,500
1781-1790	104,429	64,106	168,535	153,900
1791-1800	103,616	74,908	178,524	168,000

[a]If no slave numbers were given for a specific year, then I used the highest figure for any year within the decade as a substitute. Using this high estimate means that these decennial figures are somewhat overstated. This bias, however, offsets the possible bias due to the fact that official figures may have underestimated total slave movements because they were tax records. If the data were provided for adults only, an estimate for children of 6 percent for Luanda and 3 percent for Benguela was added.

Source: See table 2.2 and appendix tables A.2 and A.3 for sources for Luanda and Benguela figures. For missing years for Luanda in 1770, 1772, 1774, and 1775, I have relied on David Birmingham, *Trade and Conflict in Angola* ... (Oxford, 1966), p. 155. The Curtin estimates are found in Philip D. Curtin, *The Atlantic Slave Trade, A Census* (Madison, 1969), p. 207, table 62.

Although the relative importance of Benguela and Cabinda would change over time, the Luanda supplies of slave migrants remained relatively stable through most of the 18th century, ranging from 7,000 to 10,000 slaves per annum (see table 2.1). Thus the detailed annual shipping statistics for Luanda preserved in the AHU for some 27 non-consecutive years between 1723 and 1771 represent a fortuitous sample whose analysis provides a comprehensive survey of the basic features of the 18th-century Luanda trade. The sample also overlaps the period of temporary participation in the slave trade by the Pomboline monopoly trading companies.

During the period for which these detailed annual shipping records are available, there appeared no overall change in the numbers of slaves carried per vessel, or in the total volume of the migration, though annual rates tended to fluctuate (see table 2.2). The average number of slaves carried in this period, some 396

Table 2.2
Number of Slaves Shipped from Luanda, 1723-1771

Year	No. of Ships	No. of Adults	Total Slaves (Adults & Children)
1723	18	6,704	. . .
1724	17	6,108	. . .
1725	22	6,726	. . .
1726	22	8,321	8,440
1727	20	7,539	7,633
1728	21	8,418	8,532
1731	16	5,715	5,808
1734	25	8,713	10,109
1738	19	7,623	8,810
1740	22	8,075	8,484
1741	23	8,268	9,158
1742	24	10,207	10,591
1744	20	8,256	8,848
1747	25	8,328	9,869
1748	30	10,815	11,810
1749	25	8,895	9,776
1758	24	9,799	9,938
1762	22	8,268	8,415
1763	21	7,525	7,634
1764	18	7,500	7,648
1765	27	10,394	10,672
1766	25	9,237	9,420
1767	26	9,228	9,318
1769	17	5,651	5,733
1771	21	7,591	. . .
TOTALS	550	203,904	(186,646)[a]
Av. slaves per ship		371	396
St. Dev.		109	111

[a]The total number of ships for adult and children slaves was 471.

Sources: For 1723-1724 see original tables (or *mappas*) in AHU, Angola, caixa 16; for 1725-1727 see *ibid.*, cx. 17; 1728 in cx. 18; 1731 in cx. 19; 1734 in cx. 21; 1740, 1743, and 1744 in cx. 23; 1741 in cx. 22; 1747-1748 in cx. 24; 1749 in cx. 25; 1758 in cx. 27; 1762 in cx. 29; 1763-1764 in cx. 30; 1765-1766 in cx. 31; 1769 in cx. 32; 1771 in cx. 33; and 1767 in AHU, Angola, *maço* 9.

persons per vessel, seems to have been close to the norm achieved by some of the other major European powers operating off the Angolan and Loangan coasts in this period. Thus the Nantes slave traders averaged 403 persons per vessel in some 115 voyages to this region in the years 1711-1777 (see below table 8.1).

But this mid-18th century norm seems to have changed significantly by the end of the century. Thus Portuguese slave traders
leaving Angola for Rio de Janeiro in the last decade of the 18th
century and the first decade of the 19th carried on an average 454
persons per voyage from Luanda (see below, Table 3.2). Since
there are unfortunately no direct tonnage figures available for
any of the Portuguese slave trades, it is difficult to determine if
this rise in numbers was due to an increased capacity (i.e., tonnage) of the slave ships used, or if it was due to a higher concentration of slaves per ton on the existing vessels. That the former factor was most probably the case can be argued fairly
strongly from two sets of evidence. It will be seen that in all
the trades for which tonnage is available, there was a reorgani-
zation of shipping in the 18th century, which appeared to elim-
inate a large number of inefficient tonnage categories from the
trade.[6] But even more striking is the available evidence on legal
carrying capacity. Unique among all the trades, the Portuguese
as early as the 17th century had decreed formal restrictions on
the ratio of slaves to tons to be used in the Atlantic slave trade.
Such a procedure, in fact, formed a model for the British at the
end of the 18th century when they began to legislate restrictions
on slave-carrying capacities of ships. By the law of 1684 the
Crown determined that each vessel was to have its capacity to
carry slaves (or *arqueação*) recorded in its registration papers.
This capacity figure, involving different measures for different
areas of the vessel, worked out to between 2.5 and 3.5 slaves per
ton, depending on the construction of the ship.[7] The following

---

[6] See below, Chapter 7.

[7] According to the 1684 decree, which was printed and is to be found in
several collections of documents in the *AHU*, the rule was that (according
to Chapter 6): "If it is a decked ship in which there are portholes through
which the Negroes can easily receive the necessary fresh air, then capacity
below decks should be 7 adults (*cabeças*) for every two tons; not having
said portholes, the capacity should be only 5 slaves per two tons below
decks." It also allowed that for either type of ship, they could carry another
5 slaves per ton above deck. The law also provided detailed listings of the
type and quantity of food and water to be carried by the slaver in order to
provide three meals per day per slave. Provisions for housing sick slaves
apart from the rest and detailed registration by port officials for all of these
provisions were also required. See Lei 3, 18 March 1684, in *AHU*, Angola,
cx. 10. This ship's capacity law remained in effect throughout the 18th
century, and was only changed by the decree (*alvará*) of November 24,
1813, which changed the tonnage to a uniform listing of 5 slaves per

table gives the breakdown of the *arqueação* and number of slaves actually carried in both the early and late 18th-century Luanda trades.

Table 2.3

The Legal Capacity of the Ships and the Number of Slaves Actually Carried in the Portuguese Slave Trade from Luanda, 1762-1765, to Rio de Janeiro, 1795-1817

Legal Capacity by Range of Slaves Permitted	Total Legal Capacity	No. of Ships	Total Actually Carried	Percentage of Legal Capacity Achieved
1. *Luanda*				
200-299	3,286	13	3,270	99.4[a]
300-399	9,220	27	9,274	100.4
400-499	9,459	22	9,067	95.8
500-599	8,821	17	7,846	88.9
600 & above	6,252	9	5,220	83.5
TOTALS	*37,038*	*88*	*34,677*	*95.2*
2. *Rio de Janeiro*				
50-199	648	5	649	100.2
200-299	1,416	6	1,416	100.0
300-399	13,202	36	13,333	101.0
400-499	59,760	132	58,092	97.2
500-599	71,385	132	70,532	98.8
600-699	15,375	24	14,982	97.5
700-799	14,896	20	13,154	88.3
800 & above	3,465	4	2,848	82.2
TOTALS	*180,147*	*359*	*175,006*	*97.6*

[a]These percentages are averages of individual ships.

Source: Same as table 2.2 and ANRJ, Codice 242.

Using these capacity figures to determine the patterns of carrying slaves, we estimate that there was little difference between the early and late 18th-century Luanda trades. In both trades, only the smaller vessels reached full capacity (which, it should be stressed, was generous in the extreme to the ship owners), and overall the ships came in with below the numbers allowed for by law. In both cases, the larger the capacity, the less likely were the ships to carry their full complement of slaves. Although this

---

two tons. See the typical post-1813 slave ship's registration papers in *AHU*, Angola, maço 14 "Passaportes."

evidence is still indirect, the figures for capacity used here as a proxy for tonnage would seem to support the argument that it was probably increasing ship's capacity in terms of the use of larger vessels, rather than changes in crowding slaves, which determined the rise in the number of slaves carried per vessel at the end of the century. In fact, slaves-per-ton ratios probably declined somewhat during the century, since the smaller vessels that were being abandoned by the end of the century were those most likely to have the very highest ratios of slaves to tons. This phenomenon would be duplicated in all trades in which tonnage figures were provided. As will be seen in analyzing the French and English trades, the ratio of slaves per ton constantly declined as tonnage increased.

Given these universally discovered trends in carrying slaves, it can be assumed that the numbers provided by ship's captains as to the slaves actually carried are reasonably accurate even if subject to some falsification for tax or other purposes. The legal capacity figure, however, was invariably accurate, since it was a permanent part of the ship's legal papers. If the average of 421 persons legally capable of being carried is accepted as valid for these 88 ships, and the 2.5 to 3.5 slaves-per-ton ratios for below-deck capacity allowed for by Portuguese law are used, then it is evident that the average tonnage of early 18th-century Portuguese ships was between 120 and 168 tons. This figure seems to be reasonably close to known vessel tonnage in the 18th-century English trade,[8] though of course tonnage measures differed among the nations of Europe in this period.[9] Using this same formula for the 359 ships whose capacity is given for the late

[8] The modal tonnage of all British slave trades—except that to Virginia— was from 100-149 tons (see below, table 7.9). Also, it has been estimated that the average tonnage of all English shipping engaged in the Atlantic trade from Europe to North America in the mid-18th century was less than 150 tons per vessel. Douglass C. North, "Sources of Productivity Change in Ocean Shipping, 1600-1850," *The Journal of Political Economy*, LXXVI, no. 5 (Sept./Oct. 1968), p. 958.

[9] On the comparative differences between Italian, Spanish, French, Dutch, and English tonnage measures of this period, see Frederic C. Lane, "Tonnages, Medieval and Modern," *The Economic History Review*, 2d Series, XVII, no. 2 (1964), pp. 213-233. It would appear that the Atlantic shippers were relatively close to each other when using the tonnage measure (which approximated 1 metric ton burden), though differences in internal measuring standards could lead to wide variation by ports, ships, and designers.

18th and early 19th century, Luanda to Rio de Janeiro trade shows that the range had shifted upwards to a potential spread of 144 to 201 tons.

The sample mid-century data, when analyzed in terms of the direction of the trade, support all previous assumptions about the intake of the Brazilian ports. Rio de Janeiro accounted for over 50 percent of the total slaves shipped from Angola in the period 1723-1771 (see table 2.4). Together with Bahia, Rio de Janeiro

Table 2.4
Adult Slaves Shipped from Luanda, by Port of Destination, 1723-1771

Brazilian Port	No. of Adults	No. of Ships
Rio de Janeiro	104,170	282
Bahia	55,696	158
Pernambuco	37,092	95
Maranhão	2,570	5
Pará	2,161	4
Colonia de Sacramento	1,569	4
Santos	474	1
Unknown	172	1
TOTALS	*203,904*	*550*

Source: Same as table 2.2.

handled over two-thirds of the mid-century trade. Pernambuco, Maranhão and Pará received a fourth of the trade, due to the deliberate encouragement of the two Pombaline companies (the Companhia Geral do Graõ-Pará e Maranhão, and the Companhia Geral de Pernambuco e Paraíba). With the abolition of the trading monopolies, starting in the 1770s, these centers seem to have expanded their trade to Luanda and by the early decades of the 19th century they (above all, Recife in Pernambuco) had increased their share in the Angolan slave trade.[10] It should also

[10] In the total slave exports for the eight years of 1812, 1815, 1817, 1822-1826, for which surviving records provide ports of destination, Pernambuco, Maranhão, and Pará increased their share to 37 percent of exports. Rio de Janeiro continued to dominate with 54 percent of the total trade, with Bahia suffering a decline to only 6 percent. The rest was taken by southern Brazilian ports. These figures are taken from AHU, Angola, maço 16, and from Manuel Dos Anjos da Silva Rebelo, *Relações entre Angola e Brasil, 1808-1830* (Lisbon, 1970), quadro no. 2, after p. 81.

The Silva Rebelo table has several errors in it, including arithmetic ones, which I have corrected by referring to the originals of several years in the

be stressed that for most of the regions of the Brazilian northeast, the prime source of slaves remained the Guinea coast, with Angola being only a secondary supplier,[11] while, for Rio de Janeiro, the primary supplier remained Angola until the end of the slave trade.

Along with the carrying capacity, volume, and direction of the trade, the ships' registers for mid-18th-century Luanda also gives dates of departure, thus providing materials for determining if there was any seasonal variation in the movement of slaves off the African coast. An important seasonal variation in the number of slaves shipped from Luanda, in fact, does appear, with the months of July through December being the heaviest in terms of the number of persons and number of ships leaving the coast (see table 2.5). When proper allowance for voyage time is made, this approximates the seasonal arrival of slaves into the port of Rio de Janeiro at the end of the 18th century.[12] But whether this seasonal pattern is due to African or American factors is still difficult to determine. If we re-analyze the data in terms of the rainy season in Angola (the heaviest being from mid-February to the end of April), it would appear that this factor did not seriously inhibit the movement of slaves. The rainy season months on aver-

---

AHU. For 1822 he has the Ceará total incorrectly listed; it should be 465. In 1826 the original report lists no shipments to Maranhão and a year-end total of only 11,658. This makes the final total for his table 102,441, instead of 104,630, with 2 slaves shipped to Cabinda in 1822 and therefore not listed.

[11] For the very special trade that developed between Bahia and the Gold and Slave Coasts, see Pierre Verger, *Flux et reflux de la traite des nègres entre le golfe de Bénin et Bahia de todos os santos, du dix-septième au dix-neuvième siècle* (Paris, 1968), especially chapters vi and following. In the 19th century, twice as many ships went to the Guinean coast from Bahia as went to the Angolan area, *ibid.*, pp. 655-57. On the Dutch response to this special trade, see Johannes Postma, "The Dutch Participation in the African Slave Trade: Slaving on the Guinea Coast, 1675-1795" (Ph.D. dissertation, Department of History, Michigan State University, 1970), pp. 90-92, 108, 124-26. For a detailed analysis of the Upper Guinea Coast trade at the end of the century see Jean Mettas, "La traite portugaise en Haute Guinée, 1758-1797: Problèmes et méthodes," *Journal of African History*, vol. xvi, No. 3 (1975).

[12] In the late 18th century, the port of Rio de Janeiro experienced its heaviest volume of slave importations in the months from August to January (see below Table 3.3). While no sailing time figures are available before the 1820s, it can be assumed that the 34 days on average taken by ships sailing from Luanda to Rio de Janeiro (see below, table 4.2) is approximately the same for the 18th century.

Table 2.5
The Number of Adult Slaves Shipped from Luanda,
by Month and Season, 1723-1771

Month & Season	Adults	Ships
1. *Summer*	*47,775*	*129*
December	18,388	47
January	15,284	43
February	14,103	39
2. *Autumn*	*46,038*	*124*
March	15,209	43
April	16,953	44
May	13,876	37
3. *Winter*	*55,178*	*150*
June	12,694	36
July	20,165	54
August	22,319	60
4. *Spring*	*54,741*	*146*
September	17,764	48
October	18,452	48
November	18,525	50
TOTALS	*203,732*	*549*
Av. slaves per ship	371	
St. Dev.	109	

Source: Same as table 2.2.

age saw only 9 percent less slaves leaving Luanda than in the other periods; moreover, the dry season months of May and June were actually the lowest in terms of numbers leaving. Thus while the rainy season can be said to have been of some influence, it does not appear to be the predominant factor. In later chapters that analyze other trades with more extensive available material, it will be argued that it may have been American demand factors, in terms of planters' seasonal labor needs, that most dramatically affected the movement of slaves. What can be said with certainty at this point is that the different volume in the trade by season was not the result of any change in the numbers carried (which did not vary by season) but was due exclusively to the number of ships employed in the trade.[13]

[13] The simple correlation for the number of adults carried per vessel and the season of the year was insignificant at less than +0.01.

As difficult to explain as the seasonal pattern of movements is the number of adults and children participating in the slave trade. The Luanda shipping registers provide important information on the age breakdowns of the African slaves being shipped, but there are problems with the available data. Children, unlike adults, had no consistent migration trends, as the following table indicates. The annual variation could be due to any number of factors. The most obvious possibility is that there were gross errors in counting children. Since infants at the breast (*crias de peito*) went free of any export tax, and children up to a certain height (*crias de pé*) went only half taxed, there might have been a tendency to attempt to place some adults in these categories. This especially would have been the case when there was a problem over the legal capacity of a ship. As one Treasury official of Angola candidly admitted, local officials tended to consider the capacity, or *arqueação* figure, as referring to adults alone.[14] Thus the desire to avoid taxes and/or to avoid action against illegal overcrowding would have led officials consistently to overstate the number of children. The number of children reported shipped to Brazil, however, was quite low. Conversely, this low figure could be due to the lack of serious effort made to record the children since they were unimportant to royal officials in terms of taxation. Officials did not all record their observations in an identical manner, and thus entries often differed from person to person. Also, at various times children were carefully recorded, and at other times ignored, and it is often difficult to determine if no children in a given instance were shipped, or if they were simply not recorded. Thus it is probable that more children were shipped than were recorded by the port officials.

Nevertheless, I am still of the belief that children were not shipped in any large quantities in the slave trade. In the Luanda data, only 6 percent of the 156,638 slaves shipped between 1734 and 1769 were children. In the Benguela listings (see Appendix Table A.3) only 3 percent of the 57,689 slaves shipped between 1738 and 1784 were children. In the Dutch slave trade the number of children under 15 years of age shipped in the 18th century

---

[14] AHU, Angola, cx. 17, letter of Provedor de Fazenda Real (Superintendent of the Royal Treasury) of Luanda to the Crown dated 19 February 1728.

Table 2.6

Children, by Tax Category, Shipped from Luanda, 1726-1769

Year	Taxed Children[a]	Half-Taxed Children [crias de pé]	Untaxed Children at Breast [crias de peito]	Total Children	Total Slaves
1726	...	...	119	...	8,440
1727	...	...	94	...	7,633
1728	...	...	114	...	8,532
1731	...	...	93	...	5,808
1734	...	...	...	1,396	10,109
1738	...	...	...	1,187	8,810
1740	...	311	98	409	8,484
1741	...	736	154	890	9,158
1742	...	249	135	384	10,591
1744	...	426	166	592	8,848
1747	...	1,422	99	1,541	9,869
1748	...	894	101	995	11,810
1749	...	782	99	881	9,776
1758	...	...	...	139	9,938
1762	45	22	80	147	8,415
1763	31	17	61	109	7,634
1764	54	18	76	148	7,648
1765	16	62	200	278	10,672
1766	72	14	97	183	9,420
1767	13	8	69	90	9,318
1769	...	36	46	82	5,733

[a] This seems to have been a special term used only in the decade of the 1760s. Thereafter such children, since they were fully taxed, must have been placed in the adult (or *cabeça*) category.

Source: Same as table 2.2.

was anywhere from 8 percent to 13 percent of the total slaves shipped;[15] while the Pernambuco Company figures indicated children accounted for only 1 percent of the total.[16] Finally, the

[15] In some 56 expeditions financed by the Dutch West Indies Company between 1681 and 1751, the percentage of children under fifteen years of age was only 8 percent, Postma, "The Dutch Slave Trade," pp. 177-178. Postma noted that West India Company officers advised slave captains to buy children only at the last minute before sailing and only if space was left. Postma, *ibid.*, p. 179.

[16] The records of the Companhia Geral de Pernambuco e Paraiba show that of the 49,344 slaves shipped by the Company from Africa between 1761 and 1786, only 508 were listed as children, or only 1 percent. These figures probably do not include infants at the breast (*crias de peito*), which would probably have accounted for another 250 or so children. Even so, this would only bring the total up to 2 percent. António Carreira, *As companhias pom-*

registers for the port of Rio de Janeiro between 1795 and 1811 report the shipping from Africa of only 923 children out of 170,651 Africans, or 0.5 percent.

There are several possible explanations for the low number of children involved in the slave trade. One could be their higher mortality in the "Middle Passage." But an analysis of the Rio de Janeiro data shows that the children suffered less than adults, with their overall mortality at sea being 6.2 percent of those shipped from Africa, as opposed to 9.5 percent for the adults.[17] The question remains, then, why so few children were shipped. Conceivably the costs of purchase and transportation were too high to make such an enterprise profitable to the shippers, or, Africans were reluctant to supply children to the trans-Atlantic slave trade. As will be seen later in trades where sexual breakdowns of the slaves are provided, there is a systematic bias against women in the trade that cannot be explained by planter preference or shipping costs, but seems predominantly due to African restraints on the export of women. Some of these same restraints may have held for children, though transportation costs and low sale prices were obviously important considerations.

While the quantitative data in the AHU give some rough ideas of the general volume, direction, and components of the trade, other documents available in Lisbon's archives provide a glimpse into the economic underpinnings of this slave migration. In this aspect, the Portuguese differed markedly from the other major European traders along the western coasts of Africa. Instead of establishing precarious shoreline forts and trading posts, or later developing a primarily moving boat trade and leaving the interior trading and even coastal gathering of slaves to local African and mulatto traders, the Portuguese successfully attempted a different approach. They established from the beginning thriving European urban settlements to control the movement of slaves to the coast and even tried to dominate the interior sources for slaves. Thus Luanda and Benguela became important European towns in Africa and the mixed Portuguese-African traders, the *pombeiros*, became the primary movers of slaves from the interior

---

balinas de navegacão, comercio e tráfico de escravos entre a costa africana e o nordeste brasileiro (Porto, 1969), p. 261.

[17] These figures are calculated from data in the ANRJ, Policia, Codice 242.

to the coast. The Portuguese merchants of Luanda were also unique by European standards in that they controlled the movement of slaves not only long before their arrival on the coast, but long after their departure from Africa as well. So deeply involved were the Portuguese in local trade that they also played an active role in traditional African commerce, selling everything from salt and palm cloth to sea shells in the interior regions, along with the traditional European- and American-produced goods.[18]

This very unusual role as an African centered European colony also had a significant impact on the commercial organization of the Portuguese Atlantic slave trade. For unlike other European merchants, resident Portuguese traders played a significant and even a leading role in financing the movement of Africans from their home in Africa to the ports of America. In fact, a significant percentage of the slaves who were ultimately sold in America were owned by Luanda merchants. As is evident from the surviving commercial papers of the mid-18th century Luanda merchant, Captain João Xavier de Proença e Sylva, an important fraction of the slaves shipped from Angola were shipped to the account of Angolan merchants.[19] Proença e Sylva himself shipped only a few slaves with each voyage, but other merchants shipped a dozen or more, either for themselves or for the account of other Luandans. Thus, the *Galera* "Santo Antonio, Santa Anna e Almas," which left Luanda on 26 October 1727 and landed in Bahia a short time later, listed 90 owners of the 385 adults and 77 children who were shipped. This would mean an average of 5 slaves per owner. Actually the captain of the vessel, João de Tavora, was listed, along with an undesigned Company ("Capitão João de Tavora, e Companhia") as owner of 101 adults and 22 children, and the captain alone possessed another 10 adults on his own account, exclusive of the company. Presumably the captain and his company represented Bahian merchant and planter capital, which both owned the vessel and probably also purchased part of the cargo on its own account. If these 133 slaves are subtracted, the other 88 owners of slaves, all of whom appear to be residents of Luanda, would thus have averaged almost 4 slaves per owner.[20]

[18] Martin, *The External Trade*, chapter ii.
[19] These accounts are found in BNL, Colecção Pombalina, Codice 617.
[20] AHU, Bahia, cx. 37, document dated 18 December 1727.

How representative this particular voyage was of the whole 18th-century trade is impossible to say. As of the moment no other such detailed listings of owners of slaves aboard a slave vessel have come to light. From the accounts of Captain Proença e Sylva, however, some corroborative evidence to support some of the data is available. Captain Proença Sylva was involved in the trade at a much later date, his papers covering the late 1750s and early 1760s. As a resident of Luanda he shipped a large number of slaves from that port to Brazil, both on his own account and for the account of other Luandans. Though he obviously had a thriving trade, most of his shipments were in lots of only a few slaves. On the average he sent 1 or 2 slaves per vessel, his biggest recorded shipment being 7 slaves aboard one *galera* that went to Rio de Janeiro in 1762.[21]

Not only were the shipments quite small, but it appears that the captain retained ownership of the slaves from the time they were purchased in the interior of Africa to their final sale to a Brazilian planter. Thus he was required to pay not only the initial purchase price and transportation to the coast, but the sea transportation and the maintenance of the slaves in Brazil as well. He thus paid the costs of clothing the slaves in new Brazilian clothes, as well as medical expenses, and even funeral expenses, should the slave die before the sale. Finally he was required to pay his factor in the Brazilian city a sales commission, and to pay for the purchase of a letter of credit so as to remit his profits back to either Luanda or to his representative in Lisbon.[22]

[21] BNL, Colecção Pombalina, Codice 617, folio 222.

[22] To give some idea of the shipping and maintenance costs to Captain Proença e Sylva, his records note that in October of 1759 he was charged for export taxes, maintenance, passage, branding, and registration fees for shipping one slave to Recife, the sum of 16$480, with 8$000 of that figure due to transportation charges (*ibid.*, folio 174). This must have been a fairly standard set of charges, for another male adult slave he sent to Recife in February of that year also cost him 16$480 to ship to his factor in that city. In addition, the slave apparently sickened on his arrival, and medical costs added another 2$690 in expenses before he could be sold. The final sale price was 70$000 (*ibid.*, folio 114). Also in 1759 he shipped to Pernambuco another 5 slaves. Of these, 1 died at sea and another 2 were shipped as his personal property to a relative in Lisbon. This left 2 young female slaves, whom he sold for 120$000. His total costs for shipping the 5 slaves and maintaining them until their sale or shipment to Portugal was 78$955. The charge for maintaining a slave in Recife while waiting for shipment to Portugal was 60 reis per diem, which was the same charge he experienced for maintaining slaves in Rio de Janeiro until they were sold

Since I could not obtain the costs to Captain Proença e Sylva of his purchases in Portugal and Angola of goods that he used to buy slaves in the interior, nor do I have any idea of the costs to him of employing *pombeiros* and/or their commission, and finally the varying costs to him of maintaining the slaves in Luanda until the arrival of a slave ship, I cannot estimate net profits. What the captain's papers do reveal is that he had a trusted network of traders in the two major Brazilian ports, Rio de Janeiro and Bahia, and that his commercial connections also extended to Portugal. Thus, while Portugal was not a shipping base for the trade, as was England or France, it played an important role in financing the trade.[23] It would also appear that from time to time ships were built and outfitted in Portugal for the African slave trade, but that once launched they never returned to Portugal, at least from Africa.[24]

---

to local masters (*ibid.*, folios 116v, 222). In January 1762 he shipped 7 slaves to Rio de Janeiro, of which 2 died at sea and 1 after landing. His costs included an average of 14$328 per slave for taxes and transportation (always constant at 8$000 per slave whatever the age and sex), 1$500 per slave for baptism by a priest, 2$120 for medicines for a sick slave, and a sales commission of 6 percent. He sold the 6 surviving slaves for 275$600, with the shipping maintenance and commission costs coming to 131$011 (*ibid.*, folio 222).

[23] In the account papers of Captain Proença e Sylva with his factor in Rio de Janeiro, it is noted that he had bought and sold letters of credit to Brazil over the past several years, many of which seemed to have been sent to Lisbon (*ibid.*, folio 193). A similar pattern of financial activities occurred with the merchant and royal official Antonio Coelho Guerreiro when he was resident in Luanda in the 1680s and early 1690s. He was constantly shipping slaves and ivory to Bahia, either for purchase of tobacco, geribita, and other goods needed in Angola to exchange for slaves, or obtaining letters of credit for Lisbon, which in turn were used to purchase both luxury goods demanded by the resident Portuguese community in Angola and merchandise needed in the slave trade. Coelho Guerreiro also actively engaged in endorsing and discounting letters of exchange, and even provided insurance for risks of sailings for slave captains at rather high premiums. See Virginia Rau, ed., *O "Livro de Rezao" de Antonio Coelho Guerreiro* (Lisbon, 1956: DIAMANG, Publicacoes Culturais, no. 30), pp. 42ff.

[24] In 1795, for example, of the 337 Portuguese vessels that left the harbor of Lisbon (out of a total of 958 ships), only 14 went to Africa, as opposed to 51 that sailed for Brazil. At the same time, of the 348 Portuguese vessels that entered port in that year (out of a total of 1,036 ships), only 2 were listed as coming from Africa, and these 2 were from the Cape Verde Islands. At the same time, 98 were listed as arriving from Brazil. AGM, caixa "Entradas e saidas de Navios, Registro do Porto de Lisboa, 1741-1800," in undated mappa. In the same collection of port registers, there

Finally, Portuguese merchants themselves sometimes traded directly in the slave trade by shipping Portuguese food and textiles or other desired goods to Africa and then purchasing on their own account slaves for shipment to Brazil. Thus the Lisbon merchant Francisco Pinheiro in 1712 sent his cousin on a trip to Luanda and ultimately to Rio de Janeiro, the purpose of which was to sell both supplies and trade goods in Africa and then ship some 50 odd slaves on his own ship to Rio de Janeiro. Pinheiro sent several other smaller groups of slaves across the South Atlantic and also did straight trading in European foodstuffs to the Luanda Portuguese community, even selling them his ships from time to time. But from the extensive records of this one major Lisbon merchant, it would appear that even within the context of his overall trade to both Africa and Brazil, the slave trade *per se* was a relatively minor part of a general commercial trade.[25] If Pinheiro was representative, it would appear that all three merchant communities of Brazil, Luanda, and Lisbon engaged in the slave trade, but that the most active in shipping slaves were the first two, with the latter probably being more important as a supplier of ships, goods, and ultimately credit to enable the direct slave trade to function.

Thus the African slave trade from Angola, at least for the free traders, was primarily a two-way trade, rather than the more common triangular pattern that most of the other European slave-trading nations developed. Because of wind and current conditions in the South Atlantic, it was far too difficult for a ship to sail directly from Angola to Portugal, and even the trip from Brazil took from two to four months. So it was Brazilian-made ships, by and large, and Brazilian crews that maintained the Angolan slave trade. Brazilian-produced goods also formed an important part of the imports for the 2,000 persons who inhabited the town of Luanda in the mid-18th century.[26] The chief imports from

---

is a listing of sailing times for all ships from port of departure. These show that the average length of voyage from Brazil was quite long. In the registers for 1797, for example, of 4 ships that came from Bahia in April to June of that year, the average sailing time was 81 days; the 2 ships coming from Recife, Pernambuco, averaged 73 days; and the 2 ships coming from Rio de Janeiro to Lisbon averaged 109 days.

[25] Luis Lisanti, ed., *Negoçios coloniais* (*uma correspondencia comercial do seculo xviii*) (5 vols.; Brasilia, 1973), i, cdxciv ff.; and iv, 399ff.

[26] Luanda in 1773 had a population of 612 troops and 1,519 civilians. Of

Brazil were alcohol and basic foodstuffs to help feed the Luanda community.[27] It was, above all, alcohol and European and Asian imported cloth that were used by the Luanda merchants in the purchase of slaves in the interior. *Geribita*, a special type of alcoholic beverage, seems to have been a highly prized import in the Angolan hinterland.[28] But these Brazilian goods were only a part of the products used in the interior slave trade, and it seems that many African products, especially salt and palm-cloth, still played a major part in the trade.[29]

---

the troops, 140 were mulattoes and 72 were Negroes, while the civilian town population consisted of 251 whites, 138 free mulattoes, and 147 free Negroes. There were also some 983 slaves, of whom the whites owned 80 percent. *AHU*, Angola cx. 36, documents numbered 19 and 25, both dated 27 March 1773.

[27] In the wheat flour sold in Luanda in 1800 and 1801, for example, Brazilian imported sacks accounted for 22 percent and 19 percent respectively of all wheat flour sold, the rest being locally produced. AHU, Angola cx. 51, 1 April 1801, and cx. 53, 16 June 1802.

[28] In the mid-1780s, for example, the Angolans were importing 1,340 barrels of *geribita* per annum, with the bulk of this production (or 76 percent) coming from Rio de Janeiro. For three-year importation figures (1782-1784) see *AHU*, Angola maço 13, 5 January 1785.

[29] Birmingham, *Trade and Conflict*, p. 138. It would also appear that Brazil was in a deficitory trade relationship with Angola until 1808. Overall, Brazil accounted for only one-fourth of Angolan imports at the end of the 18th century. In the period from 1785-1797, for example, the value of Brazilian imports accounted for only 23% of all goods imported into Angola, and these 1.5 million reis worth of goods covered only 19% of the 6.6 million reis worth of slaves, ivory, and wax imported into Brazil from Angola. For the trade statistics for Angola from 1785-1794, see IHGB, Lata 77, document # 1 "Blança da importação e exportação . . . de Angola"; and for 1795-1797 see BNRJ, Seção de Manuscritos, 15, 3, 33, also entitled "Balanço. . . ." By the early years of the 19th century, this trade balance was changing and after 1808 Brazil as the new center of the empire became the dominant source of all American, European and Asian goods imported into Brazil. Silva Rebelo, *As relações entre Angola e Brasil*, chap. iv. There even appear some years after 1808 in which Angola had a negative balance of trade with Brazil. In 1815, for example, Luanda imported 996.9 million reis worth of goods from Brazil and Portugal (the latter accounting for only 11 million of the total), and exported only 937.5 million reis to Brazil in slaves, wax and ivory. Of the Brazilian imports, 765.9 million reis were accounted for by Rio de Janeiro, 202.7 million by Pernambuco, and 17.1 million by Bahia. Of the exports, 884.8 million reis (or 94%) was accounted for by slave exports, with wax being second at 45.5 million and ivory taking just 7.1 million reis, *AHU*, Angola, cx. 63, report dated 31 January 1816. By value, the most important products imported were textiles, followed by geribita, foodstuffs and tobacco, and gunpowder (which since 1808 was manufactured in the new Royal Powder Factory in Rio de Janeiro). For a detailed evaluation of goods, see Silva Rebelo, *Angola e Brasil*, quadro 3 following p. 179. On

It would also seem apparent from the important role played by Luanda merchants that the actual movement of slaves was closely regulated. Since the merchants could anticipate ships' arrivals, they could control local supplies so that there was little waiting at Luanda itself, which would have been an added cost.[30] Also, given the fact that Portugal remained a neutral during almost the entire 18th century, despite the series of imperial wars, the regularity of shipment also helped to maintain a rather predictable quality to the trade.

Although the bulk of the trade was in the hands of independent merchants, there were other aspects to the trade in which either the government or its representatives took an active part. In the 18th century, for example, the Crown farmed out its taxes on slave exports to private entrepreneurs. Often these men engaged in direct trading themselves, and usually they maintained a monopoly on the small ivory trade leaving Luanda.[31] Until the middle of the 18th century the Crown tended to rent out its taxes and then, as need for more funds arose, it would set up a new tax independent of the already rented ones. These new taxes were collected by royal tax officials, and from all the evidence I have seen so far it appears that the Crown never rented out all of its pre-1758 taxes to a private entrepreneur at any one time. Thus the royal tax officials were always employed, and, while the data are unclear, many of them may have also collected the taxes for the private tax farmer as well.[32] By the middle of the century some four different taxes were being collected on the export of slaves.[33] By this time, even the Crown realized that its tax struc-

---

the Rio de Janeiro gunpowder factory and its exports to Angola, see *ibid.*, pp. 155ff.

[30] Though evidence on this from Luanda is not presently available, data from Benguela would seem to support this assertion. Thus when the *Curveta* "Nossa Senhora de Agua de Lupe, e Bom JESUS dos Navigantes" sailed for Rio de Janeiro on 22 January 1763 it carried slaves purchased on its account as far back as the preceding October, with the bulk being purchased in December. AHU, Angola, cx. 30, document no. 8.

[31] Birmingham, *Trade and Conflict*, pp. 138-139.

[32] For a typical example of such a tax contract, see the printed contract given to Jacinto Dias Braga for the collection of the *novo imposto* (a tax of 1$200 per slave exported) in all the ports of Angola for a six-year period (the typical term of all tax contracts) to begin on 5 January 1742. AHU, Angola, cx. 23, dated 7 September 1740.

[33] These taxes were the *direito real, direito novo, novo imposto,* and *preferencia.*

ture was excessively complex. Thus in 1758 it abolished all the outstanding taxes and instituted a single head tax of 8$700 reis per adult slave (*cabeça*), and 3$400 for every walking child (*crias de pé*) exported from Angola.[34] This tax it also farmed out.[35]

Another area in which the government intervened as an active economic agent in the slave trade had to do with the establishment during the time of Pombal of the monopoly trade companies for Maranhão and Pernambuco. These two companies were set up in 1755 and 1759 respectively and their object was to promote the development of these respective regions.[36] Both companies were given the exclusive rights to import slaves into these Brazilian areas. Of the two companies, the most important as far as Angola was concerned was the Pernambuco & Paraiba Company. Of the grand total of 49,344 slaves this company shipped to Brazil between 1761 and 1786, 41,777 (or 85 percent) came from the port of Luanda.[37] As for the Grão-Pará & Maranhão Company, only 6,235 (or 22 percent) of its total 28,083 slaves came from this same port. The bulk of its slaves (19,666) came from the Upper Guinean ports of Cacheu and Bissau.[38] In the overall trade between 1723 and 1771, the slaves going from

[34] For these decrees see ANTT, Manuscritos Miscellaneos, no. 926, folio 252.

[35] See, for example, the contract given to Domingos Dias de Silva and his associates for the collection of the new unified head tax that was granted for a six-year term beginning on 5 January 1766. The cost to the tax farmer and his associates was the annual payment to the crown of the sum of 88:300$000. Given the estimated 12,000 slaves shipped per annum in the 1760s, this would give the tax farmer a gross income of 104:400$000, for a net profit of 16:100$000. A copy of the contract is in AHU, Angola, cx. 30, dated 6 September 1765. Portuguese currency in the 18th century was expressed in units of *reis*. The dollar sign was the standard sign used to distinguish *milreis*, or units of a thousand *reis* and thus stands where modern usage would put the comma. Finally, there was the *conto* which was equivalent to 1 million reis and was expressed as follows: 1:000$000. The colon stands for the second comma.

[36] The founding charters of the two companies will be found in Carreira, *As companhias pombalinas*, appendix, documents "E" (pp. 313-336) and "H" (pp. 347-372). A contemporary copy of the original charter for the Maranhão Company can be found in Arquivo Geral da Alfandega de Lisboa, Codice 51, libro 1, folios 8-21v. A detailed study of all aspects of the Maranhão Company, in which the slave trade assumed only a minor role, is found in Manuel Nunes Dias, *Fomento e mercantilismo. A companhia geral do Grão Pará e Maranhão (1755-1778)* (2 vols.; Para. 1970).

[37] Carreira, *As companhis pombalinas*, p. 261.

[38] *Ibid.*, p. 91.

Luanda to Pará, Maranhão, and Pernambuco totaled 41,823 persons, or 20 percent of the slaves leaving Luanda in this period. Of this total, the monopoly companies had an extremely important share. With their disappearance the movement of slaves from Luanda to the northern ports of Brazil temporarily declined, though their end as active participants in the trade had little impact on the overall movement of slaves from Angola.[39]

In important respects, the Pombaline monopoly companies operated differently from independent traders. Probably much like the classic French, Dutch, and English African trading companies of the 17th and early 18th century, they tended to operate on a much more restrictive basis, being less responsive than free traders to changing African market conditions. This seems to be reflected in their use of ships in the trade. Whereas the mean sailing for monopoly company ships was between 4 and 5 slaving voyages per ship over 32 and 27 years of activity respectively, the free traders' slave ships tended to make much fewer trips (usually between 2 and 3 voyages per vessel).[40] While this may be an artifact of the excellent quality of the company records, it would seem to argue for the idea that these company ships were on a much more fixed scheduling than the free traders and did not move in and out of particular trades or routes with as much frequency. This differential frequency appears to be a direct result of the monopoly contracts of the companies. The entrance of private traders into the trade was based on relative rates of return, whereas the monopoly companies were constrained to deliver a given number of slaves per annum to preserve their lucrative monopolies over the export trade of the slave colonies.

In terms of numbers carried, the Pernambuco company came quite close to the overall Luanda trade average of 397 slaves (adults and children) carried per vessel. It carried 49,344 African adults and children to Brazil in 125 voyages, for an average of

[39] Miller, "Legal Portuguese Slaving," pp. 151-152.

[40] Among the free traders, two six-year complete periods were analyzed, with the average sailing per ship being 1.9 trips per vessel in the 1720s (61 ships for 118 voyages) and 2.2 for the 1760s (or 63 ships for 140 trips). This same pattern is discovered later among free-slave traders arriving in Rio de Janeiro in the 1790s; the figure was 2.9 sailings, and in the Bahian shipping of the 18th and early 19th century the rate was 2.7 voyages (or 626 ships making 1,736 voyages). Klein, "The Trade," p. 544, and Verger, *Flux et reflux*, p. 658. The company experiences were, respectively, 43 ships and 175 voyages in 32 years, and 25 ships making 125 crossings in 27 years.

394 persons per vessel.[41] The Maranhão company, however, had a much smaller capacity for its ships, since in its 175 voyages it shipped only 28,083 slaves, carrying on average only 160 Africans.[42]

From the Pombaline companies' records of general costs and profits in the slave trade, it is clear that Angola was a far more profitable supplier of cheap slaves than Cacheu and Bissau. Angolan freight charges for the carrying of slaves to Brazil were half the cost (8$000 reis to 16$000 reis) of the Upper Guinean trade. Also, the average price of slaves in the two areas differed, with Guinean prices tending constantly to rise and being at least a third higher than Angolan prices. Thus, according to the Grão-Pará and Maranhão company, from which these figures are extracted, the average costs of slaves in Angola went from 33$000 to 44$000 in 1756-61 to only 40$000 to 67$000 in 1770-1788. By this later date the average price of slaves in Cacheu ran from 80$000 to 90$000. Given this difference in the prices paid to acquire slaves, the profits from the Angolan trade were consistently higher, and in fact the company never lost funds on any expedition from Angola, as it did on many trips from the Upper Guinean ports.[43]

In the records of the Pernambuco company, average slave prices in Angola fluctuated relatively little during its period of intense trade, with the median adult slave price being 74$890 in 1761 and 60$003 in 1786. The Pernambuco company paid higher prices than the Maranhão company, however, and seemed to have suffered financial loss in 12 out of the 27 years it engaged in the slave trade. But as Antonio Carreira has convincingly demonstrated, this company deliberately subsidized its slave trade in return for its control over the Pernambucan and northeastern export trade to Europe, which brought it very large profits.[44]

How profitable was the slave trade, then, to the very succesful Maranhão company, the only Portuguese private mechant or company whose records are sufficiently complete and reliable to make such a calculation? From some 9 fully documented voyages, Carreira has constructed a profit-and-loss statement. In transporting some 4,599 slaves from Angola and Benguela (between 1759-

[41] Carreira, *As companhia pombalinas*, pp. 254, 261.
[42] *Ibid.*, pp. 52-53.   [43] *Ibid.*, pp. 155, 170-175.
[44] *Ibid.*, pp. 286-287.

1777), company ships lost 1,085 slaves. The original slaves cost 170:806$030, and the 4,154 slaves finally sold in Brazil brought in 259:322$482, for a gross profit (less transportation costs) of 51:724$452.[45] This profit rate of 30 percent, which does not take into account depreciation, credit, and administration costs, etc., would seem to be quite high by general 18th-century standards. Recent studies of the various national trades in this period would seem to suggest an overall rate of about 10 percent. Thus in his very extensive study of the English slave trade between 1761-1808, Roger Anstey estimated an average rate of profit of 9.5 percent for all voyages, with the spread going from 13.3 percent in 1791-1800 to 3.3 percent in 1801-1802.[46] Equally, the detailed study by Stein of mid-18th century Nantes slaving voyages argues for a much more severely fluctuating profit margin than suggested by Anstey's averages, though agreeing that an overall profit of 10 percent was a reasonable estimate.[47] Much of the large swings in profitability depended upon three key factors: the fluctuating prices of the European or Asian goods needed to outfit the cargo used to purchase slaves in Africa; the mix of goods used to make up a standard slave unit of account in African markets; and, finally, the rate of slave mortality in the Middle Passage. Given low European prices, a mix of goods that favored cheaper imports, and low slave mortality, profits—as Stein has shown—could go as high as 57 percent on a given voyage. Given the opposite developments, loss could be as severe in the other direction.[48] From this experience, it can be assumed that the Angolan voyages of the Maranhão company on which

[45] *Ibid.*, p. 175. Carreira did not subtract the freight charges from his figures, which would have been 36:792$000 (or 8$000 per slave). See note 21, above. Subtracting this figure from his 88.5 million reis total gives the above profit figure.

[46] Roger Anstey, *The Atlantic Slave Trade and British Abolition, 1760-1810* (London, 1975), chapter ii, and especially table 1 on p. 47. Using the extensive records of 67 voyages outfitted by the Liverpool slave trader William Davenport, Richardson comes up with an overall average profit of 10 percent on investments per annum, taking all things into consideration. Individual voyage profits, however, fluctuated quite strongly with 9 ships making 100 percent and over profits and 18 voyages being deficitory, 4 of these being in the −60 to −99 percent category. David Richardson, "Profitability in the Bristol-Liverpool Slave Trade," *Revue française d'histoire d'Outre-Mer*, LXII, nos. 226-227 (1975), 301-308.

[47] Robert Stein, "The Profitability of the Nantes Slave Trade, 1783-1792," *Journal of Economic History*, XXXV, no. 4 (December, 1975), 779-793.

[48] *Ibid.*, pp. 786-787, table 2.

a 30 percent profit was achieved involved the sale of very low-cost European goods under extremely favorable terms. Since slave mortality on these company ships was unusually high (i.e., 20 percent), the implication is that the Portuguese must have been able to severely reduce their initial outfitting costs and at the same time to get excellent mixes of their trade goods accepted for the purchase of slaves. These "positive" mixes meant that in the assortment of goods that made up a standard of unit for slaves (be it piece, bar, or once, depending on the region in Africa), the Portuguese were able to weight the assortment with a large percentage of low-cost trade goods and a very low assortment of high-cost items. Whether such an arrangement was due to the monopoly company organization or to special short-term local market conditions in the Angolan trade is difficult to state at this point, and it is impossible from the currently available Portuguese data to determine the long-range trends in profitability.

This brief survey of the port registers of Luanda from 1723 to 1771 and the books of the monopoly companies reveals certain basic features of the Angolan slave trade that place it in harmony with the growing knowledge of the Portuguese and European slave trade in general. The regularity of the trade and the very high volume of shipments and large carrying capacity in rather small vessels are well revealed by the Luanda data. There is also the clear response to changes in season, and the surprisingly low number of children. Though the sexual breakdowns of slaves are not provided by Angolan sources, it can probably be assumed that here as well the Angola trade duplicated the Dutch, English, and French trades.[49] What is probably unique about the Angolan

[49] In data reconstructed from the Maranhão company records, Carreira has been able to determine the sex of some 20,141 slaves who were carried by company vessels between 1756-1788, with the resulting breakdown being 7,572 females and 12,569 males, which means a 38 percent contingent of females. (*Ibid.*, pp. 94-95.) Postma, in calculations made for 56 West India Company vessels that carried slaves from Africa in 1681-1751, found 8,629 females (or 29 percent) out of a total of 29,532 slaves who were transported. (Postma "The Dutch . . . Slave Trade," pp. 177-178.) He also notes that "as a rule, WIC [West India Company] captains had instructions to purchase a slave cargo consisting of two-thirds men and one-third women slaves." (*Ibid.*, p. 179.) Unger, in his study of a Dutch free-slave trading company, found a rather high ratio of 41 percent or 10,249 women, out of a total of 25,051 slaves carried in company vessels. (W. S. Unger, "Bijragen tot de geschiedenis van de Nederlandse slavenhandel" [part II], *Economisch-*

trade was the very important role played by African-based merchants—in this case, the Portuguese Luandans—in the carrying
trade, if our rather small sample of data is correct, as well as the
unusually steady quality of that trade. The fact that Portugal
abstained from most of the international conflicts that so disrupted the Dutch and French trades,[50] and that it controlled access to the interior and successfully defended its local monopoly
against European competitors, helps to explain the steady volume of the trade. Equally important was the seemingly inexhaustible Brazilian demand for slaves, coupled with a thriving
and largely Brazilian based merchant fleet well supported by
planter and miner capital.[51]

There were, of course, changes within the trade from Angola
during the course of the century. The major development was
the steady increase in both total volume and the average number
of slaves carried by the end of the 18th century. This new trend
continued into the next century, and also saw the increasing importance of the older port of Benguela and the opening up of
Cabinda to systematic Portuguese exploitation.[52] Reflecting this
growing volume of trade by the end of the century, there was
also a decline in the number of children being shipped from

Historish Jarrboek, xxviii [1961], 49.) Another breakdown by sex can be
found in the registers of slave ships arriving in Havana between 1790-1820.
Of the 181,909 persons who arrived, only 28 percent were women (see
table 9.8 below). In the Jamaican slave trade of the 1790s, the ratio of
women was somewhat higher at 35 percent (see below, table 7.4).

[50] Postma notes that the Dutch slave trade was virtually wiped out by
the fourth Anglo-Dutch war of 1780-1784. (Postma, "The Dutch . . . Slave
Trade," pp. 160ff.) Also, the French slave trade equally suffered a disastrous
decline as a result of international conflicts. The trade was temporarily
suppressed as a result of the wars of the French Revolution, which stopped
French slavers from operating after 1792. For the impact of the Seven
Years War, see Gaston-Martin, *Nantes au xviiie siècle: L'ère des négriers
(1714-1774)* (Paris, 1931), chapter vi; and for the developments of the
1790s see J. Meyer, "Le commerce négrier nantais (1774-1792)," *Annales:
economies, sociétés, civilisations*, xv (1960), pp. 120-129.

[51] A brief glimpse of Bahian investors in slave ships is given in the studies
of Marieta Alves, "O comercio maritimo e alguns armadores do seculo xviii
na Bahia," *Revista de Historia* (São Paulo), xxxiv, 69 (1967), pp. 91-98.

[52] By the early 19th century, average numbers carried was rapidly going
up in the movement from Angolan ports. Thus, in the five-year period 1812,
1814-1817, the average was 464 slaves per ship. Silva Rebelo, *Angola e
Brasil*, quadro no. 1, after p. 81. As for total volume, this rose to an annual
average of 14,038 in the 13 years from 1812, 1814 to 1820, and 1822 to 1826.
Ibid.

Angolan ports. If these numbers are not due simply to recording errors, they may reflect the better supply of adults available to the slave trade. Since children were considered an undesirable element by most slave traders, their diminution in the trade may be considered as an indicator of a steadier supply of the more highly priced *cabeças*, or adult slaves.

While the data presented in this chapter have resolved some of the broader questions of volume, direction, rhythm, and vessel types employed in the trade, there are many problems that they leave unresolved. The lack of sexual breakdowns, at least for the Luanda free trading vessels in the 18th century, makes it difficult to calculate this very important factor with any degree of certitude. The existence of seasonal variations, while marked, still remains a puzzling problem in terms of cause. Though the papers of Captain Proença e Sylva give a hitherto unsuspected picture of an extremely vital Luanda merchant community, the data are still too fragmentary to detail the importance of this community in the financing and maintenance of the slave trade over time.[53]

Finally, the role played by European and Portuguese merchants in the supply of textiles, trade goods, and capital is a subject as little studied as the financial arrangements made by the Luanda merchants with their own trading agents, the *pombeiros*. The costs of transportation to and from the interior, of commissions paid to the *pombeiros*, along with actual costs of imported goods, remain to be determined before profit figures can be fully ascertained. While the unanswered questions thus remain formidable, the systematic exploitation of the port registers of Luanda, along with the detailed records of the Pombaline slave-trading companies, have at least provided the broad outlines of the 18th-century Portuguese slave trade from Angola to Brazil.

[53] Nevertheless, some 19th-century data give the impression of a rather thriving merchant community in the early years of the century. Thus the Luandan merchant Francisco Luis Vieira (who was also a colonel in the local militia) claimed in official documents before the Crown that he had exported 11,074 adult slaves and 13 children to Brazil in the period from 1822 to 1825. Another militia officer and local merchant, Jose Severino de Sousa, officially swore to the Crown that he had shipped 20,018 adult slaves to Brazil between 1811 and 1816; and a third sought admission to the Order of Christ on the basis of having sent 4,825 slaves to Brazil between 31 October and 31 January 1805. *Ibid.*, p. 94.

Chapter Three

The Trade in African Slaves to Rio de Janeiro, 1795-1811

To turn from the analysis of the mid-18th century movement of slaves from Angola to the arrival of slaves in the port of Rio de Janeiro at the end of the century, is to shift focus from questions relating to the removal and loading of Africans onto oceangoing vessels, to their experience once they left African waters. This new focus involves questions about the flow of slaves into the receiving port of Rio de Janeiro from all the regions of Africa, as well as the causes for the variations in these movements. It involves analyzing the participation by local merchants in the commercial organization of the trade. But, above all, it concerns the problem of the incidence and cause of mortality in the Middle Passage.

The sources for the analysis of the late-18th- and early-19th-century slave trade to Rio de Janeiro are the naval lists of all slave ship arrivals kept by the royal officials for purposes of obtaining full information on the payment of royal export taxes on slaves from Portuguese Africa. By the decree (*alvará*) of 13 March 1770 the Portuguese Crown ordered the port officials at Rio de Janeiro to investigate all incoming slave ships' registers and determine if the actual number of persons landed by these ships was consistent with the number recorded in their registers. These latter lists were based on figures supplied in the Portuguese African ports from which the slavers came, and were also to include a "death book" kept by the captain for slaves who died on each trip. Thus a captain of a slaver was required, before he left Brazil, to register as his own property or that of the ship's any slaves purchased for use in his crew. Then when he landed in Africa his registry books were signed by the Portuguese port officials, listing the number of adults and children placed on board. During the voyage he kept a "death book" giving the number of slaves who died at sea. Upon arrival in Rio de Janeiro, royal notaries (*escrivaes*) inspected the ship and determined the number of slaves actually landed in Brazil and compared these with the figures provided in the African registers and death book.

Though the law was probably put into practice in the 1770s, the only surviving records of these royal notaries come from a bound folio volume in the Arquivo Nacional in Rio de Janeiro, which covers 375 ships' landings from 24 July 1795 to 18 March 1811.[1] On the fronts and backs of each of the folios appears a standard formula of which the following is an example:

On the 24 day of the month of July of 1795 in the City of São Sebastião do Rio de Janeiro, aboard the Bergantim Venus of which the Master is José Francisco M. which came from Benguela, to which I, Notary by Order and Commission of the Chief of the Squadron, Intendant of Marine José Caetano de Lima, along with the Notary of the Marine of the Royal Treasury João Marques Ribeiro, come in order to see if the number of slaves transported in the said Bergantim exceeds its records. And attending to the said counting of the slaves themselves after examining the Book of Deaths, and making the other necessary Investigations in accordance with Chapter 11 of the Alvara of March 13, 1770, I found that there were 494 live slaves and one female child of one-half rights, and 11 children at the breast, in which figure are included 12 who come as members of the crew, since they are needed for lack of sailors, and that 13 had died at sea and two within this Port; that together they add up to the number of 494 cabezas, 1 standing child [½ duties] and 11 children at the breast, its *Arqueação* giving the figure of 509. And in order to register this information forever, I made this document in which signed their names the said ship's Master, the Notary of Marine of the Royal Treasury, with me Valentim Antonio Vilella, Notary of the Royal

[1] ANRJ, Codice 242. Other lists of ships which came from Rio de Janeiro to Luanda and returned exist for the period 1736 to 1830 in the archives of Luanda, Angola. But, unfortunately, all these Angolan originated shipping lists lack information on slaves carried. See Corcino Medeiros dos Santos, "Relações de Angola com o Rio de Janeiro (1736-1808)," *Estudos Historicos*, XII (1973), pp. 7-68; and Joseph C. Miller, "Legal Portuguese Slaving from Angola. Some Preliminary Indications of Volume and Direction, 1760-1830," *Revue française d'histoire d'Outre-Mer*, LXII, nos. 226-227 (1975), pp. 135-176; and "Sources and Knowledge of the Slave Trade in the Southern Atlantic," unpublished paper.

Warehouses of the Intendencia of Marine who writes the document, and signs.

Valentim Antonio Villela

João Marques Ribeiro   José Francisco M.[2]

How accurate these 375 ships' landings are in terms of mortality figures is difficult to say. Using only the internal evidence from this one collection, it appears that very high mortality caused no problem whatsoever to the captain of the vessel and such cases are recorded often enough to indicate at least a minimum degree of honesty. The notaries raised formal complaints only when the African exit registries or death books did not exist, indicating some type of illegal transportation and thus avoidance of the royal taxes on the slave trade.[3]

As to the actual recordings of the notaries, either due to illegibility, torn pages, or lack of data presented by the captains, I have complete materials for only 351 cases. Partial data in the form of totals landed alive exist for another 20 cases, with no totals whatsoever in 4 other cases (though these latter do provide the year and month of arrival and in some cases the port of origin).

The following tables have therefore been constructed on the

[2] This is a composite formula document, with the data taken from several different entries in *ibid.* As for the official Portuguese titles, the two notaries are listed as follows: Ribeiro is Escrivão de Marinha da Real Fazenda; Villela is Escrivão dos Armazéns Reaes de Intendência da Maranha. Caetino de Lima is Chefe de Esquadra, Intendante de Marinha. As for the designation of children, standing children (*crias de pé*) were defined in a 1758 tax law as being of a height of four palm lengths or below, and were required to pay only half the usual export tax to the Portuguese Crown on exiting from Africa. The children at the breast (*crias de peito*) were considered as tax free when accompanied by the mother. This decree of 25 January 1758 is reprinted in Mauricio Goulart, *Escravidão africana no Brasil* (*das origenes a extinção*) (São Paulo, 1949), p. 197.

[3] Though comparable mortality figures are unavailable, there do exist alternate figures on total importations. Using a different set of documents, Mauricio Goulart, in his study of the Brazilian slave trade, gives import figures for Rio de Janeiro for the six-year period from 1801 to 1806 which add up to 53,797. (Goulart, *Escravidão africana*, p. 267.) This compares to my own codice calculations of 58,782 for the same period, with the difference probably being accounted for by the failure of the Goulart figures to account for Costa da Mina and Mozambique imports. This data, as in many other cases, comes from the Goulart study, which is unquestionably the best single work to date on the African slave trade to Brazil and supersedes the traditional study of Affonso de E. Taunay, "Subsidios para a história do tráfico africano no Brasil," *Anais do Museu Paulista*, x (1941).

basis of 351 complete cases, unless otherwise indicated. In all enumerations of slave arrivals, I have eliminated the slaves listed as members of the crew, since these were Brazilian-purchased slaves who remained with the ship and were not sold, and whose deaths were not recorded in the slave death books.

The evidence of the naval lists clearly indicates that Rio de Janeiro had already achieved its predominant role as Brazil's leading slave importing port by the end of the 18th century. Whereas the ports of the northeast, especially Bahia and Recife, had predominated until well into the 18th century, with the end of the special role of the Pombal monopoly companies, the Rio de Janeiro trade unqualifiedly became the most important for Brazil.[4] In conjunction with this shift of the trade southward in Brazil, there was a corresponding shift in emphasis southward in the African ports of origin for the arriving slaves. By the second half of the 18th century the Congo-Angolan coast ports were increasing their flow of slaves for Brazil, and even the northeastern Brazilian ports were obtaining a significant share of their slaves from south of Cape Lopez.

In terms of the numbers carried by the Brazilian-bound slave ships, the port of Rio de Janeiro also showed itself to be a significant American importing zone. Not only did the average of 480 slaves shipped (see table 3.1) compare to similar figures for Bahia, its leading rival Brazilian port, but, as will be seen in the later trades, it had the highest volume-per-ship rates for all American ports. Furthermore (see table 3.1), after 1809 the volume of the trade dramatically increased. The pre-1809 trade seems to have been of approximately the same volume as in the period 1731-1735 when slave arrivals into Rio de Janeiro fluctuated between 5,839 and 10,536 per annum, with an average for the five years of 7,422.[5] After 1809, however, there occurred a steady secular increase in the volume of slaves arriving in the port, who by the late 1820s numbered some 34,000 per annum.[6]

[4] For a detailed estimate of the numbers of slaves going to each of the major ports at this time, see Herbert S. Klein, "The Trade in African Slaves to Rio de Janeiro 1795-1811: Estimates of Mortality and Patterns of Voyages," *Journal of African History*, vol. x, No. 4 (1969), pp. 545-546.

[5] ANTT, Manuscritos da Livraria, Brasil, Livro 2, f. 240; for the details of this early Rio de Janeiro trade, see below, table A.1.

[6] See below, Chapter 4.

Table 3.1
The Number of Slaves Arriving in the Port of Rio de Janeiro,
1795-1811, and Their Mortality Experience

Year	No. of Slaves	Ships	Average Rate of Mortality (per 1000)	Ships for Which Mortality Known	St. Dev.
1795	5,318	12	58	(12)	61
1796	9,873	26	117	(26)	85
1797	9,267	23	106	(21)	67
1798	6,780	16	65	(15)	44
1799	8,857	19	38	(19)	19
1800	10,368	22	48	(21)	29
1801	10,011	19	25	(19)	18
1802	11,343	24	81	(24)	112
1803	9,722	20	63	(20)	30
1804	9,075	20	59	(20)	36
1805	9,921	22	86	(22)	35
1806	7,111	21	171	(19)	98
1807	9,689	23	164	(23)	109
1808	9,602	23	139	(23)	94
1809	13,171	30	114	(28)	74
1810	18,677	42	98	(32)	57
1811	3,440	9	114	(6)	48
TOTALS	*162,225*	*371*			
Av. slaves per ship	437		93	(350)	79
St. Dev.	119				

Source: ANRJ, Codice 242.

Prior to 1809, however, important structural changes were occurring within the relatively unchanging total volume of trade. By the end of the century, Rio de Janeiro seems to have been receiving far more slaves directly from Africa and fewer transshipped slaves from the northern Brazilian ports. Also there was a shift in emphasis in African sources. In the late 18th century, not only was the Congo-Angola coast beginning to play a more predominant role, but the East African ports were now also being opened fully to Portuguese Atlantic interests. Whereas Mozambique accounted for only 120 slave arrivals in the 1730s, by the 1795-1811 period the figure had risen to over 6,000 slaves. This was still a small percentage of the total number of arriving slaves, and the early nature of the trade was reflected in a still quite low average number of persons carried around the Cape to Brazil.

But both volume and carrying capacity would change rapidly in the following decades, and by the 1820s East Africa was shipping the largest number of slaves per vessel of any African region.

Table 3.2
Origin of Slaves Arriving in the Port of Rio de Janeiro,
1795-1811

Port & Region	No. of Slaves Arrived	Ships	Average Rate of Mortality (per 1000)	Ships for Which Mortality Known	St. Dev.
1. West Africa	2,761	12	63	(7)	28
São Tome	1,198	7	83	(3)	10
Costa da Mina	934	3	28	(2)	25
Calabar	629	2	68	(2)	19
2. Southwest Africa	155,385	344	89	(330)	72
Malembo	452	1	—	—	—
Cabinda	5,020	11	33	(2)	34
Rio Zaire	549	1	184	(1)	—
Luanda	73,689	163	103	(162)	77
Benguela	75,675	168	74	(165)	63
3. East Africa	4,079	15	234	(13)	135
Mozambique	4,079	15	234	(13)	135

Source: Same as table 3.1.

In both the pre- and post-1809 periods, there was a marked seasonal variation in the pattern of slave arrivals into Rio de Janeiro, a pattern that would be repeated in most of the major New World ports of arrivals for African slaves. In the case of Rio de Janeiro, the spring and summer months from August to January seem to have been a particularly important period for arriving slaves, while the fall and winter period from February through July were low-arrival months. Since there was no difference in the numbers of slaves per ship carried by season, the change in total numbers was exclusively due to the number of ships arriving.[7] Given the fact that there were no significant weather and wind patterns that could account for this seasonality,[8] the key factors would seem to be either African supply con-

[7] The simple correlation between the average number of slaves and the seasons was insignificant, +0.009.

[8] A complete discussion on these factors is found in Klein, "The Trade in Slaves," pp. 537-538.

ditions or American demand considerations. While the data for Rio de Janeiro trade are insufficient to answer fully the questions relating to African supply, there is no question that the high season of importation to Rio de Janeiro roughly approximates the sugar-harvesting season in Brazil, which lasted from late July or August until the following May.

Table 3.3

The Number of Slaves Arriving in the Port of Rio de Janeiro, by Month and Season, for the Complete Years 1796 to 1810

Season & Month	Slaves	Ships	Average Rate of Mortality (per 1000)	Ships for Which Mortality Known
1. *Summer*	*43,274*	*96*	*70 (52)* [a]	*90*
December	16,853	35	66	32
January	17,754	40	69	37
February	8,667	21	81	21
2. *Fall*	*33,991*	*82*	*119 (92)*	*80*
March	11,026	26	109	25
April	11,319	27	121	26
May	11,646	29	125	29
3. *Winter*	*32,841*	*75*	*112 (96)*	*73*
June	8,104	19	145	18
July	9,747	22	95	22
August	14,990	34	106	33
4. *Spring*	*43,361*	*97*	*82 (68)*	*89*
September	10,545	25	72	22
October	13,512	30	88	29
November	19,304	42	83	38
TOTALS	*153,467*	*350*		*332*
Av. slaves per ship	439		94	
St. Dev.	120		80	

[a]Standard deviation in parentheses.

Source: Same as table 3.1.

A rather unusual feature of the Brazilian naval lists, as in those for Portuguese Africa, is the consistent recording of children and infants. In this respect, the findings from Rio de Janeiro are compatible with those found for the mid-18th century Angolan migrations figures. In both the child and infant categories there is

57

a surprisingly low number. In only 27 percent of the total ships arriving were children even listed in the manifests, and they made up less than 1 percent of the total of arriving slaves. This is an even lower proportion than that found for the early 18th-century Atlantic slave migration from Angola.[9] It was not the higher likelihood of death that caused so few children and infants to be taken, since those who crossed the Atlantic suffered approximately the same mortality rates as the adults. Again, one is forced to propose either low American demand and relatively high purchase and transportation costs, or African refusals to permit children to enter the trade.[10] Why the number of children should have declined in the 18th-century Rio de Janeiro trade is even more of a problem to resolve. For, by all the indices, any falsification of records that would have occurred would have encouraged the over-registration of the less taxed children to the very end of Portuguese control over the African slave trade. Either the number of adults was more than sufficient to discourage the turn toward less profitable children, or the constraints on their participation on the part of Africans may have been increasing.

Even more unusual and unique to the Brazilian trade than the low number of children was the large number of American slaves who made up the crews of the slave ships. As was indicated in the standard registers, the use of Brazilian-purchased slaves to make up crew complements was always justified by the lack of free sailors. This crisis in sailors must have been considerable

[9] See above, Chapter 2.

[10] There is no question, however, that there was a positive price paid for all children in American slave societies prior to the closing of the Atlantic slave trade. For the slave price data on provincial Rio de Janeiro coffee plantations in 1873, see Pedro Carvalho de Mello, "The Economics of Labor in Brazilian Coffee Plantations, 1850-1888" (Workshop in Economic History, Department of Economics, University of Chicago, 1974, Report #7475-8), pp. 39-40. In his dissertation, "The Economics of Brazilian Slavery" (Department of Economics, University of Chicago, 1975), figure 24, he indicates that prices in 1858, compared with those in the later periods, were consistently higher at all age groups, but especially in the younger years, strongly supporting the hypothesis that even before the abolition of the trade, prices were positive for children. A similar age and sex price profile for slaves was discovered in a sample of over 2,500 slave sales from Bahia in the period 1838-1882, see Maria Luiza Marcilio et al., "Considerações sobre o preço do escravo no periodo imperial: Uma analise quantitative" *Anais de Historia* (Assis, São Paulo), no. 5 (1973), pp. 179-194.

since 42 percent of the 350 ships that have complete data indicate slaves in their crew. This also meant that the average of 14 slave crewmen per vessel probably made up between one-third to one-half of the crew.[11] While the total number of sailors was not recorded, it can be assumed that the Portuguese probably were carrying approximately the same number of crewmen as the French slavers at the peak of the 18th-century trade. This would have meant an average of 35 sailors per vessel. Since the trading practices of the Portuguese were quite distinctive, in that local merchants were responsible for assembling most of the slaves to be shipped, the need for sailors to trade on the coast was smaller, though, of course, sailors were still needed to control the slaves.

The detailed recordings of ships' and captains' names that appear in the port registers also make it possible to work out a pattern of frequency and a degree of specialization for ships employed in the Rio de Janeiro trade. The frequency of voyages made by individual ships in the trade can be seen from a breakdown of 280 consecutive landings between 1799 and 1810. Over half the ships (see table 3.4) made only two voyages or less. Thus it appears that there was a major turnover of ships in the trade. Why this should have been the case and what other activities the ships might have undertaken is difficult to determine. However, from evidence gathered by Pierre Verger, it is clear that the Rio de Janeiro to Africa trade was not unique in this rapid turnover. In the Bahia trade to Africa, Verger found that the 1736 voyages he studied before 1815 were carried out by 626 ships, with over half of the ships making 2 voyages or less, and with no ships having undertaken more than 12 voyages. For the period 1815-1830 there were 338 voyages made by 201 ships, this time with over half making less than 1 voyage and the maximum total being 7 voyages.[12]

The multi-voyage experience of the longest traders shows that the majority were highly specialized within the trade to Rio de

[11] The average number of slaves in the crew for the 148 vessels that had them on arrival was 14, with the mean and modal figure both being 12 slave sailors. The standard deviation was 7 sailors, and the minimum was 1, with the maximum being 35.

[12] Pierre Verger, "Mouvements des navires entre Bahia et le Golfe du Bénin (xviie-xixe siècle)," *Revue française d'Histoire d'Outre-Mer*, 56 année, LV, No. 198 (1968), pp. 18-19.

Table 3.4
Frequency of Voyages of the Ships That Landed at
Rio de Janeiro between
3 March 1799 and 24 December 1810

No. of Voyages Made per Ship	Total No. of Ships by Frequency of Voyages	Total No. of Voyages
1	35	35
2	20	40
3	12	36
4	5	20
5	4	20
6	7	42
7	6	42
8	1	8
9	3	27
10	1	10
TOTALS	94	280

Source: Same as table 3.1.

Janeiro. This is evident from the fact that these multi-voyage ships made almost exclusive use of certain African ports to obtain slaves. In the cases of the two curvetas *Santo Antonio Portilhão* and *Rainha dos Anjos*, which had the longest consecutive runs for these types of ships to the ports of Benguela and Angola (Luanda) respectively, and in the experiences of two *navios* which accounted for 38 percent of the total voyages from East Africa, such specialization was obvious. The reasons for this specialization are most probably due to the very special nature of the Portuguese-Brazilian slave trade. The prominent role played by local merchants and their close association with Brazilian factors, the fixed nature of the port facilities, and the availability of locally secure trading arrangements would also seem to suggest an intimate long-term contact that would make for the high degree of specialization in the trade shown by the longer multiple-voyage shipping. How the majority of the single-voyage ships fit into this pattern is difficult to discern, but it would seem most likely that they tended to trade through established and well-known Portuguese African merchants, much as the multiple-voyage traders. Given the short-term nature of most trading partnerships and the desire to spread the risks over many ventures,

Table 3.5
Rio Landings of the Curveta *Santo Antonio Portilhão*

Date of Landing [a]	African Port	No. of Slaves Shipped	Died at Sea	Died on Landing	Total Sold in Rio	Slaves in Crew
13 Mar. 1799	Benguela	532	11	0	521	12
6 Dec. 1799	Benguela	532	7	0	525	18
30 Nov. 1800	Benguela	547[b]	8	1	538	0
11 Jul. 1801	Benguela	532	7	0	525	3
20 Apr. 1802	Benguela	532	10	0	522	8
21 Mar. 1803	Benguela	532	22	1	509	12
27 Sep. 1804	Benguela	533[c]	39	2	492	0
17 Mar. 1806	Benguela	532	93	4	435	15
13 Sep. 1807	Benguela	533[d]	22	0	511	0
13 Aug. 1809	Benguela	532	61	7	464	0

[a]This is the date of inspection, which occurred any time from a day or two to a week after the actual port entry of the ship.

[b]This total includes 15 children.

[c]This total includes 1 child.

[d]This total includes 1 child.

Source: Same as table 3.1.

Table 3.6
Rio Landings of the Curveta *Rainha dos Anjos*

Date of Landing [a]	African Port	No. of Slaves Shipped	Died at Sea	Died on Landing	Total Sold in Rio	Slaves in Crew
30 Oct. 1800	Angola	564	5	0	559	28
22 Feb. 1807	Angola	472	82	3	387	17
8 Mar. 1808	Angola	576[b]	157[b]	2	417	0
4 Jan. 1809	Angola	521	88	5	428	0
5 Jan. 1810	Angola	598	79	3	516	0
5 Feb. 1811	Angola	695	86	6	603	0

[a]This is the date of inspection.

[b]This total includes one child.

Source: Same as table 3.1.

Table 3.7
Rio Landings of the Navios *Ninfa do Mar* and *Restaurador*

Date of Landing [a]	African Port	No. of Slaves Shipped	Died at Sea	Died on Landing	Total Sold in Rio	Slaves in Crew
		Ninfa do Mar				
13 Jun. 1802	Mozambique	445	228	0	217	0
21 Mar. 1804	Mozambique	431	67	2	362	14
25 Apr. 1807	Mozambique	193	63	0	130	0
		Restaurador				
26 Jan. 1808	Mozambique	423	70	0	353	0
8 Mar. 1809	Mozambique	514	71	1	442	0
24 Sep. 1810	Benguela	630	80	2	548	0

[a]This is the date of inspection.

Source: Same as Table 3.1.

it can be assumed that most of the single-voyage ventures followed the practices of the ships that were constantly in the trade and probably relied on the same merchant base and connections.

Because of the very highly specialized nature of the Portuguese Atlantic slave trade, the movement of slaves occurred in ships that almost exclusively concerned themselves with the transportation of persons across the Atlantic. Thus only a relatively few ships were needed to move a very large number of people from Africa to America. This meant that slave ships accounted for a relatively small number of the ships entering the port of Rio de Janeiro during this period. But the economic importance of the slave trade far outweighed its numerical importance in the total volume of shipping. In the total volume of trade entering the port of Rio de Janeiro between 1795 and 1811, the sales of the arriving slaves represented approximately a third of the value of all items, goods, and persons brought into the city for sale by trans-Atlantic shipping.

In actual fact this figure is somewhat higher than it should be because of the crisis in international trade that Brazil suffered as a result of the fall of Portugal to France in 1808. But even in the days of normal European trade, from 1796 to 1807, the value of slave sales represented 23 percent of total value of all slave and non-slave imports, and the slave trade ranked approximately third in importance after manufactured goods and imported textiles. After 1807, its importance increased dramatically, as a result both of the crisis in European trade and the long-trend increase in the number of arriving slaves. It became the single most important factor in Rio de Janeiro's international trade and accounted for 64 percent of the total value of slave and non-slave imports in the period from 1808 to 1811.[13] Once the European trade crisis was resolved, however, this figure probably fell again to about one-third in the following decades.

Aside from information on the type of shipping, the manner of carrying slaves, and even age characteristics of slaves, the Rio de Janeiro port registers provide a detailed recording of the Africans' mortality both in the Middle Passage and upon landing in the port. This material is one of the first and one of the most complete documentations to be discovered for any of the major trades. It thus provides one of the first sets of materials for analyzing the mortality in the Middle Passage, a theme that will be explored in several subsequent chapters.

Along with other quantitative aspects of the trade, the incidence and causes of the mortality of Africans in the Middle Passage have been seriously neglected not only for the South Atlantic Slave trades but in all the other major slave trades as well. Although some statistics were gathered for the 17th, 18th, and 19th centuries for various parts of the trade, until recently there were few attempts to explore this material systematically. Scholars have, of course, made educated guesses on the mortality of the Middle Passage, but these estimates have varied from a low of 8 percent to well over 30 percent or even higher, and have rarely been substantiated with detailed statistics.[14]

[13] The figures for the total value of all imports (except slaves) is taken from José Jobson de Andrade Arruba, "O Brasil no comércio colonial (1796-1808)" (Ph.D. thesis, Departamento de Historia, Faculdade de Filosofia, Letras e Ciências Humanas, Universidade de São Paulo, 1972), p. 133. Jobson cites the value of the average slave in Rio de Janeiro at 89$600 in 1803 (*ibid.*, p. 291). I have used this figure as a multiplier for all slave imports, and then I have added these totals to the total non-slave imports given by Jobson, to arrive at a new total values figure that now includes the slave trade.

[14] The low estimate was made by the leading U.S. scholar on slavery, U. B. Phillips, who declared that "the mortality on the average ship may be roughly conjectured from the available data at eight or ten percent." (U. B. Phillips, *American Negro Slavery* [New York, 1940 ed.], 38.) At the other end were the old estimates first made by the Belgian scholar Dieudonné Rinchon, who took the unusual position that mortality was actu-

The oldest published data on slave mortality are provided by the Royal African Company records for the years 1680 to 1688. In that period it sent 249 ships to America from the African coast, with a total of 60,783 slaves. The mortality rate for these slaves was 23.6 percent.[15] On figures not supplied by the author, Westergaard estimated that "the percentage loss on the Guinea-West India slave ships varied from about 10 to about 25 percent of those taken on" and notes that these are the rates for the years 1698-1700, 1707, 1714, and 1733.[16] Though he refused to make an estimate, Gaston-Martin provided data for a total of 239,525 slaves shipped from Africa to the West Indies by Nantes merchants between 1715 and 1775, and found that 35,927 Africans died at sea, which yields an over-all average mortality rate of 14.9 percent.[17] For 1791 the House of Lords published documents showing 15,754 Africans shipped to America with an average mortality of 8.7 percent, and 31,554 being shipped in 1792 at a loss of 17 percent.[18]

---

ally higher in the 19th century than in earlier periods. Largely basing himself on the erroneous estimates of James Bandinel, Rinchon estimated a 20 percent mortality rate prior to 1800 and a 50 percent mortality rate at the apogee of the trade in the 19th century. (Dieudonné Rinchon, *La traite et l'esclavage des congolais par les européens* [Bruxelles, 1929], 209.) Bandinel, in a much-cited memorandum he presented to the House of Commons, calculated that from 1778 to 1815 some 363,000 Africans were imported into all the Americas and estimated the loss, by extrapolation from extremely fragmentary evidence, at 14 percent per annum. With little serious justification, he then claimed that annual losses from 1814 to 1847 were 25 percent, with total imports being 872,000. (Great Britain, Parliament, House of Commons, Select Committee on Slave Trade, *Second Report* [30 May 1848], Appendix, no. 2, 179.)

[15] C.S.S. Higham, *The Development of the Leeward Islands Under the Restoration, 1660-1668* (Cambridge, 1921), 158, table v.

[16] Weldemar Westergaard, *The Danish West Indies Under Company Rule (1671-1754)* (New York, 1917), p. 144.

[17] Gaston-Martin, *Nantes au XVIIIe siècle*, p. 115. A detailed analysis of these and other Nantes slave trade mortality data is provided below in Chapter 7.

[18] Cited in Thomas Fowell Buxton, *The African Slave Trade and its Remedy* (London, 1840), pp. 172-173. Buxton also provides various educated guesses made by contemporary "experts" that varied from 20 percent to 33.3 percent. In the Bandinel memorandum on the mortality in the slave trade from Africa to the West Indies there was provided a rather detailed summary of contemporary expressions on the trade. It was noted by many slave captains that, excluding extraordinary mortality due to epidemics such as smallpox, the prime cause of mortality was dysentery, and that length of

In the 1840s the House of Commons published the most extensive printed data on slave mortality available anywhere. These detailed compilations covered imports into selected American ports (principally Rio de Janeiro, Bahia, and Havana) from the late 1810s on, with listings of over 700 ship arrivals, based on reports of local British consuls. In about half the cases mortality data were given, and the average rate of loss was 9.1 percent.[19]

In the specific case of the Brazilian trade, no such detailed statistics on such an extended base have ever been published. The leading Brazilian scholar on this subject, Mauricio Goulart, though offering no concrete examples, did estimate a 10 percent mortality for the 18th and 19th centuries in the trade to Brazil. Interestingly, in the light of some of the 16th- and 17th-century estimates above, Goulart noted in his conclusion on the mortality question that "the percentage of deaths has been greater [than the 10 percent for the 18th and 19th centuries], notably in the early years of the traffic . . ." and estimates a rate of mortality between 15 percent and 20 percent for the 16th and 17th centuries.[20]

In analyzing the port registers on the question of mortality, we need to establish the causes for this mortality as can be measured by the relevant available statistics. Traditionally the argument has been advanced that "tight packing" was the principal cause of slave mortality in the Middle Passage. This argument presumes that the slave captains carried aboard the highest number possible so that even with high mortality enough would survive to make a profitable voyage.[21] The best way to measure the impact

---

stay along the coast to pick up cargoes usually increased the mortality rates. (Select Committee on Slave Trade, *Second Report* [30 May 1848], Appendix, no. 1, 175-177.) For a more detailed analysis of slave mortality rates aboard English slave ships, based on data unavailable to Buxton, see below, Chapter 7.

[19] Great Britain, *Parliamentary Papers*, XLIX (1845), 73, pp. 593-633; and Philip Curtin, *The Atlantic Slave Trade: A Census* (Madison, 1969), chapter 10. Also see David Eltis' revisions of these data in "The Direction and Fluctuation of the Transatlantic Slave Trade 1821-43: A Revision of the 1845 Parliamentary Paper," MSSB Conference Paper, Colby, Maine, 1975; and "The Export of Slaves from Africa, 1821-43," unpublished paper.

[20] Goulart, *Escravidão Africana*, p. 278.

[21] For the thesis of "tight-packers" and the supposed willingness to accept high rates of mortality, which they claim was the predominant philosophy of the trade in the post-1750 period, see Daniel P. Mannix and Malcolm

of "tight packing" is to see if there is an increase of mortality with the number of slaves arrived. Since the Rio de Janeiro data lack information on tonnage figures, a test can be made by comparing the numbers carried against mortality rates, as is done in table 3.8. It is immediately evident that there is no significant

Table 3.8
The Mortality of African Slaves Arriving in
Rio de Janeiro (1795-1811)
by Number of Slaves per Ship Leaving Africa

No. Leaving Africa	Average Rate of Mortality in the Middle Passage (per 1000)	Ships
50-99	66	3
150-199	118	3
200-249	172	9
250-299	56	2
300-349	126	14
350-399	87	33
400-449	99	50
450-499	86	69
500-549	80	82
550-599	118	44
600-649	83	17
650-699	88	8
700-749	92	7
750-799	44	6
800-849	84	2
850-899	27	1
Mean mortality per ship	94	
St. Dev.	79	
TOTAL		350

Source: Same as table 3.1.

correlation between the number of slaves carried and the rate of mortality. If anything, the smaller vessels have slightly higher rates of mortality. This is a result that, as will be seen, is consistent with every other major source of data on mortality in the 18th- and 19th-century trades.

To refute the "tight packing" hypothesis, of course, will require tonnage data, which, though unavailable for the Portuguese

Cowley, *Black Cargoes. A History of the Atlantic Slave Trade, 1518-1865* (New York, 1962), pp. 105-106.

material, is available from the French and English trades of the 18th century. But given the similarity of the results on this question for all trades, it can be assumed that, with the tonnage available, the same results would occur for the Rio de Janeiro trade. If the manner of carrying the slaves was not influencing slave mortality, then what other factors can be seen as having a significant impact?

It would appear, at least, that there were significant differences in the mortality recorded by port of exit from Africa. The first factor to note is the important distinction between East and all of Western Africa (see above, table 3.2). While no data are available for the time of crossing from the Rio de Janeiro port registers of this period, we know from later 19th-century newspaper reports, that on average the sailings from East Africa took a month longer than those from Angola. It would seem evident that time at sea was somehow correlated with mortality, though the difference between Benguela-originated ships and their mortality, which contrast with those from Luanda—both within the same traveling time from Rio and relatively near each other on the African coast—is difficult to explain.[22]

Finally, just as there was a marked seasonality in the number of ships arriving, there is also a positive correlation between season of arrival and mortality, with the low months of overall movement being those with the higher mortality.[23] This phenomenon, which does not seem to have occurred in other trades where mortality data are available, is difficult to explain. It may be that

[22] For an analysis of these sailing times, see below, Chapter 4. It might be argued that these Angolan port differences in mortality rates were due to differing catchments for their respective slave migrating populations and to differing local food and climatic conditions.

[23] As can be seen in table 3.3, the difference in the mean mortality between the lowest and highest season is over 100 percent. This sharp difference in average mortality is, interestingly enough, caused by a relatively small number of ships diverging around normal mortality experience, which seems to be relatively constant throughout most of the year. In the summer and fall months—the two extreme examples in mortality—virtually the same ratio of ships (40 percent and 37 percent respectively) had mortality rates in the range of ½ standard deviations around the mean (which range accounted for 40 percent of the observations). However, the summer had 47 percent of the ships with mortality rates of 55 per thousand or below, while, for the fall, the figure was only 26 percent. Conversely, only 13 percent of the ships arriving in summer (the lowest mortality period) had death rates above 134 per thousand, as opposed to 26 percent in this range in the winter season and 36 percent in the fall.

the harvest cycle in Africa itself (a possibility recently suggested by Miller in his study of Angola) might be related to this factor of mortality. Also, such a factor may account for the regional variations along the Angolan coast itself. Given the relatively weak influence of these various factors upon the incidence of mortality in this Rio de Janeiro sample and the lack of information on sailing times, only the clearly negative hypothesis of the failure of "tight packing" as a primary cause of mortality seems acceptable in this discussion of mortality.

A much more satisfactory solution, however, exists for determining the incidence or level of mortality. Here the traditional guesses can be tested against reliable concrete data, and the result shows a mortality rate of 9.3 percent. The interesting fact about this number is that it is an average of several years, and that in any one year the rate can fluctuate quite markedly around this mean. This fluctuation can be related to a host of factors, from the local outbreak of communicable diseases that reach epidemic proportions, to food, weather and other economic and ecological crises, and finally such factors as rebellion, piracy, and warfare among the Europeans themselves. While mortality rates appear to have declined over a century, even over a fifteen-year period the rates can fluctuate from half to double the mean. This, as will be seen in the French slave trade, was even the pattern of experiences of the multiple sailings of individual captains and their ships.

But what of the figure of 9.3 percent? Is it large or small? Evidently it is much lower than the rates that have often appeared in the traditional literature. But is it a "normal" rate? Here the answer quite obviously is "no." First of all, the data indicate that 98 percent of the transported slaves were over the age of approximately 12 years. From the information from other trades, most notably the Cuban and Spanish trades, it appears that the overwhelming majority of transported slaves were in the prime age group of 15-40. For such a population, a monthly age specific death rate of 93 per thousand is unqualifiedly a rate above even the most extreme epidemics. Even if this rate were to be compared to a crude death rate for the entire population (which would include the much higher rates for children and aged averaged in), it would be considered in late-18th-century European terms an extremely high mortality rate. Crude death rates for

England and Wales for the period 1780 to 1810, for example, varied from a high of 28 per thousand to a low of 23 per thousand.[24] In France, during the period of the 1770s and 1780s, mortality is estimated to have gone as high in some areas as 44 per thousand and as low as 27 per thousand.[25] But these were stable communities in normal periods. To determine the outer limits of crude death rates, it should be noted that an epidemic in France in the 17th century was estimated to have caused a rise in the death rate in a given area from the normal 34 per thousand to 253 per thousand in one year's time.[26]

But what of age-specific death rates, and death rates of non-stable populations in the same period? In France in 1770, for example, the age-specific death rates for a population that was overwhelmingly rural and peasant was for males and females of ages 15-24 on the order of 11.6 per thousand persons; for those between 25-34 it was 15.2 per thousand, and for persons 35-44 years of age the figure reached only 19 per thousand.[27] This same pattern prevailed in Great Britain, where in the period 1817 to 1836 the mortality of civilians of military age was 11.5 per thousand. This age-specific group was also fairly close to the age groups selected for the slave trade, though of course females were also included in the latter population. When such men of military age actually served in the army, their mortality rate in Great Britain went up to 15.3 per thousand. For troops serving overseas, however, the rates were extremely high. In the Mediterranean and temperate zones of the world, the rate was between 12 and 20 per thousand. In the tropical areas of the Indian Ocean, it ranged from 30 to 75 per thousand. In the American tropics, the rate rose to a level between 85 and 138 per

[24] D. V. Glass, "Population and Population Movements in England and Wales, 1700 to 1850," in D. V. Glass and D.E.C. Eversley, eds. *Population in History* (London, 1965), 241, table 8.

[25] Jacques Dupaquier, "Sur la population française au XVIIe et au XVIIIe siècle," *Revue historique*, 92ᵉ année, ccxxxix (Janv.-Mars 1968), 65.

[26] J. Meuvret, "Demographic crisis in France from the sixteenth to the eighteenth century," in *Population in History*, p. 513. On the other hand, Louis Henry has indicated that mortality rates during the plague in Amsterdam in the 17th century were in the 125 per thousand to 170 per thousand range. Louis Henry, *Manuel de démographie historique* (Geneve-Paris, 1967), p. 54.

[27] J. Bourgeois-Pichat, "The General Development of Population of France since the Eighteenth Century," in D. V. Glass and D. E. C. Eversley, eds., *Population in History*, p. 497.

thousand. Finally, West Africa showed a disastrous mortality range from 483 to 668 per thousand mean strength per annum.[28]

Comparable rates to those suffered by the slaves in the trans-Atlantic crossing seem to have been the experience of European immigrants crossing to America from Europe in the 18th century. Though the materials are far more scattered and incomplete than the slave trade statistics, the general impression for the indentured servant and immigrant trade to North America is one of very high epidemic rates in this early period. Thus, in 1710, 10 ships carrying German immigrants to Philadelphia experienced a 25 percent mortality in their 4 to 5 month crossings.[29] Other quite small samples of early 18th-century North Atlantic shipping also report mortality rates of between 15 percent to 20 percent.[30] These common trends, however, appear to have sharply diverged in the 19th century, when immigrant mortality rates appear to have declined much more rapidly than the slave mortality figures.[31] It should also be stressed that immigrant ships probably contained a higher proportion of aged and children than did the slave ships, and thus had a population more susceptible to mortality. More directly comparable populations who were forced to

[28] Philip D. Curtin, "Epidemiology and the slave trade," *Political Science Quarterly*, LXXXIII, no. 2 (June 1968), 202-203. The mortality rate of Englishmen working for the Royal African Company on the African coast between 1684 and 1732, though quite high at 269 per thousand resident population, was not quite as high as the 19th-century English troop rates. K. G. Davies, "The Living and the Dead: White Mortality in West Africa, 1684-1732," in Stanley L. Engerman and Eugene Genovese, eds., *Race and Slavery in the Western Hemisphere, Quantitative Studies* (Princeton, 1975), p. 89. Also, there seems to have been a much lower rate of mortality experienced by Dutchmen in the employ of the West India Company who worked on the Gold Coast between 1719 and 1760. Their mortality rate was only 185 per thousand, though again this is an abnormally high figure, given the age and sex structure of the population. (H. M. Feinberg, "New Data on European Mortality in West Africa: The Dutch on the Gold Coast, 1719-1760," *Journal of African History*, xv, no. 3 [1974], p. 367.)

[29] Frank R. D. Diffenderfer, *German Immigration into Pennsylvania* (Lancaster, Pa., 1900), pp. 45-49, 258-259. It would appear that the average number of immigrants carried in the mid-18th-century trade to North America was on the order of 300 immigrants per vessel, in ships averaging just under 200 tons. The resulting average of 1.5 immigrants per ton was probably on the high side, and is, in any case, quite obviously much lower than corresponding figures for the 18th-century slave trades.

[30] See e.g., K. F. Geiser, *Redemptioners and Indentured Servants in . . . Pennsylvania* (New Haven, 1901), p. 50.

[31] See below, pp. 90-93.

migrate, for example, were the British and German troops who were sent to the West Indies and North America. Of 14 regiments consisting of 8,437 men sent from England to the West Indies in the period from 1776 to 1780, the average mortality was 11 percent, with the range on individual ships going from a low of 2 percent to a high of 25 percent.[32] It has been estimated that similar troop movements to the port of New York during the American Revolution suffered on average a mortality rate of at least 8 percent.[33]

Thus the 93-per-thousand rate experienced by the Africans transported by the Portuguese across the Atlantic was a rate that was unusual by European standards. Even when Europeans were forced to live in close quarters, as was the case with the military, their rates did not reach the high epidemic numbers experienced by the Africans. Only when faced with new epidemiological zones, or when experiencing a short-term mortality crisis, did these local epidemic rates for Europeans begin to approximate those for the African slaves.

The picture of the trade as seen from a major American port of disembarcation thus adds a new dimension to the materials that have been analyzed up to this point. We have seen that the flow of slaves and ships experienced a marked seasonal variation, that new routes had begun to develop on the East African coast just as traditional routes in the Upper Guinean Coast had ceased to function as a major source of supply. As yet the East African route was still a minor and relatively newly developed area, as its low average numbers of slaves per ship and still minor participation indicated. Nevertheless in the new century both the volume of the East African trade as well as the carrying capacity of the ships would grow.

Finally, the Rio de Janeiro material provides systematic information on the pattern of mortality suffered in the Middle Passage. Hitherto traditional estimates of trans-Atlantic mortality rates

[32] BM, Additional Manuscripts, 38345, folio 17. I am indebted to David Syrett for calling my attention to this source.

[33] David Syrett, *Shipping and the American War, 1775-83* (London, 1970), p. 191. In contrast to the slaves, however, the manner of carrying troops was considerably more spacious. Thus it was customary on British transports since the time of the Seven Years War to estimate between one and two measured tons per soldier (*ibid.*, pp. 183-184).

have been challenged, just as traditionally assumed causes for mortality have been questioned. These issues, however, have only just begun to be analyzed, and in the following chapters all of these questions of cause and incidence will be explored from the perspective of a number of major American trades.

Chapter Four

Shipping Patterns and Mortality in the African Slave Trade to Rio de Janeiro, 1825-1830

Having established the parameters for the incidence of mortality in the late-18th-century slave trade to Rio de Janeiro, I will now attempt to use an alternative body of data to determine the nature of that mortality and larger aspects of the trade in the changed conditions of the late 1820s. In analyzing this trade, I have utilized the detailed shipping news reports in the two leading commercial daily newspapers of Rio de Janeiro in the early 19th century, the *Diario do Rio de Janeiro* and the *Jornal do Comercio*. Unfortunately, detailed records of ships' arrivals were published by the Brazilian newspapers beginning only in mid-1825, and ending early in 1830 with the official—though not real—termination of the trade by the Brazilian government in response to British pressure. Between these two dates, some 430 ships are listed as having arrived in the port of Rio de Janeiro, carrying slaves from Africa. These detailed notices provide the name and type of ship, the port of African embarcation, time at sea, merchant in Rio to whom the slaves were consigned, and, most important, both the number of slaves shipped and the number who died at sea. These materials thus can be used to determine the origin and numbers of the slaves arriving in the port of Rio de Janeiro, the year and season of their arrival, the types of ships used, the role of the importing merchants, and the mortality suffered in transit by the African slaves.

In dealing with such printed sources, the question immediately arises as to their reliability. Because they were written primarily for businessmen interested in purchasing slaves, concerned about mortality aboard ship and therefore demanding accurate accounts, it can be assumed that there is no inherent reason that the printed notices should be deliberately distorted. These newspaper listings were, also, apparently the chief source of data in the period for the British Foreign Office report of 1845.[1] As such they have not only been accepted as useful by subsequent historians, but they were also widely used by contemporaries in the debates on the slave trade at that time.[2] While the data used pertain only to the slaves brought into Rio de Janeiro, this accounts for over three-quarters of all African slave arrivals listed for this period.[3] The basic omission from these data relate, of course, to the possibilities of smuggling slaves into Brazil without there being any record left. While this may mean that the overall magnitude of the African slave migration is too low, there are, again, no reasons to anticipate any major biases in the various accounts of slave origins, seasonal patterns, and shipboard mortality.

The most immediate factor to note in analyzing the overall trade statistics (see table 4.1) is that the steady growth of slave arrivals begun around 1809 continued unabated in the interval from 1825 to 1830. The annual level of slave migrations during this period exceeded that in the preceding years of the slave trade, and was exceeded only by the high levels of the period immediately prior to the final closing of the Brazilian slave trade, the years 1846 to 1849.[4] The years 1827 to 1830 were abnormally

[1] This list, reprinted in Great Britain, *Parliamentary Papers*, LXIX (1845), 73, "Slave Trade-Slave vessels" report dated 25 February 1845. This report was used by Philip Curtin, *The Atlantic Slave Trade: A Census* (Madison, 1969), for his 19th-century estimates, and has been revised and modified for various sectors of the trade by Leslie Bethell, *The Abolition of the Brazilian Slave Trade* (Cambridge, 1970), pp. 389-390; and most recently by D. Eltis, "The Direction and Fluctuation of the Transatlantic Slave Trade 1821-43: A Revision of the 1845 Parliamentary Paper," MSSB Conference on the Atlantic Slave Trade, Waterville, Maine, 1975.

[2] See, for example, Thomas Foxwell Buxton, *The African Slave Trade and Its Remedy* (London, 1839), pp. 16-29.

[3] For the period from 1817 to 1843, Rio received 73 percent of the slaves arriving in Brazil that were known to the British Foreign Office. (Curtin, *The Atlantic Slave Trade*, p. 69.) There is no reason to believe that the Rio de Janeiro sample is a biased sample of the known Brazilian trade. Using more detailed Foreign Office data than the official published lists, David Eltis has recently recalculated the volume of the slave migration into Brazil, obtaining figures substantially higher than those estimated by Curtin. Nevertheless, the relative importance of the slave trade to Rio de Janiero remains the same, accounting for approximately 70 percent of all slaves landed in Brazil in this period. David Eltis, "The Export of Slaves from Africa, 1821-43," unpublished ms., diagram 8.

[4] See Curtin, *The Atlantic Slave Trade*, p. 234, and Bethell, *The Abolition*, pp. 388-395.

high, a characteristic that has been attributed to the rush to meet demands prior to the prohibition that began in 1830.[5] Nevertheless the legal prohibition was ineffective, and by the mid-1830s trade was again returning to normal levels.[6]

The changing sources of African slaves within this period also continue trends that began earlier in the century. Whereas the East African ports provided less than 3 percent of Rio's slaves in the period from 1795 to 1811, they provided one-quarter of the slaves during the period from 1825 to 1830. There were also shifts in the sources of West African supply. Whereas almost all slaves imported in the 1795-1811 period came from the region of Angola, split evenly between the two major ports of Luanda and Benguela, in the 1825-1830 period Angola provided only 44 percent of Rio's imports. Growing in importance on the West Coast were the ports north of the Congo River (Rio Zaire), particularly Cabinda (see table 4.2). By this later period Cabinda had become the major supplier of slaves to Rio, while the Angolan coast port of Ambriz had become as important a supplier as Benguela. Benguela and Luanda, which had dominated the trade at the start of the 19th century, now provided only 12 percent and 21 percent of Rio's slaves, respectively.

These shifts in the African sources of Rio's slaves did not, generally, represent an opening of new areas of slave trading in Africa, but rather a shift in the destination of the slaves sold from each area. Prior to the start of the 19th century the East African

[5] March 1830 was the date by which the Anglo-Brazilian anti-slave-trade treaty went into effect. (See Bethell, *The Abolition*, p. 60.) That the treaty had some immediate impact is evident from the newspaper notices. Only a few ships leaving Africa with slaves after the end of March 1830 are recorded; all but one of the ships arriving in Rio de Janeiro from April to September were ships that sailed from Africa before the expiration date. Evidently Brazilian traders expected the British navy to start seizing ships with the enactment of the treaty. But needed enabling legislation was much delayed and official Brazilian criminal prosecutions did not begin until November 1831 (*ibid.*, p. 69). Even then, effective prosecution was difficult and the trade rapidly revived. But as far as the newspaper reportings are concerned, the treaty date of March 1830 terminates all listings of slave shipping. Thereafter, all ships recorded as coming from Africa give no information as to slave arrivals.

[6] By 1835, it is estimated that slave arrivals for all Brazilian ports south of Bahia were back to their pre-treaty levels, and in fact exceeded even the frenetic 1828-1830 period. (David Eltis, "The Direction and Fluctuation of the Transatlantic Slave Trade 1821-43: A Revision of the 1845 Parliamentary Paper," paper presented at the MSSB Conference, Colby, Maine, 1975, diagram 1).

Table 4.1

Number of Slaves Shipped from Africa to Rio de Janeiro, 1825-1830, by Region

	REGIONS OF AFRICA								
Period of Arrival	From Congo[a]		From Angola		From Mozambique		Total	
	Ships	No. of Slaves	Ships	No. of Slaves	Ships	No. of Slaves		No. of Slaves
Dec. 1825 - May 1826	5	1,819	19	8,389	6	3,262		13,470
June 1826 - May 1827	21	8,809	39	16,189	11	6,329		31,327
June 1827 - May 1828	36	12,262	35	13,422	13	7,998		33,682
June 1828 - May 1829	38	13,804	42	17,561	25	14,180		45,545
June 1829 - May 1830	41	14,244	65	25,973	28	15,407		57,097[b]
June 1830 - Sept. 1830					4	1,472		1,472
TOTALS	141	50,938	200	81,534	87	48,648		182,593[b]

[a]Congo refers to the region from the Rio Zaire north under Portuguese control, which presently forms a part of Angola.

[b]Includes 4 ships, carrying 1,473 slaves, with unknown Africa origin.

Source: Diario do Rio de Janeiro and Jornal do Comércio (1825-1830).

Table 4.2
Number of Slaves Shipped to Rio de Janeiro, 1825-1830,
by Regions and Ports of Africa
(standard deviations in parentheses)

Ports[a] and Regions of Africa	No. of Ships	No. of Slaves	Average No. of Slaves per Ship	Average Sailing Time from Africa
1. *Congo*	*141*	*50,938*	*361 (138)*	*33.5 (7.3)*
Molembo	26	5,479	211	34.0
Cabinda	95	39,452	415	33.9
Rio Zaire[b]	20	6,007	300	31.0
2. *Angola*	*200*	*81,534*	*408 (128)*	*33.5 (6.3)*
Ambriz	59	20,934	355	33.6
Luanda	86	38,940	453	34.1
Benguela	55	21,660	394	32.4
3. *Mozambique*	*87*	*48,648*	*559 (164)*	*60.8 (11.8)*
Lorenço Marques	7	4,031	576	57.1
Inhambane	6	3,408	568	58.2
Quelimane	31	15,608	503	58.3
Mocambique	43	25,601	595	63.5
TOTALS[c]	*428*	*181,120*	*423 (157)*	*39.2 (13.7)*

[a]The ports are listed consecutively from north to south for West Africa and from south to north for East Africa.

[b]Rio Zaire, called until recently the Congo River, was the name used in the period under study by the Portuguese.

[c]There were four ships, carrying 1,473 slaves, whose African ports of exit are unknown.

Source: Same as table 4.1.

slave trade, smaller in magnitude than that of the West African coast, was dominated by the French, used mainly for their Indian Ocean colonies, and by Arab traders. Although the French did start trans-Atlantic shipments in the last decades of the 18th century, it was only with the slave trade to Brazil in the 19th century that the area became a part of the Atlantic slave system.[7]

[7] See Edward A. Alpers, *The East African Slave Trade* (Nairobi, 1967), and his "The French Slave Trade in East Africa (1721-1810)," *Cahiers d'études africaines,* x (1970), 80-124. See also Curtin, *Atlantic Slave Trade,* p. 242. The Mozambique trade was greatly influenced by governmental regulation. Prior to 1752, Portuguese East Africa had been a subordinate jurisdiction within the colonial government of Portuguese India and its trade mostly controlled by monopoly companies. It was estimated that Portuguese slave exports at mid-century were only some 1,000 persons per annum. But

The Brazilian expansion into the area north of the Congo River similarly reflected a decline in the French and Dutch trades from this area.[8] While it has been claimed that trade from this area declined from its peaks in the last decades of the 18th century, the annual slave movements in the period studied were equal to the 18th-century peaks. The Angolan trade, while falling in its relative importance as a Brazilian supplier, was maintained at about the same absolute level as earlier periods. Miller claims that a "greater number of slaves than ever left the Congo-Angola coast during most of the period of the 'suppression of the slave trade' in response to demand from Brazil and the Spanish colonies."[9] The major change in trading patterns between the 18th and 19th centuries was the expansion of the Brazilian slave trade

---

the creation of an independent Capitania Geral in 1752 changed the tempo of Mozambique affairs. Trade was eventually made free to all Portuguese subjects from that date onward, though the port of Mozambique was given monopoly status in all commerce. In 1786, however, the Mozambique monopoly was broken, and the ports of Quelimane, Sofala, Inhambane, and Lourenço Marques were given the right to free trade. While Quelimane established its own customs house (*alfândega*) in the following year, it took several more years before the other ports were able to overcome Mozambique opposition and establish their own independent trade. (José Justino Teixeira Botelho, *Historia militar e politica dos portugueses em Mocambique* [2 vols.; Lisbon, 1934], I, 405-414, 507-522; and Fritz Hoppe, *A Africa Oriental Portuguesa no tempo do Marques de Pombal, 1750-1777* [Lisbon, 1970], pp. 226ff.) Thus it was only by the last decade of the 18th and first decades of the 19th century that the southern Portuguese East African ports were finally permitted to participate in the slave trade. Even so, their full involvement in the trade did not take place until after the end of the Napoleonic wars in 1814, when general peace and the development of interior regional markets finally brought major commercial expansion.

[8] See Phyllis Martin, "The Trade of Loango in the Seventeenth and Eighteenth Century," in Richard Gray and David Birmingham, eds., *Pre-Colonial African Trade*, (London, 1970), 139-161, and her *The External Trade of the Loango Coast, 1576-1870* (Oxford, 1972). Eltis argues that between 1826 and 1830 there may have been a bias against reporting ships north of Cape Lopez (Eltis, "The Export," pp. 7-8). But this does not seem to have been a significant source for Rio de Janeiro bound slaves even before or after this period.

[9] See Joseph C. Miller, "The Slave Trade in Congo and Angola," in Martin L. Kilson and Robert I. Rotberg, eds., *The African Diaspora* (Cambridge, Mass., 1976), p. 111, "Legal Portuguese Slaving from Angola, Some Preliminary Indications of Volume and Direction, 1760-1830," *Revue française d'histoire d'Outre Mer*, LXII, nos. 226-227 (1975), pp. 135-176; see also Martin, *External Trade*, pp. 117-135, and Curtin, *The Atlantic Slave Trade*, pp. 251-264.

northward and eastward, filling gaps left by the disappearance of traders from other European nations.

There were also some apparent changes in the nature of the trade with African ports. Whereas in the period from 1795 to 1811 the average number of slaves carried by ships from East Africa was 345, less than three-quarters the amount carried by vessels from Angola, by the 1820s the ships from East Africa were carrying nearly 560 slaves. This was 27 percent more than ships from Angola.[10] The number of slaves carried per ship from Angola declined by about one-fifth in this period, for reasons that are difficult to determine. As seen in table 4.2, ship sizes varied within regions as well, and there seems to be some correlation between the total number of ships coming from a port and the average number of slaves carried.

The distinct patterns of seasonality in the timing of arrival into Rio in the period from 1796 to 1810 are also noted in the 1825-1830 period. While there was a quite sharp difference in the East African trade between the first and the last six months of the year, a similar pattern exists for shipments from West Africa. There are only minor differences in the number of slaves carried per ship from each port in the different seasons, and about two-thirds of all slaves arrived during the months of summer and fall. The causes of this seasonal pattern seem, in the case of Mozambique, to be more related to sailing conditions from Africa and to conditions of supply within Africa, than they do to seasonal demands for labor in the Brazilian market. Sailing conditions from East Africa were very difficult during the winter and spring months.[11] In the case of the Congo and Angolan ports, there is a similar pattern of seasonal shipping, as was noted a decade earlier in the slave-ship arrivals into Rio de Janeiro. Again the question of the impact of African or American causal

[10] When classified by ship type, the most frequently cited was the *bergantim*, which was used in over one-half the voyages. Used in over 10 percent of voyages were both *galeras*, carrying above-average numbers of slaves, and used disproportionately in the East African trade, and *escunas*, with small numbers carried, used almost exclusively in the West African trade. Unfortunately I do not yet have any tonnage data for these ships.

[11] In private correspondence Philip D. Curtin has written: "Not only is the southeastern coast of Africa one of the roughest in the world, the marine conditions in this area are at their worst in the winter months, and on into the spring, when gales are almost constant."

Table 4.3
Seasonal Pattern of Ship Arrivals in Rio de Janeiro,
1825-1830, by Regions and Ports of Africa

Ports and Regions of Africa	Season[a]			
	Winter	Spring	Summer	Fall
1. *Congo*	26	25	46	45
Molembo	4	8	6	8
Cabinda	20	12	32	32
Rio Zaire	2	5	8	5
2. *Angola*	34	52	55	60
Ambriz	8	17	22	12
Luanda	14	24	20	29
Benguela	12	11	13	19
3. *Mozambique*	7	5	51	26
Lorenço Marques	1	2	2	2
Inhambane	1	–	4	1
Quelimane	1	1	20	10
Moçambique	4	2	25	13
TOTALS	67	82	152	131

[a]December, January, February are the months of summer;
March, April, May, the months of fall; June, July, August are
winter; and September, October, November, are spring.

Source: Same as table 4.1.

factors in accounting for this seasonal pattern is difficult to determine. There was the approximate correlation between the peak seasons of sugar harvest and the arrival of slaves into the port. Nevertheless, the problems of the rainy season in West African ports have often been cited as a factor in determining migrations, while African harvesting and planting seasons must surely have had an influence as well.

The maritime notices of the *Jornal do Comercio* and the *Diario do Rio de Janeiro* also provide information previously lacking on the marketing of the slaves imported. While over 100 merchants were listed as receiving slaves from Africa during this period, there was a concentration in the marketing of these Africans. The leading 10 merchants accounted for 40 percent of the total shipments, while 41 percent obtained only one shipment. Even so, the average merchant still accounted for just over 4 shipments of slaves.[12]

[12] A comparison has been made for one year, 1829, between the number

Table 4.4
Number of Merchants of Rio de Janeiro Who Received
Shipments of Slaves, 1825-1830, by Number of Consignments

No. of Slave Cargoes	No. of Merchants Receiving Consignments	Total No. of Shipments Consigned
1	42	42
2	10	20
3	12	36
4	9	36
5	10	50
6	1	6
7	4	28
8	5	40
9	2	18
10	1	10
18	1	18
19	1	19
20	2	40
26	1	26
39	1	39
TOTALS	*102*	*428*[a]

[a]There were 8 shipments of slaves for whom no merchants were listed.

Source: Same as table 4.1.

Just as there was a concentration in ship trading to selected African ports, so too these leading merchants also tended to specialize in slaves from specific regions of Africa. Thus only 4 of these merchants received slaves from both East and West Africa (see table 4.5), and 2 of these were principally involved with the trade from one of these regions. Given the complex credit arrangements and rather intimate relationship between African merchant exporters and Rio factors, it is relatively easy to understand why there was such concentration and specialization by area for the majority of merchants.[13]

---

of traders receiving slaves and the size of the total merchant community. Of the 173 Brazilian merchants listed in the 1829 *Almanak imperial do comércio e das corporações civis e militares do imperio do Brasil,* 28 were listed as having imported slaves. It is thus clear that the participants in the African slave trade were not a minor element in the merchant community. This almanac is also listed as "Segundo anno" of "PLANCHER-SEIGNOT para 1829," and is found in the BNRJ, Seção dos Livros Raros, L, 6, 8.

[13] Within West Africa, a similar pattern of specialization, though not as pronounced as that shown in table 4.5, existed.

Table 4.5
The Ten Leading Merchants of Rio de Janeiro Who Participated
in the Slave Trade from Africa, 1825-1830

No. of Slave Shipments	Merchants	Total No. of Slaves	Sources of Slaves
39	Joaquim Antonio Ferreira	15,209	Only two shipments were from East Africa
26	Joaquim Ferreira dos Santos	11,371	All were from West Africa
20	Miguel Ferreira Gomes	9,060	All were from West Africa
20	João Alves da Silva Porto	8,303	Ten shipments were from East Africa
19	Lourenço Antonio do Rego	8,134	All were from West Africa
18	Antonio Jose Meirelles	5,920	Only two shipments were from East Africa
10	Francisco José dos Santos	4,967	Six shipments were from East Africa
9	João Rodrigues Perreira de Almeida	4,915	All were from East Africa
9	Miguel Guedes Pinto	3,931	All were from West Africa
8	Joaquim José de Rocha	3,008	All were from West Africa
178		*74,818*	

Source: Same as table 4.1.

The actual role that these merchants played in the African slave trade and in the internal distribution within Brazil is extremely difficult to assess at the present time. In the mid-18th century the Rio merchants who received consignments of slaves were generally working for Luandan and other Angolan merchants. These merchants seemed to control the bulk of the slaves moved from Angola to Brazil. These Angolans carried out the initial purchase of the slaves from the Africans in the interior kingdoms, transported them to the coast, paid for the shipment for Brazil, clothed and housed them in Rio and the other Brazilian ports, and finally sold them to Brazilian planters and other slave owners. In this transaction, the Rio merchant probably imported some slaves in his own name or with other local merchants, but did most of his business for an Angolan exporter, simply getting a commission on the sale price. But this relationship was changing rapidly by the beginning of the 19th century. The relative decline of Angola and its increasing dependence on Rio for imports and capital was probably reflected in the shift of the role of the Rio merchants in relationship to their Angolan counterparts.[14] While African-based merchants must still have played an important role by the 1820s, it would seem that the Rio merchants by this time were importing the bulk of the slaves in their own names. The fact that a given merchant was handling such large numbers of slaves, plus the more important role played by Brazilian capital in Angolan affairs, all point in that direction. Nevertheless, until further studies are undertaken, the exact relationship of the two groups of merchants remains to be clarified.

Also unexplained is the relative infrequency with which individual ships appeared on the list of Rio's arrivals. Despite the relatively short sailing time from the African ports to Rio, only one-half of the vessels recorded appeared more than once, and only 10 percent averaged as much as one arrival per year. This infrequency cannot be explained solely on the basis of turn-around time, and suggests that a strict bilateral trade between Africa and Rio did not exist for the slave trade in this period.

The newspaper advertisements can also be used to analyze factors in the mortality of slaves in transit from Africa to Rio. While the data on mortality are less complete than those for other variables, there is sufficient evidence to provide some useful basis for explanation. In the 390 cases where there were deaths recorded on the voyage from Africa, the mortality rate was 66 slaves died at sea per 1,000 shipped. This compares favorably with the rate of 93 per 1,000 recorded in Rio's trade at the beginning of the 19th century—more favorably than these aggregate ratios would suggest, since there was a shift to the higher mortality shipments from East Africa over this period. The causes of the decline are not clear, since it is doubtful that sailing time could have decreased sufficiently, and it would be expected that longer inland journeys to the coast would have been required.

Before examining the mortality rates further, we must note that not only do they vary systematically and rather dramatically by port of embarcation from Africa, but the variation from any port is quite large (see tables 4.7 and 4.8). The distribution of

[14] Manuel dos Anjos da Silva Rebelo, *Relações entre Angola e Brasil, 1808-1830* (Lisbon, 1970).

Table 4.6

Mortality Rates of Slaves Shipped from Africa to Rio de Janeiro, 1825-1830, by Region[a]

Period of Arrival	REGIONS OF AFRICA			TOTAL		
	From Congo	From Angola	From Mozambique	Av. per Ship	St. Dev.	No. of Ships
Dec. 1825 - May 1826	14	68	48	57	(59)	24
June 1826 - May 1827	15	65	92	56	(62)	62
June 1827 - May 1828	36	54	104	55	(54)	77
June 1828 - May 1829	35	57	136	69	(70)	95
June 1829 - May 1830	39	66	125	72	(72)	128[b]
June 1830 - Sept. 1830			252	252	(91)	4
TOTAL SHIPS	117	186	87	66	(69)	390
Av. per ship	33	62	121			
St. Dev.	42	47	99			

[a]The mortality rates are computed as the ratio of slaves who died at sea to total slaves shipped, and are expressed as deaths per 1,000 shipped.

[b]There were two ships included in this total whose African origin was unknown.

Source: Same as table 4.1.

Table 4.7
Mortality Rates of Slaves Shipped to Rio de Janeiro, 1825-1830,
by Regions and Ports of Africa[a]

Ports and Regions of Africa	No. of Ships with Deaths Recorded	Average Mortality Rate per 1,000	Standard Deviation
1. *Congo*	*117*	*33*	*42*
Molembo	17	47	59
Cabinda	84	32	40
Rio Zaire	16	24	19
2. *Angola*	*186*	*62*	*47*
Ambriz	47	32	42
Luanda	84	71	46
Benguela	55	73	44
3. *Mozambique*	*85*	*121*	*99*
Lorenço Marques	7	103	98
Inhambane	6	52	62
Quelimane	30	107	99
Moçambique	42	145	98
TOTALS	*388*	*66*	*69*

[a]The mortality rates are computed as the ratio of slaves who died at sea to 1,000 slaves shipped.

Source: Same as table 4.1.

mortality rates for ships from the three major regions is quite skewed, with the median below the mean. This means that the high average death rates reflect the influence of the smaller number of ships with above-average mortality experience. Nevertheless the year-to-year changes shown in table 4.6 are based upon shifts in the distribution of the experience of many ships, and not to the unusual experience of only one or two ships.[15] The distribution of mortality rates in table 4.8 can explain, also, the frequent citation of what are, by average experience, unusually high rates. Mortality rates of over 20 percent of the slaves aboard ship were not unknown and are to be found for all regions of Africa. Yet these rates occurred on only 5.6 percent of ships for which data was recorded, and on less than 2 percent of shipments from West Africa. Thus the attention paid to abnormal cases is

[15] The measure used was the percentage of ships in each year with a mortality rate above the all-period average for the zone. Sharp increases in the average death rate were concomitant with a rise in the percentage of ships with "above average" mortality rates.

Table 4.8
The Distribution of Mortality Rates of Ships Carrying Slaves to
Rio de Janeiro, 1825-1830, by Regions of Africa

Mortality Rate per Ship (per 1,000)	REGIONS OF AFRICA			
	From Congo	*From Angola*	*From Mozambique*	*Total*
1 - 19	65	41	9	115
20 - 39	22	32	17	71
40 - 59	14	31	6	51
60 - 79	9	28	7	44
80 - 99	1	17	5	23
100 - 119	—	18	4	22
120 - 139	1	5	3	9
140 - 159	2	6	6	14
160 - 179	1	4	7	12
180 - 199	1	1	4	6
200 - 219	—	1	3	4
220 - 239	—	2	3	5
240 - over	1	—	11	12
TOTALS	*117*	*186*	*85*	*388*

Source: Same as table 4.1.

misleading, since in this sample the average (median) ship had a
mortality rate of under 5 percent.

The causes for these rates of slave deaths in the Middle Passage
in this sample seem to be highly correlated with sailing time and
port of origin in Africa.[16] While there was a significant difference
between the mortality experiences of ships coming from the two

[16] Regressions, both arithmetic and logarithmic, were run for ships from
all regions together, as well as for each region separately. When all regions
were grouped together, the regression equation was:

Mortality Rate $= -.047 + .0028$ Sailing Time $\qquad R^2 = .330$
$\qquad\qquad\qquad\quad (13.8)$

The number below the coefficients is the *t*-ratio
When separate variables were introduced for each region, the equation was:

Mortality Rate $= -.078 + .0033$ Sailing Time $+ .028R_2 - 002R_3 \quad R^2 = .363$
$\qquad\qquad\qquad (9.7) \qquad\qquad\qquad\quad (4.4) \quad (0.2)$

where R_2 equals one if the port was in Angola, and R_3 equals one if the
port was in Mozambique.

Curtin's discussion (*The Atlantic Slave Trade*, p. 281) of a sample of
ships involved in the slave trade between 1817 and 1843 emphasizes the
"marked correlation between mortality rates at sea and length of voyage."
In his unpublished thesis, LeVeen has used regression analysis on this data
to argue that about one percent of the slaves died each four days at sea.
(See E. Phillip LeVeen, "British Slave Trade Suppression Policies, 1820-
1865: Impact and Implications," unpublished Ph.D. dissertation, University
of Chicago, 1971.)

West African regions, the higher mortality rates for those from East Africa seem consistent with their longer sailing time. The number of slaves carried per ship was not, however, an important influence on mortality rates, being non-significant in regressions including sailing time, and not itself having an independent influence on sailing time.[17] There was some seasonal pattern in the mortality rates. Ships arriving in the summer—the most frequent season of arrival—had the lowest rates; while those for winter arrivals—the least frequent season of arrival—tended to be higher than average.

The importance of sailing time has several noteworthy dimensions. The pronounced difference in mortality experience for slaves shipped from the Congo and from Angola, despite the similarity in sailing times to Rio, indicates the importance of the source of origin of the slaves. This, of course, could reflect differences in the length of time involved in transit from source of capture to the port, as well as possible differences in the time between arrival at the port and the onset of the voyage.[18] Since the supply of slaves close to the coast was becoming exhausted as a result of prolonged periods of shipment, it is possible that not only were longer trips from the interior required, but also that the condition of those enslaved was becoming poorer over time.

Another crucial aspect of the sailing time is obscured when no differentiation is made for the different African regions of origin, as is clear from table 4.9. There is some increase in the mortality rate with increased sailing time for each of the major zones, although there is no difference between 30-39 and 40-49 day voyages from either of the West African regions. Yet what is particularly striking is the sharp increase in the rate after some

[17] This evidence does not bear directly on arguments relating to "overcrowding," since data on the tonnage of the ships is unavailable. Preliminary analysis of data for the slave trade from 1817 to 1843 (kindly provided by Philip Curtin), and for the British trade at the end of the 18th century (see below, Chapter 7) indicate that there was no systematic relationship between slaves per ton and mortality rates, although there was a negative relationship between ship tonnage and mortality rates. The number of slaves carried per ton, in fact, declined systematically with ship tonnage.

[18] See Martin, *The External Trade*, pp. 93-115, 136-137. She quotes an estimate by Unger, of mortality rates in Dutch shipments from the Loango Coast of 10.6 percent in the period from 1732 to 1808 (p. 104). If so, the mortality rate from this region declined rather sharply, by over two-thirds in the early 19th century.

Table 4.9

Relationship between Mortality Rates of Ships and Length of Voyages, 1825-1830, by Regions of Africa

Length of Voyage	REGIONS OF AFRICA						TOTAL		
	From Congo		From Angola		From Mozambique				
	No. of Ships	Mortality Rate	No. of Ships	Mortality Rate	No. of Ships	Mortality Rate	No. of Ships	Average Mortality Rate	Standard Deviation
20-29	34	29	51	47			85	40	37
30-39	64	32	107	64			171	52	49
40-49	14	31	21	62	12	64	47	53	42
50-59	2	87	4	145	30	84	36	91	69
60-69	2	111	1	215	20	104	23	109	86
70-79					15	200	15	200	87
80-89					7	231	7	231	112
Over 90					1	349	1	349	

Source: Same as table 4.1.

specific length of voyage, which differs by region.[19] For the West African ports the sharp increase occurs for those ships with voyages of over 50 days, whereas for East Africa the "cut-off" point is at 70 days. For those ships from East Africa with sailing times below 70 days, the death rates are comparable with, and frequently below, those of West African ships. While these samples are small, it might be tentatively suggested that slave captains had fairly definite expectations about the length of crossing, allowing for some anticipated excess above the average, and that they adequately supplied themselves with food and water for their routes on this basis. There was a trade-off in the use of the space on board ship, between the carrying of additional slaves and the provisioning of food and water for the crew and the slaves. Some allowance needs to have been made for above-average voyage times, but an excessive allowance would have meant too great a reduction in the number of slaves carried to markets in Rio. Thus there was an "optimum" number of slaves to be carried per ship, dependent upon expectations as to the sailing time between Africa and Rio. The excessively high mortality rates that have attracted attention are characteristic of those voyages in which, for whatever reason, the actual sailing time exceeded the length of the voyage for which captains found it profitable to prepare themselves.

It should be stressed that even though the mortality rates among Rio's slave imports had declined over a quarter-century from 93 per 1,000 slaves to 66 per 1,000, even the lower rate was an extraordinarily high ratio for the predominantly young adult population that the African slaves represented. While age and sex data are not given for the imported slaves, from previous studies we can presume that the bulk of the slaves were young adults between the ages of 15 and 40, and primarily male. Their age-specific death rates, if they had remained in Africa, would have been considerably below those experienced on the sailing from Africa to Rio.[20]

[19] Regressions were run for each region separately, partitioning between ships with below average sailing time and those with sailing times above the average. There is generally no relationship for the former category, with some positive relationship for the latter group. Other partitioning levels and the results indicate that for sailing times within the range of "normal expectations," mortality was more related to random influences than in any systematic way to the length of the voyage.

[20] A high mortality rate for males of about twenty would be in the range

These rates would also appear high for other comparable migrant population movements by sea in the 19th century. Of these movements, the best studied so far is the convict labor transportation to Australia. These convict ships, despite their much lower ratios of persons carried to tonnage (averaging less than .5 persons per ton), experienced mortality rates not dissimilar to the slave trade. Thus in the period from 1787 to 1800, some 10.4 percent of the total of 7,547 convicts on 41 ships (whose crossing averaged 191 days) perished on the high seas. This rate, however, quickly dropped to 4.1 percent for the 8,778 convicts who left in some 55 ships in the period from 1810 to 1815 (with average sailings of 168 days). Thereafter, though the volume of convict migration kept increasing, reaching its maximum level in the late 1820s and the 1830s (averaging some 4,785 per annum), the rate of mortality was consistently below 1 percent of those who left Europe.[21] It should be recalled when comparing these rates, that these were longer voyages, and may have had much higher numbers of elderly persons subject to higher risks of mortality. But what is most impressive about these data is that the death rates fell so rapidly in this trade and then remained consistently low for the rest of the century. They were in fact somewhat lower than the regular emigrant movements from Europe to America in the same period.

Although the more useful comparison for the slave trade would be with the 18th- and 19th-century data from the European peasant migrations to America, surprisingly, much less systematic data is currently available than for the slave or convict migrations. What little that does exist, however, would seem to suggest that the 18th-century immigrant mortality rates were similar to the slave mortality rates in the same period.[22] That these rates

---

25-50 per 1,000 for one year. Roberts has estimated that for slaves in the West Indies, of both sexes in the years 1820-1832, mortality was below 20. See G. W. Roberts, "A Life Table for a West Indian Slave Population," *Population Studies*, V (1951), 238-243.

[21] A.G.L. Shaw, *Convicts and the Colonies. A Study of Penal Transportation from Great Britain and Ireland to Australian and Other Parts of the British Empire* (London, 1966), pp. 116, 363ff. The calculations for the pre-1800 period were made from the more extensive list on p. 116.

[22] See above, pp. 70-71. This is also suggested by Oliver MacDonagh, *A Pattern of Government Growth, 1880-1860. The Passenger Acts and their Enforcement* (London, 1961), pp. 50-51, 129; who argues that high rates of 10 percent mortality may have been common prior to the adoption of

may not be quite comparable should be stressed here, since it is possible that among the emigrants there were larger ratios of very young children and older persons, which would mean that the emigrant population had a higher proportion of its members at risk than among the slaves.[23] Nevertheless, though these mortality rates were similar in the 18th century, immigrant mortality dropped as dramatically as convict mortality in the early decades of the 19th century, reaching the consistently low figure of 2 percent mortality and under in the mid-century crossings. Thus the 132,246 emigrants who shipped from Liverpool to New York in 1854 experienced a death rate of 1.2 percent.[24] A year earlier, American records show that the mortality of 96,950 immigrants in 312 vessels arriving in New York in the four-month period from September 1 to December 1 was 2.0 percent, while the 395,325 immigrants who arrived in all American ports in the year 1853 reported a rate of under 1 percent.[25]

---

more stringent legislation. Unfortunately, no systematic data is currently available for the decades before and after the various regulatory acts.

[23] What little data that exists giving age and sex breakdowns among the immigrants would suggest a somewhat higher representation of persons over 40 than among the slaves. Thus, among the 167,444 Danish immigrants to North America between 1868-1900, some 10 percent were 40 years of age or over and some 20 percent were 14 years or under. (Kristian Huidt, *Flight to America. The Social Background of 300,000 Danish Immigrants* [New York, 1975], p. 73.) Although no breakdown exists for adult slaves, it can be assumed that the low sale value of persons over 40 reduced their participation in the trade. As for children, the data are conflicting. Thus only 7 percent among the slaves landed in Jamaica in the 1790s were children (see below, table 7.4), whereas among the slaves arriving in Cuba in the 1790-1820 period the number of children is comparable, if not slightly higher than the Danish data (see table 9.7). As to the sex ratio, it would appear that immigrants and slaves were not too dissimilar in their high representation of males, though in this convicts were even more heavily male than either these two migrant groups. Thus in most of the slave trades in the 18th and 19th centuries males were between 60 percent and 70 percent of the total immigrants (see below, tables 7.4 and 9.7). In the total of 1.4 million emigrant arrivals to the United States between 1844 and 1850, 60 percent were males. (U.S. Congress, Senate, *Report of the Select Committee on the Sickness and Mortality on Board Emigrant Ships* [Washington, D.C., 1854], p. 24.) The ratio of males among the convicts was close to 90 percent. (Shaw, *Convicts and the Colonies*, pp. 363ff.)

[24] Great Britain, House of Commons, Parliamentary Papers [Reports from Committees], *Second Report from the Select Committee on Emigrant Ships*, vol. xii (1854), no. 349, pp. 8-9.

[25] U.S. Congress, Senate, *Report of the Select Committee*, pp. 26-30. There appears to be a discrepancy between reports by quarantine medical

Until the late 1850s, sailing ships predominated in the carrying trade of immigrants, and their rates of mortality in the sea voyage was consistently higher than steam vessels. Thus, of the 950,916 steerage passengers who arrived aboard steamers between 1864 and 1869 in the port of New York, the average mortality was only 0.18 percent, and this was for an average of 425 steerage passengers per voyage. At the same time, the sailing vessels on average carried only 219 steerage passengers, yet their mortality was 0.9 percent for the sea voyage. This average mortality, just as in the slave trade, covered a high degree of variance. But even in the seemingly epidemic year of 1866, steamers experienced a mortality rate of only 0.5 percent while sailing ships went to a high of 1.1 percent.[26] What these figures would seem to suggest is that time at sea was as important an indicator of immigrant mortality as it was in the earlier slave mortality. Also, it can be assumed, at least until the early 1860s, that the average immigrant mortality on the trip to America in the 19th century remained at the 1 percent to 2 percent level, since sailing vessels continued to predominate.[27] Thus as late as 1856, only 3 percent of the immigrants arriving by steerage to America came by steamer; and in the port of New York, sailing vessels still predominated in the immigrant trade until 1864, a year in which they accounted for 57 percent of the landed immigrants.[28] The big killers in the mid-19th-century immigrant trade were somewhat different from those in the slave trade, being, in order of importance, "ship's fever" or typhus, cholera, and smallpox. Unlike the slave trade, there also appeared to be a sharp difference in

---

officers and ship's captains—the former reporting 2,158 deaths, or a mortality rate of 2.2 percent. The Senate Committee, while giving both sets of figures, uses the captain's reports as the standard ones.

[26] Frederich Kapp, *Immigration and the Commissioners of Emigration* (2d ed.; New York, 1969; 1st ed. 1870), p. 241. In his general study of the Atlantic migration of Europeans in the 19th century, Taylor suggests that by the 1860s the overall mortality rate for the approximately 35-day voyage by sail from Europe to America was under 1 percent. (Philip Taylor, *The Distant Magnet* [New York, 1971], pp. 139-140.)

[27] Individual year rates could go much higher than this average figure, of course. Thus, largely as a result of the crisis of the Irish famine and the high incidence of disease and malnutrition among them, the 90,105 poor Irish who emigrated to Canada during the summer of 1847 experienced a mortality rate of 5.4 percent in the crossing, with an even higher mortality rate among those hospitalized after landing. (Kapp, *Immigration*, p. 23.)

[28] *Ibid.*, pp. 38, 241.

the mortality experience of the European shipping engaged in the trade, with the English immigrant ships consistently having the highest disease and mortality rates in the trade.[29]

In comparing these samples of mortality in the convict and immigrant trades with those which emerge from the study of the slaves reaching Rio de Janeiro in the period from the 1790s to the 1830s, we can offer some tentative conclusions. It would seem that while general mortality rates for these different migrating populations were comparable in the 18th century, the immigrant and especially the convict rates dropped far more rapidly than the slave rates and remained consistently below them by the 1820s and 1830s. The causes for this change in the 19th century are difficult to explain. Certainly the ratios of persons carried to tons of shipping were much lower in the immigrant and convict trades. But this was the case in both the 18th and 19th centuries. Also, in all three trades it would appear that communicable diseases were the prime cause of the very high death rates and that contagion and the spread of these diseases was not directly linked to the number of persons carried per ton. Moreover, the descriptions of neglect in terms of the supply of fresh provisions (especially among the English immigrant shippers) do not suggest healthier or more abundant supplies of food than those carried for slaves. Until more abundant quantitative data is available for the early decades of the 19th-century immigrant trade, the causes for these different trends cannot be fully elucidated. As to the tentative conclusions about the slave mortality experience based on the Rio de Janeiro data, these will be more fully tested in the comparative chapters that follow on the French and English slave trades in the 18th century, where several of the variables missing from the Portuguese data could be computed.

But before we deal with the comparative experiences of other slave trades, it would be useful to complete this survey of the Portuguese trade with a study of the question of the impact of the African slave populations within Brazil itself. Unfortunately for this purpose, the quality of the Brazilian census materials prior to the close of the Atlantic slave trade is such that no direct effort can be made to measure the mortality and natality experience of the Africans after their arrival. Nevertheless, there is a

[29] *Ibid.*, chapter ii.

body of data that can be explored tangentially to this theme, and that ultimately leads back into the broader question of the response of the resident slave population to the closing of the Atlantic slave trade. The following chapter, therefore, will consider the internal slave trade that began to develop as a result of the closing of the Atlantic slave trade to Brazil in 1850.

Chapter Five

The Internal Slave Trade
in 19th-Century Brazil

With the successful termination of the Atlantic slave trade to
Brazil in 1850, the internal slave trade expanded within the
Brazilian empire, just as it did within all the major American
slave regimes that ended the slave trade prior to emancipation.[1]
Though both contemporaries and later historians were fully
aware of the new slave trade, its dimensions and characteristics
have not been fully explored. This failure of analysis has been
due to the scarcity of published quantitative and qualitative data.
As a result, historians have been unable to assess the dynamics
of the trade in terms of the types of slaves shipped between the
provinces, their place of origin, and their impact on the importing
and exporting zones. It is especially within the context of this
latter area that the most controversy has developed on the internal slave trade.

The key question relating to this trade, which developed just
as coffee was achieving its dominance within the Brazilian economy, was the extent of its impact on the supply of slaves for the
new coffee plantations of Rio de Janeiro and São Paulo. Did
these slaves, in fact, come from the declining sugar plantations
of the northeast, or did they come from the natural growth of
the already heavily slave populated zones of these central and
southern coffee provinces?

The traditional view has been that the native slave class was
unable to maintain itself because of natural rates of population
decrease; therefore the only recourse was to attract slaves from
the less economically vital sugar industry of the Brazilian northeast.[2] This in turn explains the rapid decline of slavery as an

---

[1] On this development in English-speaking America, see D. Eltis, "The
Traffic in Slaves between the British West Indian Colonies, 1807-1833,"
Economic History Review, Second Series, xxv, No. 1 (Feb. 1972), and
Frederic Bancroft, *Slave Trading in the Old South* (Baltimore, 1931).

[2] For the latest statement of this traditional view, see Robert Conrad, *The
Destruction of Brazilian Slavery, 1852-1888* (Berkeley, 1972), chapter iv.

institution in the northeast—through the losses of slaves to the more economically viable plantations of the coffee zones of Rio de Janeiro and São Paulo of the center and south. But was the Brazilian slave population able to reproduce itself? This could have occurred if the declines in total population that occurred were simply due to the temporary impact of the older and more male flow of Africans into the slave labor force. If this was the case, then the booming center-west coffee zones may have been able to supply their own slave needs out of natural population growth and local redistribution, and therefore would have relied only moderately on the inter-provincial long-distance, sea-routed internal slave trade to fulfill its needs. In turn, this would mean that the decline of the institution of slavery in the northeast of Brazil and to a lesser extent that of the far south, was due to increased rates of local manumission and the progressive shift to more economic forms of cheap and competitive free labor. The only way to test such hypotheses in the absence of detailed pre-1872 national censuses is to analyze the inter-provincial slave trade between the northeast and the south and the key center-west receiving port of Rio de Janeiro, which was the primary port for the coffee economy at this time. The sources for this study will be data available from the registers of the port of Rio de Janeiro in 1852.

Before we analyze this material, some general discussion of the nature of the trade is necessary. Clearly, internal migration of slaves, even seaborne inter-regional movement, was not a new phenomenon in 1850. A steady, widespread inter-provincial trade had gone on while the Atlantic slave trade was at its height. Also, an important part of the internal trade, both before and after 1850, was quite local, involving the land transfer of slaves within provincial borders, or between contiguous provinces. However, long-distance seaborne trade, the concern of this study, developed most fully after the Atlantic slave trade was terminated. While it still had elements of intra-regional movement, especially among the northeastern ports, it was primarily a trade in slaves from northeastern and southern ports to the central coffee zones of Brazil.

The principal destinations were Rio de Janeiro and Santos, the former being the more important. In 1852, for example, Rio de Janeiro was reported to have received over 4,400 slaves, and its average per-annum arrivals for 1852 to 1859 was estimated at 3,430.[3] Though no figures are available this early for Santos, its annual intake of slaves over a decade later was in the 1,000-to-2,000 range. Thus, in 1867, 904 slaves came to the city, 1,229 arrived in 1868, and 2,129 in 1869.[4] Considering that these were the primary ports of entry for slaves transported from the south and northeast by sea, the movement of slaves may have reached as high as 5,000 to 6,000 per annum in these two decades. One contemporary Brazilian authority, in fact, estimated in 1860 that in the decade of the 1850s some 5,500 slaves were annually being shipped to the central states from the north alone.[5]

This pattern of some 5,000 to 6,000 slaves transported by sea

[3] One contemporary source reported that 26,622 slaves were imported into Rio de Janeiro between 1852 and 1859, which would give an annual average of 3,327 slaves. This source stated that slave imports into Rio de Janeiro were as follows:

1852	4,409	1856	5,006
1853	2,909	1857	4,211
1854	4,418	1858	1,993
1855	3,532	1859	963

(Sebastião Ferreira Soares, *Notas estatísticas sôbre a produção agrícola e carestia dos gêneros alimenticios no Império do Brazil* [Rio de Janeiro, 1860], pp. 135-136.) The British Minister to Rio de Janeiro, W. D. Christie, reported that 34,688 slaves were imported by sea into Rio de Janeiro between January 1852 and July 1862, which would give a rate of 275 per month or 3,300 per annum. (W. D. Christie, *Notes on Brazilian Questions* [London, 1865], p. 93; cited in Bethell, *Abolition*, pp. 375-376.)

[4] For the respective importation figures see: Joaquim Saldanha Marinho, *Relatorio apresentado á assembléa legislativa provincial de São Paulo . . . no dia 2 de fevereiro de 1868 pelo presidente da mesma provincia . . .* (São Paulo, 1868), p. 15; Barão de Itauna, *Relatorio com que s. exc. o sr. . . . passou a administração da provincia ao exm. sr. . . . 3° Vice-presidente* (São Paulo, 1869), Annexo no. 1, Mappa n. 7; and Antonio Candido da Rocha, *Relatorio apresentado á assembléa legislativa provincial de São Paulo pelo presidente da provincia . . .* (São Paulo, 1870), pp. 65-66. It should also be noted that slaves were exported from this same port and that the net gain for the port was 580 slaves in 1867, 780 in 1868, and 1,746 in 1869.

[5] Ferreira Soares, *Notas estatísticas*, pp. 135-136. It should be noted here as well, that while southern ports such as Santos exported as well as imported slaves, northern ports such as Salvador da Bahia also imported as well as exported. Thus, in 1855 Bahia exported 1,699 slaves and imported 471 for a net loss of 1,228. In 1856 its net loss was 1,794, with 2,388 slaves exported to other ports of the empire and 594 imported. (Alvaro Tiberio de Moncouro e Lima, *Falla recitada na abertura da assembléa legislativa da Bahia . . .* [Bahia, 1856], Mappa n. 48; Jõao Lins Vieira Cansansao de Sinimbu, *Falla recitada na abertura da assembléa legislativa da Bahia . . .* [Bahia, 1857], Mappa n. 24.)

in the 1850s and 1860s would also seem to hold for the early 1870s. Between 1872 and 1876 some 25,711 slaves were imported into Rio de Janeiro and São Paulo provinces. This number, however, must have included a considerable inland and intra-regional element, since Minas Gerais lost slaves through migration during this same period.[6] Increasingly severe export taxes and other provincial government restrictions seem to have curtailed the trade seriously by the later 1870s and the early 1880s, even before its final abolition with emancipation in 1888.

Given the increasing restrictions of the last decades, and the shifting demands for slaves in Rio de Janeiro and São Paulo throughout the existence of the trade, it is difficult to determine the exact volume for the 1850-1888 period. Basing themselves on alternative sources, two recent scholars have placed the parameters of the inter-regional slave trade in the range of 100,000 to 200,000 persons between 1850 and 1881.[7] Accepting the 200,000 figure as an upper bound limit still means that the inter-regional trade was much less important as a migratory movement than the Atlantic slave trade. In the last years of the trade, that is from 1831 to 1850, the trans-Atlantic slave merchants are estimated to have moved some 24,000 slaves per annum into Brazilian ports, or over 482,000 for the twenty-year period.[8]

[6] Directoria Geral de Estatística, *Relatorio annexo ao do Ministerio dos Negocios do Imperio de 1878* (Rio de Janeiro, n.d.), p. 120.

[7] Using British consular reports as his source, J. H. Galloway estimates the total loss of the northeast to Rio de Janeiro due to shipments by sea at 90,000 slave migrants between 1850 and 1880, or 3,000 slaves per annum. (See Galloway's "The Last Years of Slavery on the Sugar Plantations of Northeastern Brazil," *Hispanic American Historical Review*, LI, No. 4 [Nov., 1971].) His estimate may be considered the lower limit, since it excludes southern slave movements and any post-1880 figures. Primarily basing his analysis on the 1873 and 1887 slave matriculas, and using alternative sets of information, Robert Slenes has estimated that the inter-regional slave trade from northeastern and southern ports to the center-west coffee zones brought some 200,000 migrants between 1850 and 1881. (Robert W. Slenes, "The Demography and Economics of Brazilian Slavery: 1850-1888" [Ph.D. dissertation, Department of History, Stanford University, 1976], p. 138.) Thus the internal inter-regional seaborne slave trade from the south and the north to the center-west probably can be safely estimated to fall in the range of 100,000 to 200,000 persons between 1850 and 1888.

[8] Bethell, *Abolition*, p. 390. It was also smaller than the internal slave trade in the United States. An early estimate presented by Gray notes that the United States internal slave trade between 1820 and 1860 involved some 942,000 persons. (Lewis Cecil Gray, *History of Agriculture in the South-*

Although a rough idea can thus be obtained about the volume of the internal slave trade, ascertaining the nature of that trade is another matter. The deliberate destruction of the enormous mass of slave censuses, masters' registration lists, and individual slave passports, which could have provided the answers, forces the researcher to seek alternative documentation. One of the few such documentary sources remaining is an early register, kept by the police of the imperial court, of slaves imported into the city of Rio de Janeiro in 1852.[9] It is from these detailed demographic, social, and economic statistics, as well as from analysis of other relevant demographic materials, that some initial hypotheses concerning the internal slave trade will be proposed.

The legal recording of the arrival of these slaves in Rio de

---

ern United States to 1860 [2 vols.; 2d. ed., Gloucester, Mass., 1958], II, 651.) Using an alternative method, known in demographic analysis as "survivor technique," Fogel and Engerman have recently estimated the internal slave trade in the United States from the end of the Atlantic slave trade to Abolition (1808-1860) at 793,200 persons. (Robert W. Fogel and Stanley L. Engerman, *Time on the Cross, The Economics of American Negro Slavery* [2 vols., Boston, 1974], I, 46; II, 43ff.) These figures cover a longer period of time, but, even broken down into yearly averages, are at least three times the maximum yearly estimate for the internal Brazilian slave trade. It should be recalled, however, that there were 3.9 million slaves in the United States in 1860, compared to 1.5 million slaves in Brazil in 1872. Thus Slenes ("The Demography and Economics," pp. 171-172) argues that the ratio of migrating slaves to total population (1840 to 1860 in U.S. and 1870s in Brazil) is approximately equal at 1 percent of the total slave population of the two nations.

A separate question has to deal with the nature of the two contrasting inter-regional migrations, that of Brazil and the United States. Recently Fogel & Engerman (*ibid.*, 1, 48) estimated that 84 percent of the inter-regional internal slave trade was composed of slaves moving with their masters and only 16 percent of slaves were sold across regions. This estimate has been challenged by Richard Sutch and Herbert Guttman, who argue that the lack of data makes such estimates impossible at the present time. (See their discussion in Paul A. David et al., *Reckoning with Slavery, A Critical Study in the Quantitative History of American Negro Slavery* [New York, 1976], pp. 99-103.) From somewhat more general data for Brazil, Slenes was able to show that the majority of slaves estimated to have migrated in the inter-regional internal slave trade were sent *a entregar* (that is on consignment of second parties for ultimate sale). (Slenes, "The Demography and Economics," pp. 123, 131.)

[9] In the ANRJ are preserved the manuscript reports of the police of the port of Rio de Janeiro on all the slaves arriving in the city between 18 July 1852 and 17 November 1852, a list that includes 978 slaves (see ANRJ, Policia, Codice 397).

Janeiro derives from legislation associated with termination of the old Atlantic slave trade. As part of the extensive related legislation, the Brazilian government passed a series of acts requiring registration of the national slave population. One of these supplemental decrees was a law of July 8, 1852, which required that the secretariat of police of the court district (which was by definition the municipal limits of Rio de Janeiro) inspect all slaves imported into the city by ship. The object of this inspection, which required an interview with each slave and examination of the relevant ownership papers and slave "passports" (i.e., identity cards), was to determine if the slaves had originally entered the empire illegally.[10] The results of this inspection form a very complete body of information on the age, sex, color, occupation, and nativity of each slave imported by ship into the city during the months in question, as well as a listing of the type of vessel in which the slave had been transported and that ship's last port of call. The major deficiencies of this body of data, of course, are that it is only a small sample of the whole trade (less than 1 percent of the maximum estimated total volume), that it represents less than one year's importation even in one port, and, finally, that it comes at the very earliest period of the trade. Unfortunately, no other registration lists for this trade could be found in the Arquivo Nacional of Brazil, and, until other sources can be discovered, this non-random sample of the internal seaborne slave trade will have to serve as a basis for the establishment of some tentative hypotheses about the trade.

An analysis of this sample (see table 5.1) shows that well over two-thirds of the 978 slaves imported into Rio de Janeiro between July and November of 1852 were Brazilian born, or *crioulos*, and almost as large a proportion were male. A preponderance of males is to be expected for a migrating group in 19th-century America. Such a high male contingent, as well as a concentration of ages in the adult category, was fairly common among European migrants to America throughout the 19th and well into the 20th century, and was also typical of the trans-Atlantic slave trade.[11] Because of the very heavy volume of the trans-Atlantic

---

[10] For the typical formula of inspection, see the examination of the steamship *Conceição* on 29 July 1852, in *ibid.*, folios 44-45v.

[11] See above, Chapter 2, note 49, for a detailed breakdown of sex ratios in the slave trade, all of which showed a very high incidence of males. For

Table 5.1
Sex and Origin of Brazilian Slaves Arriving in
Rio de Janeiro in 1852

Sex	Native-Born	African-Born	Totals
Male	458	196	654 (67%)
Female	251	73	324 (33%)
TOTALS	709 (72%)	269 (28%)	978 (100%)

Source: ANRJ, Policia, Codice 397.

slave trade in the 19th century, the slave population of Brazil in 1852 was weighted toward males. Nevertheless, the male/female ratio of the 1852 slave group is even higher than one would expect. Males represented 67 percent of the total group, or 201 males per 100 females. In the province of Rio de Janeiro as a whole in 1850, the sex ratio of the slaves was 151 males per 100 females; while two years earlier in a separate census for the city of Rio de Janeiro, the sex ratio was 145 male slaves to 100 females. Another importing province, São Paulo, in an 1836 census, had 126 males per 100 females.[12]

a similar pattern among 19th- and 20th-century migrating Europeans, see United Nations, Department of Social Affairs, *Sex and Age of International Migrants: Statistics for 1918-1947* (Population Studies, no. 11, New York, 1953), p. 10. In contrast to these very high rates of male participation in the inter-regional and inter-continental transfers of population, the internal slave trade in the United States seems to have been more sexually balanced. Sutch estimated that in the period 1850 to 1860 only some 52 percent of the slaves arriving in the new cotton areas were males (Richard Sutch, "The Breeding of Slaves for Sale and the Westward Expansion of Slavery, 1850-1860," in Stanley Engerman and Eugene Genovese, eds., *Race and Slavery in the Western Hemisphere: Quantitative Studies* [Princeton, 1975], p. 180, table 4.1); while a study of the New Orleans slave market found that 59 percent of the slaves arriving from the older plantation areas for sale in New Orleans were male (Lawrence J. Kotlikoff, "Towards a Quantitative Description of the New Orleans Slave Market," Report no. 7475-24; Workshop in Economic History, University of Chicago, 1975, p. 69, table ix). This may be due to the influence of the supposedly higher percentage of the United States slaves moving with their families and that of their owners in the internal slave trade. The importance of this type of migration, however, is seriously debated in the literature, as was noted above (see note 8).

[12] The census will be found in Joaquim Norberto de Souza e Silva, *Investigações sôbre os recenseamentos da população geral do Império* (Conselho Nacional de Estatística, Serviço Nacional de Recenseamento, Documentos Censitários, Série B, Numero 1, Rio de Janeiro, 1951, original edition 1870, pp. 84, 95, 99). Although individual areas of dense and recently

The ratio of males transported in the slave trade would then appear to have been higher than in the general slave population at mid-century. A much sharper difference between this group and the non-migratory slave population can be found, however, in age distributions. Though strictly comparable data are not available, we can learn much through comparison of the age structure of the 1852 group (given in table 5.2) with that of the

Table 5.2
Age Breakdown of the Slaves Arriving in
Rio de Janeiro in 1852

Age	Males	Females	Total
Under 1	6	6	12
1-4	9	9	18
5-9	18	15	33
10-14	79	31	110
15-19	99	49	148
20-29	235	134	369
30-39	137	57	194
40-49	53	17	70
50-59	14	5	19
60-69	1	—	1
70-79	3	—	3
80 & over	—	1	1
TOTALS	*654*	*324*	*978*

Source: Same as table 5.1.

urban population of São Paulo in 1836 and the entire slave population in 1872. In each case the 1852 group had a much higher proportion of males and females in the adult grouping (the over-19 or over-15 group in the respective tables). The 1852 group with over 73 percent in the 15-40 age group exceeded even the 62 percent of the Vassouras county slaves in 1840-1849, the boom

---

imported slave populations, such as the county of Vassouras (Rio de Janeiro) in the 1850-1859 decade had a high ratio of males, some 63 percent in this case, as seen in Stanley J. Stein, *Vassouras, a Brazilian Coffee County 1850-1890* (Cambridge, Mass., 1957), p. 77, figure 2, overall provincial averages seem to have been much lower, and considerably lower by the 1872 imperial census. By this date the sex ratio among slaves was 114 males to 100 females (or 53 percent male). Directoria Geral de Estatística, *Recenseamento geral da população do Brasil a que se procedeu no dia 1° de agosto de 1872* (21 vols., Rio de Janeiro, 1872-1876).

Table 5.3
Comparative Age Structure of the Slaves Arriving in Rio in 1852
and the Slave Population of São Paulo in 1836

Age Groups	1852		São Paulo, 1836	
	Males	*Females*	*Males*	*Females*
	%	%	%	%
0-9	5	9	23	25
10-19	27	25	28	29
20-49	65	64	38	35
50 & over	3	2	11	10
TOTALS	*100%*	*100%*	*100%*	*100%*
	(N = 654)	(N = 324)	(N = 2,751)	(N = 2,568)

Source: For the São Paulo census of 1836, see Maria Luiza Marcilio, *La Ville de São Paulo, peuplement et population, 1750-1850* (Rouen, 1968), p. 214.

decade when that "black belt" coffee county had its highest ratio of adult working force slaves.[13]

In terms of occupation too, this imported slave group varied from the sedentary national slave population of 1872, though here the archival data are not sufficiently complete to be very affirmative. As can be seen in table 5.5, the registration lists fail to indicate the occupations of a large number of the imported slaves. Together with the children too young to have occupations and the officially designated *sem professão* group, the slaves without an established occupation or with unknown occupations make up 41 percent of the total of 978 slaves. This considerably reduces the sample and may distort the relative weight of the other factors.

Nevertheless, the table gives some approximate idea of the relative importance of various categories of occupations. What is not clear is to what extent this distribution of occupations reflects the rest of the slave population. Here, fortunately, there exists the rough occupational breakdown contained in the 1872 census. When we compare the percentage importance of occupations between these two groups, as is done in table 5.6, certain characteristics of the 1852 imported slave group stand out. The percentage importance of artisans among the imported slaves, for example, was over double the national norm in 1872, and the per-

[13] Stein, *Vassouras*, p. 79, figure 3.

Table 5.4

Comparative Age Structure of the Slaves Arriving in Rio in 1852
and the Slave Population of the Empire in 1872

	1852		Empire, 1872	
Age Groups	Males	Females	Males	Females
	%	%	%	%
1-15[a]	18	19	34	33
16-50	81	80	57	58
51 & over	1	1	9	9
TOTALS	100%	100%	100%	100%
	(N = 648)	(N = 318)	(N = 802,962)	(N = 703,813)

[a]From both the 1872 and 1852 data I have excluded all children 11 months or under, since these were not counted in the 1872 census. I have also excluded from the total *N* in the 1872 census, all persons whose age was listed as unknown.

Sources: ANRJ, Policia, Codice 397; and Directoria Geral de Estadistica, *Recenseamento da populacao do Imperio do Brazil a que se procedeu no dia 1° de agosto de 1872* (21 vols; Rio de Janeiro, 1872-1876).

Table 5.5

Occupations of Slaves Arriving in Rio in 1852, by Sex

Occupation	Males	Females	Total
Agricultural laborers	172	14	186
Domestic servants	90	94	184
Skilled workers & artisans	112	22	134
Cattlemen & shepherds	31	—	31
Fishermen & seamen	25	—	25
Unskilled non-agricultural laborers	14	—	14
Children 10 years & under	28	31	59
"Without occupation[a]	128	5	133
Not given[b]	54	158	212
TOTALS	654	324	978

[a]"Without occupation" is a translation of the standard occupational category *sem professão*.

[b]Includes all cases where no occupation was given, nor *sem professão* indicated. In this figure are also included the 12 males and 2 females whose occupations were listed, but illegible.

Source: Same as table 5.1.

Table 5.6

Comparative Occupational Distribution of the Slaves Arriving in
Rio in 1852 and the Slave Population of Brazil in 1872

Occupation	1852		Brazil, 1872
	N	%	%
Skilled workers & artisans	134	14	5
Fishermen & seamen	25	3	—[a]
Agricultural & pastoral laborers	217	22	54
Domestic service	184	19	12
Unskilled laborers	14	1	6
Without profession	133	14 ⎱	24
Children under 10 years	59	6 ⎰ 42%[b]	—
Not given	212	22 ⎰	—
TOTALS	978	100%[c]	100%

[a]Less than 1 percent (actual percentage was .02).

[b]Since the 1872 census classified everyone by profession, I assume
that they placed my categories "children under 10 years" and "not
given" in the "without profession" listing. Thus I would assume that
the two percentages (42 percent and 24 percent) are roughly representative of the same groups.

[c]Columns do not add up to 100 because of rounding.

Source: Same as table 5.4.

centage of domestic servants was slightly higher. On the other
hand, less than half the percentage number of agriculturalists and
pastoral workers was to be found in the 1852 group. All this
would seem to suggest that the imported slaves, as a group, were
far more skilled and far less oriented toward rural occupations
than would have been expected if they had been representative
of the national slave population. Thus it would appear that skilled
and more urbanized slaves were the ones being transported in
the internal slave trade. Given the equal costs of transportation,
it could be expected that higher-priced slaves were more likely
to be transported than the cheaper fieldhands.

As to the last major characteristic of the 1852 population,
nativity, this group seems to be reasonably representative of the
mid-century Brazilian slave population as a whole. Though statistics of Africans within the slave population before the first
national census of 1872 are difficult to obtain, some scattered
numbers would seem to suggest that the 28 percent of the 1852

group who were Africans may not have been too far from the average. In the late 1830s, for example, São Paulo had an African-born slave group that was 45 percent of the total slave population, and Pernambuco also had 45 percent of its slaves listed as foreign-born.[14]

Given the general scarcity of pre-1872 census materials on Africans in Brazil, the detailed statistics on the 269 Africans of this group provide a valuable glimpse of the African element in the Brazilian slave society. When compared to the native-born slaves in the 1852 sample, they are more heavily male, much older, and much less skilled than the native-born descendants of African slaves. Thus, for example, the median ages of Africans, 33 and 30 respectively for males and females, compares to a median age of 20 for both sexes of the Brazilian-born slaves. In the matter of the sex ratio, whereas the African group's ratio is 268 males per 100 females, that of the native-born is 182 per 100.

As could be surmised, the African slaves, having been older when they first arrived,[15] and less easily trained because of the initial language barriers, were less frequently encountered among the skilled occupations than were the creole slaves (see table 5.7).[16] Whereas Africans formed 28 percent of the total of 978 slaves, they held only 17 percent of the skilled trades, and in the five leading skilled occupations they surpassed their total group percentage importance in only one occupation, stonemasonry.

The police records also provided the specific birthplace for a large number of slaves, in addition to distinguishing them as to native and African birth. As can be seen in table 5.8, almost the entire African population was accounted for in this manner, whereas only half of the creoles were so placed. For the Africans, it appears that this imported group was fairly representative of the rest of the African population in Brazil. The two major areas of Guinea and Portuguese West Africa (Angola, Benguela, Ca-

[14] Joaquim Norberto de Souza e Silva, *Investigações*, pp. 48, 99. The city of Rio de Janeiro itself had an extraordinarily high African-born slave population which represented 60 percent of its slave labor force in 1849 (*ibid.*, p. 95).

[15] Of the 351 slave ships that landed in Rio de Janeiro in the 1795-1811 period, for example, only 28 percent held any children.

[16] Africans were also much more reduced among the free colored. For a survey of the available statistics on this, see Herbert S. Klein, "The Colored Freedmen in Brazilian Slave Society," *Journal of Social History*, 3:1 (fall, 1969), 40.

Table 5.7
Occupation of Skilled and Artisan Workers by Place of Birth
Among the 1852 Slave Arrival Sample

Occupation	Africans	Creoles	Totals
Seamstresses (*costureira*)	1	20	21
Carpenters (*carpinteiro*)	5	15	20
Shoemakers (*sapateiro*)	1	15	16
Tailors (*alfaiate*)	1	15	16
Stone masons (*pedreiro*)	5	10	15
Coachmen (carters)[a] (*carreiro*)	—	7	7
Sawyers (*serrador*)	1	5	6
Caulkers (*calafate*)	—	4	4
Blacksmiths (*ferreiro*)	—	4	4
Barbers (*barbeiro*)	1	2	3
Hatmakers (*chapeleiro*)	1	1	2
Muleteers (*tropeiro*)	1	1	2
All other skilled occupations (having only one person per occupation)	5	11	16
Skilled	22	110	132
Unskilled	247	599	846
TOTALS	*269*	*709*	*978*

[a]I have restricted this term to teamsters. All other types of coachmen (i.e., those who carried passengers in their vehicles) I have subsumed under the domestic servant category.

Source: Same as table 5.1.

binda, and the Congo) were the best-represented group here, as they probably were in the whole of the African-born population in 19th-century Brazil.[17] As for the creole population, the preponderance of northeastern-born slaves clearly reflected the north-south movement of the internal slave trade.

[17] While "more than 50 percent" of the Africans from Stein's Vassouras sample came from South West Africa, he claims that the next largest group came from Mozambique (Stein, *Vassouras*, pp. 76-77). Stein, however, provides no exact statistics and he also confuses the location of several African groups. Thus his data, except for the Angolan area, are not quite comparable. According to Philip D. Curtin (*The Atlantic Slave Trade, A census* [Madison, 1969], p. 207, Table 62), Angolan slaves accounted for some 68 percent of the volume of the 18th-century slave trade to Brazil, slaves from Costa da Mina making up the remaining 32 percent. The Mozambique slave trade did not develop on a major scale until the 19th century, and even then accounted for no more than one-fifth of all African exports to 1843 (*ibid.*, p. 258, table 74). On the dominance of Costa da Mina and Angola in the 18th- and 19th-century trade see also Mauricio Goulart, *Escravidão africana no Brasil (das origens à extinção do tráfico)* (Rio de Janeiro, 1950), p. 186.

Table 5.8
Birthplace of Slaves Arriving in Rio in 1852

Location or Ethnic Group	Males	Females	Total	%
AFRICA	200	78	278	100
1. West Africa	77	44	121	44
Mina[a]	54	22	76	
Yoruba [Nago][a]	14	16	30	
Hausa	2	1	3	
Djolas [Monjolla]	4	3	7	
Gege (Dahomey)	1	1	2	
Calabar	1	0	1	
São Tomé	0	1	1	
Cabo Verde	1	0	1	
2. Southwest Africa	97	28	125	45
Angola	34	12	46	
Congo	23	4	27	
Cabinda	21	3	24	
Benguela	12	7	19	
Cassange (Angola)	3	0	3	
Quissama (Angola)	1	0	1	
Libolo [Rebolho] ('')	3	1	4	
Amaca [Ambaia] ('')	0	1	1	
3. Southeast Africa	19	4	23	8
Mozambique	17	3	20	
Inhambane	1	1	2	
Amakua [Amagui]	1	0	1	
4. Unknown[b]	7	2	9	3
BRAZIL	454	246	700	100
1. North[c]	13	8	21	3
2. Northeast[d]	186	103	289	41
Maranhao	36	15	51	
Piauí	3	0	3	
Ceara	27	11	38	
Rio Grande de Norte	15	8	23	
Paraíba	2	2	4	
Pernambuco	39	23	62	
Alagoas	1	7	8	
Sergipe	8	9	17	
Bahia	55	28	83	
3. Southeast	9	4	13	2
Rio de Janeiro	6	4	10	
Minas Gerais	3	0	3	
4. South	16	7	23	3
Parana	1	0	1	
Rio Grande do Sul	8	4	12	
Santa Catarina	7	3	10	
5. Unknown[e]	230	124	354	51

[a]*Mina* was a generic term indiscriminately applied to different peoples of Dahomey and the Slave and Gold Coasts. According to Arthur Ramos, the term strictly should apply to the Fanti-Ashanti

Table 5.8 (Continued)

peoples. Equally, according to Ramos, *Nago* stands for the Yoruba nation. Arthur Ramos, *Introdução à antropologia brasileira* (Rio de Janeiro, 1943), I, 352, 353. I am indebted to Philip Curtin for the identification of the *Monjolla* as the Djolas. The names in brackets are 18th-century spellings.

[b]Of the 9 Africans listed as unknown, 5 were classified simply as *Africana*, with the rest coming from groups whose modern names and locations I have been unable to locate.

[c]All the slaves from the northern region came from the single state of Para.

[d]I have adopted the regional divisions of the Brazilian Planning Ministry (EPEA), which seem more relevant from a socio-economic viewpoint than the usual IBGE breakdown. For the regional-state divisions, see: Escritório de Pesquisa Econômica Aplicada, *Plano decenal de desenvolvimento economico e social: Demografia, diagnóstico preliminar* (Rio de Janeiro: Ministerio do Planejamento e Coordenacão Econômica, 1966), p. 73n.

[e]Among the unknown were large numbers of slaves for whom unlocated towns were listed, rather than provinces.

Source: Same as table 5.1.

Though the port records show that the slaves arrived aboard ships coming from every major port in Brazil, the majority of the ships, as well as slaves, came from ports north of the province of Rio de Janeiro (table 5.9). Within the northern provinces, Bahia was, at least in this sample, the most important source of slaves, being four times greater than its nearest competitor, Pernambuco, though its provincial slave population at the time of the 1872 census was only twice as great. Its larger participation in the trade may have been the result of re-exporting slaves from other regions in the north, rather than an actual higher ratio of removing slaves from its own population.

The place of the slave arrivals from Rio Grande do Sul, the second largest provincial source of slaves for Rio de Janeiro in this period, is another important finding. Rio Grande do Sul was, of course, the largest slave province of the southern region. But this migration also reflected the mid-century economic crisis in the jerked beef trade, which caused a major selling of the province's investment in slaves to the "north."[18] The province's loss of slaves seems to have continued throughout the period of the internal slave trade and was especially severe after the mid-1860s.

[18] Fernando Henrique Cardoso, *Capitalismo e escravidão no Brasil meridional* . . . (São Paulo, 1962), pp. 68-69.

Table 5.9
Brazilian Ports of Origin of Slaves Arriving in Rio in 1852

Port and Region	Numbers	Percentage
1. *Northern Ports*	*740*	76
Bahia	374	
Pernambuco	78	
Rio Grande do Norte	51	
Paraiba	48	
Maceio (Alagoas)	34	
Vitoria (Espirito Santo)	13	
Caravella (Bahia)	4	
São Mateus (Espírito Santo)	2	
"Portos do Norte"[a]	136	
2. *Southern Ports*	*152*	16
Rio Grande do Sul	102	
Santa Catarina	19	
Ubatuba (São Paulo)	6	
Iguape (São Paulo)	4	
Santos (São Paulo)	4	
São Sebastiao (São Paulo)	1	
Pôrto Alegre	5	
Laguna (Santa Catarina)	4	
Paranaguá (Parana)	4	
Itajaí (Santa Catarina)	3	
3. *Ports of the Province of Rio*	*80*	8
Campos	41	
Rio de Sao Joao de Barra	7	
Macaé	9	
Angra dos Reis	9	
Niteroi	5	
Ilha Grande	4	
Mangaratiba	2	
Cabo Frio	1	
Parati	2	
4. *Unknown Ports*[b]	*6*	1
TOTALS	*978*	*100*

[a]"Portos do Norte" seems to have been an indiscriminate term applied to vessels which had visited several northern ports.

[b]This included two ports which were illegibly written.

Source: Same as table 5.1.

In 1863 the province counted over 77,000 slaves, a figure that dropped to some 67,000 by 1872.[19]

As regards the mechanics of the internal slave trade, the relatively small number of slaves transported in relation to the rather large volume of shipping kept the individual lot of slaves, even in this relatively high arrivals' year of 1852, to a very small number. The average shipment was 4 slaves per vessel. This compares to the figure of over 480 slaves per vessel in the trans-Atlantic slave trade from Africa to Rio de Janeiro at the beginning of the 19th century.[20] Clearly, the post-1850 internal slave trade was only part of a diversified trade in which the shipping of slaves on merchant vessels represented only a minor element. Though a wide variety of ships entered this trade during the four months of 1852, the bulk of the slaves (or 87 percent) were carried in only three types of vessels, pinnaces (*patachos*), brigs (*brigues*) and steamships (*vapores*), each equally accounting for over a quarter of the slaves transported.

These data on ports and slaves appear to confirm long-held beliefs that slaves were being drained from the northern states to the central region. But not all of the large, expanding slave states of the latter area were attracting slaves in equal magnitude. Of the three major central-southern slave states—Minas Gerais, Rio, de Janeiro, and São Paulo[21]—the first seemed able to supply most of its slave labor needs by internal growth and redistribution of the slave force within the vast confines of the province. The two smaller slave states of Rio de Janeiro and São Paulo, however, were far less able to meet their labor needs from internal growth and redistribution, or at least so the leading planters of these two

[19] *Ibid.*, pp. 80-81.

[20] The average shipment carried for the beginning of the 19th century in Rio de Janeiro had been 486 slaves per vessel. (Klein, "The Trade," p. 538.)

[21] In 1872 Minas Gerais was the largest slave state in Brazil, with 370,459 slaves. This compared to 341,576 for Rio de Janeiro (city and province) and 156,612 for São Paulo. Between the population estimate of 1819, which was based on fairly reliable church data, and the census of 1872, the slave population in Brazil as a whole had grown by only 0.57 percent per annum. For the provinces of Minas Gerais, São Paulo, and Rio de Janeiro, the per-annum growth rates of slave population in these 53 years were respectively: 1.47 percent, 1.30 percent, and 1.59 percent. The 1819 estimate of Conselheiro Antonio Rodrigues Velloso de Oliveira, recalculated to fit the 1872 provincial boundaries, is found in Joaquim Norberto de Souza e Silva, *Investigações*, p. 152, bottom table. This table is also reprinted in vol. i of the 1920 census.

regions thought. Throughout the second half of the century, the legislatures of the two states were constantly petitioning for the importation of slaves from outside the provincial boundaries and demanding imperial government support for some type of internal slave trade, or alternative supplies of contract labor.[22]

But from the data provided by the 1852 slave imports, it would appear that the internal inter-regional slave trade was relatively small, at least compared to the old Atlantic slave trade, and specialized in small shipments of domestic, skilled, and field-hand slaves being moved south. How these slaves, many of whom were not field hands, could fill the enormous demand for agricultural laborers is difficult to see. If this 1852 group is representative, and if in later years the trend was not systematically reversed, then it may even be questioned whether the internal slave trade seriously fulfilled the need for agricultural laborers in the coffee fields of Rio de Janeiro and São Paulo over any extended period of time.

Fortunately, a fairly accurate analysis of the impact of this internal slave trade can be made from data supplied in the 1872 census. In that census, Brazilian-born slaves were listed as to their place of birth. For the three major importing states, the birthplace of their resident *crioulo* slaves is given in table 5.10. As is evident from this table, the impact of imported slaves was quite minimal in Minas Gerais and Rio de Janeiro, being less than 1 percent in the former and less than 3 percent in the latter. Even in Rio de Janeiro, if we separate out the city of Rio de Janeiro, with its 37,966 native-born slaves, then the provincial total rises to 99 percent provincial born. Only the figures for São Paulo offer a significant number of slaves born out of the state, and then the figure is only 16 percent of the *crioulos*. Added to this—if we observe where these three importing states got their slaves—it is clear that their immediate neighbors, themselves importing states, were often as important as the states of the old northeast. Thus in São Paulo, of the 18.29 percent born out-of-province slaves, a third, or 6.27 percent, came from Minas Gerais and Rio de Janeiro.

It could be argued from this evidence, as Emilia Viotti da Costa has already concluded about Minas Gerais, that the bulk

[22] Emilia Viotti da Costa, *Da Senzala a colonia* (São Paulo, 1966), pp. 60-61.

Table 5.10
Place of Birth of Brazilian-Born Slaves in the Provinces of
Minas Gerais, Rio de Janeiro, and Sao Paulo in 1872

Province	Minas Gerais		Rio de Janeiro		São Paulo	
	No.	%	No.	%	No.	%
1. Same as place of residence	341,515	(99.78)	266,611	(97.18)	121,501	(84.35)
2. From one of the other two states	192	(0.06)	1,515	(0.55)	9,041	(6.28)
3. Northeastern states, plus Bahia, Sergipe and Espírito Santo	525	(0.15)	5,046	(1.84)	11,815	(8.20)
4. Southern states, excluding São Paulo	46	(0.01)	973	(0.35)	1,178	(0.82)
5. Center-West	22	(ᵃ)	73	(0.03)	427	(0.29)
6. North	10	(ᵃ)	123	(0.04)	89	(0.06)
TOTALS	342,310	(100.0%)	274,341	(100.0%)	144,051	(100.0%)

ᵃIndicates less than 0.01 percent.

Source: Diretoria Geral de Estatistica, *Recenseamento da população ... de* 1872.

of the field-hand slaves needed in the coffee and sugar fields were stripped from declining areas within the major expanding states themselves, or were brought in from contiguous areas. Thus, while the internal seaborne slave trade may have been supplying skilled slaves to the central Brazilian slave markets, it was too costly a system to supply cheap field-hand laborers on a large scale. The transportation costs, despite discounts for slave passengers, were still quite high.[23] To this were added the sales taxes, and, beginning in the last years of the 1850s, increasingly prohibitive migration taxes levied by the exporting states, which substantially raised the price of northern slaves in center-west markets.[24] Furthermore, evidence from one of the declining re-

[23] In the steamship service run from Rio de Janeiro to Santos, for example, slaves over 20 went for half the fare of a second-class passenger; slave children and youths up to 19 years for some unknown reason paid a slightly higher fare than the adult slaves. (Eduardo von Laemmert, *Almanak administrativo, mercantil e industrial da Côrte e Provincia do Rio de Janeiro para a anno de 1861* [Rio de Janeiro, 1861], p. 405.)

[24] Paulista legislators complained about municipal and imperial taxes im-

The Internal Slave Trade in Brazil

gions in the expanding province of Rio de Janeiro, that of the county of Vassouras, clearly demonstrates a very rapid decline of slaves in the adult work-force category as the region's own coffee fields declined.[25] It would appear that such sources as Vassouras were the chief suppliers for the Western Paulista plantations.

This hypothesis of a heavily urbanized and/or skilled labor force migration from the north is also supported by some evidence from the northern exporting provinces. In 1855 the president of the province of Bahia reported that of the 1,835 slaves exported from the province in 1854, 836 came from urban centers, and only 583 had been in agricultural labor, with 416 unknown.[26] Three years later, the president of the province of Ceará also reported on the export of slaves from his district. He wrote to the central government that "the major part of these exported slaves are not employed in agriculture, the majority in fact being in skilled occupations which are today filled by free laborers who have withdrawn from agriculture. . . ." He also noted that many of the exported slaves were also "employed in domestic services or in cattle raising."[27]

On the basis of the birth data from the 1872 census, and the partial occupational data of the 1852 migration sample, some initial hypotheses about the broad impact of this trade on the importing and exporting provinces can be proposed. To begin with, it would appear that the seaborne inter-regional trade was not the main supplier of field-hand labor for the expanding coffee plantations of Rio de Janeiro and São Paulo, or the coffee and mixed commercial agriculture of Minas Gemais.[28] Their demands

---

posed on slave sales, which, they charged, seriously impeded this trade. (Viotti da Costa, *Senzala*, p. 132.)

[25] Stein's figures on the dramatic decline of slaves in the working-age category 15-40 (from 62 percent of the total age group in 1840 to 1849, to 40 percent by 1860-1869 and 35 percent by 1880-1888) clearly illustrate this draining of a labor force into an intra-regional trade. (Stein, *Vassouras*, pp. 78-79.)

[26] João Mauricio Wanderley, *Falla recitada na abertura da assembléa legislativa da Bahia* . . . (Bahia, 1855), p. 38.

[27] Marquez de Olinda, *Relatório da Repartição dos Negocios do Imperio, 1858* (Rio de Janeiro, 1858), Annexo G, p. 6.

[28] It should be noted that the heaviest concentration of slaves in Minas Gerais was in the southern area and *zona da mata*, both areas being the center of Minas' important coffee plantation zone. (Francisco Iglesias,

for agricultural labor were in all likelihood met primarily from intra-provincial and intra-regional sources. This in turn would suggest that there was rapid change going on within the three largest slave states of the southeastern region in terms of labor demands and agricultural activity. It might also suggest, as an alternative explanation to the Vassouras model of economic collapse leading to selling off of adult workers, a situation in which slave birth rates in the older coffee plantations and contiguous areas were sufficiently high that they were able to meet not only local needs but also increasing demands for labor in the newer coffee regions. This alternative model, however, can be tested only when basic research on the parish registers finally produces the needed vital statistics of the slave population.

There remain to be considered the questions of the relation of the slave trade to the decline of slavery in the northeast, and its effect, if any, on the shift of black population from the older sugar regions to the southeastern states. Fortunately, a recent survey of the post-1850 sugar economy in Pernambuco provides an initial answer to the first question. According to this study, the province lost some 22,000 slaves to the inter-provincial seaborne slave trade between 1850 and 1881. However, it also lost an almost equal number, some 21,000, to the free black class through private manumission, and another 49,000 through various forms of public manumission before 1888. It would thus seem that for Pernambuco, at least, the internal slave trade accounted for some 24 percent of the total number of individuals removed from the slave population during the period from 1850 to 1888.[29]

As to determining the impact of the internal slave trade on the redistribution of the total black population, data are difficult to obtain. The extremely poor quality of pre-1872 demographic sta-

---

Política economica do govêrno provincial minero [1835-1889] [Rio de Janeiro, 1958], pp. 70, 131.)

[29] Peter Eisenberg, "From Slave to Free Labor on Sugar Plantations: The Process in Pernambuco" (paper read at the 1970 meetings of the American Historical Association), Table v. Even in a major year of slave arrivals in 1879, it was reported that the province of Rio de Janeiro sold 27,879 slaves outside the province and brought in 43,875 migrating slaves, for a net gain of only 15,996 slaves (or only 5% of the total slave population). Even this small net gain was offset by deaths and manumissions that totaled 40,888. Ismêria Lima Martins, "Os problemas de mão de obra da grande lavoura fluminense. O tráfico intra-provincial (1850-1878)" (M.A. thesis, Universidade Federal Fluminense, 1974), p. 23.

tistics makes anything but very rough estimates difficult. But, if we compare the slave population in the 1819 census of Conselheiro Velloso de Oliveira (for which no free colored figures are provided), to the total black population in 1872, and assume that the 1819 distribution of slaves closely resembled the distribution of the total black class (given the smaller size of the free colored group in 1819), then it would appear (see table 5.11) that there was only moderate change in the distribution of Afro-Brazilians between these two national censuses. The change in the relative distribution of the slave population can be accounted for by heavier African arrivals in the southeastern provinces in the period from 1819 to 1850,[30] by higher manumission rates in the older sugar regions of the northeast, or by a combination of the two factors.[31]

While the analysis up to this point has been based primarily on materials from the period from 1872 and earlier, a recent study of the Campinas slave market and the special slave matriculas of 1873 and 1887 has shown that the combination of a suddenly booming coffee industry and a comparatively declining export trade in sugar, cotton, and jerked beef, all created a uniquely hectic finale to the internal slave trade in the period from 1875 to 1881.[32] If this recent study is correct, then it would appear that

[30] Between 1817 and 1843, according to British statistics, Rio de Janeiro and Santos imported 80 percent of the total slaves shipped to Brazil from Africa. (Curtin, *The Atlantic Slave Trade,* p. 240, table 69.)

[31] That Brazilian slave manumissions predominantly involved women, with a very significant representation of children, was an argument I advanced in my article "The Colored Freedmen in Brazilian Slave Society," *Journal of Social History,* III, No. 1 (fall, 1969). This hypothesis was based on an analysis of aggregate census data. Since then, detailed studies of local regions have confirmed these assumptions and supported the idea that manumission had a major impact on the negative growth rates of the Brazilian slave population.

For these recent studies see: Stuart B. Schwartz, "The Manumission of Slaves in Colonial Brazil: Bahia 1648-1745," *Hispanic American Historical Review,* LIV, no. 4 (November, 1974); Katia M. Queiros Mattoso, "A proposito de cartas de alforia na Bahia, 1779-1850," *Anais de Historia,* IV (1972); Arnold Kessler, "Bahian Manumission Practices in the Early Nineteenth Century," paper presented to the American Historical Association, San Francisco, December, 1973; Mary Karasch, "Manumission in the City of Rio de Janeiro, 1807-1851," paper presented at *ibid.*; and James Patrick Kiernan, "The Manumission of Slaves in Colonial Brazil: Paraty, 1789-1822" (Ph.D. dissertation, Department of History, New York University, 1976).

[32] The discussion in this paragraph is based on Slenes, "The Demography and Economics," chapter iv.

Table 5.11
Distribution of the Slave and Total Colored Population of Brazil
by Region and Province, 1819 and 1872

Region & Province	Slave 1819	%	Slave 1872	%	Total Colored 1872	%
1. *North*	*39,040*	(4)	*28,437*	(2)	*147,585*	(2)
Amazonas	6,040		979		9,571	
Pará	33,000		27,458		138,014	
2. *Northeast*	*567,213*	(51)	*480,409*	(32)	*3,045,387*	(53)
Maranhão	133,334		74,939		244,584	
Piauí	12,405		23,795		145,322	
Ceará	55,439		31,913		400,013	
Rio Grande do Norte	9,109		13,020		120,475	
Paraiba	16,723		21,526		221,938	
Pernambuco	97,633		89,028		538,575	
Alagoas	69,094		35,741		252,847	
Sergipe	26,213		22,623		123,378	
Bahia	147,263		167,824		998,255	
3. *Southeast*	*412,542*	(37)	*891,306*	(59)	*2,184,756*	(38)
Minas Gerais	168,543		370,459		1,176,426	
Espírito Santo	20,272		22,659		50,026	
Rio de Janeiro[a]	146,060		341,576		593,847	
Sao Paulo	77,667		156,612		364,457	
4. *South*	*47,616*	(4)	*93,335*	(6)	*229,634*	(4)
Paraná	10,191		10,560		47,937	
Santa Catarina	9,172		14,984		30,968	
Rio Grande do Sul	28,253		67,791		150,729	
5. *Center-West*	*40,980*	(4)	*17,319*	(1)	*148,872*	(2)
Goiás	26,800		10,652		114,216	
Mato Grosso	14,180		6,667		34,656	
TOTALS	1,107,391	(100%)	1,510,806	(100%)	5,756,234	(100%)[b]

[a]Includes the population of the city of Rio de Janeiro.

[b]Does not add up to 100 because of rounding.

Source: For the 1819 census, which is a recalculation of the original numbers of Conselheiro Antonio Rodrigues Velloso de Oliveira in accordance with 1870 political divisions, done by Norberto de Souza, see [Joaquim Norberto de Souza e Silva], *investigaçoes sobre os recenseamentos da população geral do imperio*, p. 152.

in the very last few years of the trade, the important increases in slave prices in the center-west coffee regions, combined with coffee prices high enough to keep even such marginally productive zones as Vassouras in heavy production, meant a sudden turning of the seaborne trade into a field-hand labor trade. At most this trade accounted for only 90,000 slaves, many of whom came from the southern cattle areas by overland routes into São Paulo. Though this last movement was quantitatively and qualitatively different from the earlier trade, it probably was not sufficient to change the long-range trends that had been firmly established in the preceding years. By 1881 taxes in the emigrating zones were so severe that this entire movement was brought to a close, while the fall in coffee prices in the 1880s ended the temporary boom in production in the older coffee zones, thus permitting a full return to intra-regional sources, which until 1875 had been the primary sources for slaves even in that most long-distance of slave markets, that of Campinas.[33]

Other aspects of the inter-regional trade revealed in the 1852 sample also seem to have been the norm for the entire period of the trade. Since 1852 seems to have been a high year for slave arrivals, the fact that average numbers carried were so small even then clearly indicates the relatively diffuse nature and minor role of this trade within the broader commercial relations between the northeastern and southern ports and those of Rio de Janeiro and Santos. This low number suggests that the slave sales on land were in relatively small groups. The seaborne trade also moved overwhelmingly from ports north of Rio de Janeiro into the center, with only minor migrations from the south. The majority of slaves from this region apparently moved by land routes, especially in the late 1870s. The migrant slave group was predominantly adult and male, and higher-priced skilled and urban slaves seem to have been a greater proportion than in the population as a whole. This pattern probably continued throughout most of the period. Since transportation and other costs (such as export taxes) were equal for all slaves, regardless of their market price, it was more economic to ship the higher-priced slaves to the Rio de Janeiro market insofar as field-hand prices remained comparatively lower than skilled slave prices. Finally, the 1852 sample provides a rare glimpse into the African element within the slave population of Brazil at mid-century. It shows that the Africans exhibited all the disabilites that could be expected of older individuals, less acculturated to Brazilian society, who thus constituted a severely disadvantaged minority within the Brazilian slave force.

[33] *Ibid.*, p. 136.

The findings from this extremely limited sample of the post-1850 inter-provincial seaborne slave trade are in some ways comparable with those recently reached in a study of the largest internal post-Atlantic slave trade market in the United States, that of New Orleans in the 19th century. From a sample total of 9,778 slaves covering the years 1804 to 1862 it was concluded that 75 percent of the slaves sold in this port city originated from within the state of Louisiana.[34] Even during the period of greatest seaborne and overland importations in the 1820s, local slaves still accounted for 54 percent of the slaves sold, with probably an estimated 27 percent of all slave sales coming from eastern coastal states, with most of them probably arriving by sea.[35]

Thus, even in the prime inter-provincial (or inter-state) slave market of the United States, intra-regional trading remained the most important source for slaves. In fact, it would seem that planters preferred (as expressed in price differentials) locally originated slaves over inter-regionally imported ones, largely because of prior acclimation to living and working conditions in the given region. Thus New Orleans seems to have been similar to Rio de Janeiro as well as to interior Brazilian city markets in that arriving inter-provincial slaves formed only a small part of total slave sales. These southern Brazilian slave markets also probably experienced a concentration upon slaves in the prime age groups. In the New Orleans slave market 78 percent of sales were of slaves aged 15 to 39. Where the New Orleans statistics differ from the inferences generated from the 1852 sample, is in the relative occupational distributions. Given the higher costs of the inter-regional trade as opposed to the intra-regional and local trades, I would have expected that the higher priced artisans would be over-represented and children under-represented in the former markets. But this does not appear to have been the case in New Orleans, and it seems difficult to explain. However, the same dominance of males as revealed in the 1852 Rio de Janeiro sample is also apparent in New Orleans. Whereas males represented only 49 percent of in-state sales at New Orleans, they represented 59 percent of the slaves arriving from upper south coastal states.[36]

[34] This systematic sample was generated by Robert Fogel and Stanley Engerman and has been analyzed by Lawrence J. Kotlikoff, "Towards a Quantitative Description of the New Orleans Slave Market," *loc. cit.*

[35] *Ibid.*, p. 65, table VII.

[36] *Ibid.*, pp. 67, 69, tables VIII and IX. In alternative estimates taken from

While some characteristics of the New Orleans slave market differed in important ways from the Rio de Janeiro slave market, they were essentially similar in the greater use of local and intra-regional sales than has been traditionally assumed. It is also evident that the Rio de Janeiro market differed substantially from internal markets within the interior. Along the West Paulista frontier, for example, the early years of coffee development were associated with local and intra-regional slave movements, and also a high percentage of planters migrating with their slaves. Only as the frontier moved on and the various regions became settled plantation communities did the local slave markets begin to reflect inter-provincial sales.[37]

But if the sample from 1852 is any indication, then even with the development of longer-distance trading, the source of slaves for the coffee plantations came primarily from the central and southern states and from intra-regional sources. It would appear that the combination of the boom-and-bust cycle of early coffee production and the end of the Atlantic slave trade both contributed to this phenomenon. For, in the former case, there seemed to be a rapid decline of some regions as exemplified by Vassouras, which promoted local shifts in slave concentrations. Finally, the end of African immigration on a massive scale permitted the creole slave population birth rates to overcome the distorted age and sex structure of the arriving Africans and thus kept the local populations either stable or diminished their natural decline. As a result, the combination of more creole slaves and rapid soil depletion was probably sufficient to keep local coffee slave markets supplied with the bulk of their field-hand labor force. It was thus the primary role of the inter-provincial seaborne slave trade to supply a relatively limited number of skilled slaves to the southern markets.

---

the decennial federal U.S. censuses, however, Richard Sutch has calculated total net imports into the lower south importing states for the decade from 1850 to 1860 as being some 269,000 slaves, of which 18 percent were under 10 years of age, and only 58 percent were in the prime age categories. This compares with a 4 percent figure for all 19th-century New Orleans slave sales and 78 percent in the prime age categories 15 to 39. This estimate of Sutch for the 1850-1860 decade means that less than 1 per cent of the total slave population in 1860 migrated in this ten-year period. (See Richard Sutch, "The Breeding of Slaves for Sale," p. 180.)

[37] Warren Dean, *Rio Claro, A Brazilian Plantation System 1820-1920* (Stanford, 1976), Ch. III.

Chapter Six

Slaves and Shipping in 18th-Century Virginia

Having outlined the broader questions involved in the development of the South Atlantic slave trade and its impact on Brazil, I would now like to examine the various aspects of the complex trade that Great Britain developed in the 18th and early 19th centuries. I will concentrate on two contrasting trades: in this chapter, on the British slave trade to the small importing zone of Virginia in British North America in the early 18th century, and in the following one, on the more intense British slave trading to the West Indies at the end of the 18th and beginning of the 19th centuries. The Virginian and British West Indian trades differed markedly from the South Atlantic African migrations. Both involved intra-Caribbean slave movements, were primarily 18th-century trades, and were less intimately linked to specific African regions, as were the Portuguese and Brazilian trades.

The first part of this study of the British slave trade concerns the rather small trade in the middle of the 18th century that was involved in bringing Africans as well as slaves from other Caribbean and American regions to the North American colony of Virginia. In the context of the other Atlantic slave trades, the trade to North America was of a shorter duration, less intense and involved direct African shipments for a much shorter time.

The three most important North American zones of importation throughout most of the 18th century were Virginia, South Carolina, and Georgia. Although Virginia was the largest of the continental slave societies, it ranked second in importance to South Carolina as an importer of slaves. Nevertheless, the abundance and quality of the available data make this colony the best with which to begin a comprehensive study of the dynamics of the slave trade to the region that would form the United States. The sources for this study are the materials gathered over forty years ago by Elizabeth Donnan in her documentary collection on the Atlantic slave trade. Although scholars have had access to her study for some time, there has been no comprehensive analysis undertaken of the records that she has reprinted.[1] The aim of this study is to analyze these records, both to determine the internal dynamics of the slave trade to Virginia in terms of routes and shipping, and to place that trade with its sources, volume, ship's slave-carrying capacity, frequency of voyage, and tonnage patterns within the context of the general structure of the entire Atlantic slave trade in the 18th century.

The listings for Virginia provided by Donnan cover a large part of the 18th century; however, the most complete registrations are for the period 1727 to 1769.[2] The 644 voyages recorded during these 42 years may not be the total number of slavers that arrived in this period in Virginia ports, but they provide a large enough sample from that universe to make detailed analyses about the basic outlines of the Virginia trade a reasonable undertaking. Moreover, the complete nature of these listings, the best for any Southern continental colony in that century, enable Virginia's shipping to be compared in its tonnage, carrying capacity, and trade route patterns with the other major plantation slave societies.

Until the end of the 17th century, the slave trade to Virginia remained small, with the majority of slaves coming directly from the British West Indies.[3] With the ending of the Royal African Company's monopoly of African sources after 1698, the number of direct shipments of slaves from Africa to Virginia began to rise rapidly.[4] By the period 1710 to 1718, 42 percent of all of the

[1] Scholars have constantly cited this work since it was first published in 1935, but few have systematically analyzed the data. In terms of the slave trade to Virginia, some preliminary calculations were undertaken by Arthur Pierce Middleton, *Tobacco Coast: A Maritime History of Chesapeake Bay in the Colonial Era* (Newport News, 1953), esp. ch. 5; Philip D. Curtin, *The Atlantic Slave Trade, A Census* (Madison, 1969), pp. 143-145; Melville J. Herskovits, *The Myth of the Negro Past* (Boston, 1958), pp. 46-47.

[2] Elizabeth Donnan, *Documents Illustrative of the History of the Slave Trade to America* (New York, 1965; 4v), IV, 188-234.

[3] Middleton, *Tobacco Coast*, p. 136. A recent analysis of the head rights granted for the importation of Negro slaves shows that from the mid-1630s until the end of the 1680s, the average number of slaves for whom head rights were granted fluctuated from 42 to 62 per annum, and only rose to 184 per annum by the 1690s (Wesley Frank Craven, *White, Red and Black* [Charlottesville, 1971], pp. 85-86).

[4] Free traders, following the 1698 repeal of the Royal African Company's

Table 6.1
Origin of Slaves Arriving in Virginia,
10 December 1710 to 10 December 1718[a]

Region of Origin	No. of Slaves	No. of Ships
British West Indies	2,399	105
Africa	1,892	17
Continental Br. America	101	32
England	6	5
Unknown[b]	130	5
TOTALS	*4,528*	*164*

[a]Indian slaves were excluded from these figures.

[b]Includes several named ports for which no location can be determined. However, given the average number of slaves carried by these vessels, it can be assumed that they were West Indian in origin.

Source: Donnan, *Documents,* IV, 175-182.

slaves imported into Virginia were coming directly from Africa, though West Indian sources still accounted for 53 percent of the totals. Thereafter, direct African slaving expanded rapidly.

Whereas in the 1710-1718 period the average annual importation from Africa was 236 slaves, compared with 300 from the British West Indies, the number of slaves of African origin rose to 1,228 per annum in the period from 25 March 1718 to 25 March 1727.[5] By the third decade of the 18th century, African slavers were monopolizing the trade, and the basic patterns, which remained constant for the rest of the century, had been fully established.

In analyzing the complete returns from all sources for the period from 12 April 1727 to 26 December 1769, we find that the total number of slave arrivals in any given year was relatively small. The largest annual importation was, in fact, only 3,116 slaves in 1736. Even more impressive is the large number of ships

---

trade monopoly, brought in nine times as many slaves to Virginia from Africa as did the Company. (K. G. Davies, *The Royal African Company* [London, 1957], 143.) The same processes, periodization, and routes found in the Virginia slave trade were replicated in the smaller Maryland trade. (See Darold D. Wax, "Colonial Maryland and the Slave Trade," unpublished ms.)

[5] Donnan, *Documents,* IV, 183-187.

used to transport this relatively small number of slaves. In 1736, for example, it took 40 ships to bring the total number of slaves, or 78 slaves per vessel. In the entire period from 1727 to 1769, some 39,679 slaves were imported in 644 ships, for an average of 62 slaves per vessel.

Table 6.2

Number of Slaves Arriving in Virginia Ports by Region of Origin, 1727-1769
(number of ships in parentheses)

Quinquennium[a]	British North America[b]		British West Indies		Africa[c]		Total[d]	
1727-1732	3	(1)	112	(15)	1,377	(8)	2,239	(29)
1733-1737	253	(11)	1,228	(97)	9,111	(44)	10,592	(152)
1738-1742	407	(28)	1,382	(122)	5,498	(28)	7,287	(178)
1743-1747	260	(9)	790	(80)	3,048	(15)	4,298	(105)
1749-1753	226	(4)	865	(47)	6,281	(28)	7,372	(79)
1754-1759	6	(2)	279	(24)	625	(4)	913	(31)
1760-1764	261	(7)	185	(13)	5,735	(31)	6,196	(52)
1765-1769	1	(1)	142	(13)	639	(4)	782	(18)
TOTALS	1,417	(63)	4,983	(411)	32,314	(162)	39,679	(644)
Av. slaves per ship	22		12		199		62	
St. Dev.	50		28		99		99	
Mean tonnage per ship	43.7		51.9		91.0		61.2	
St. Dev.	28.6		34.9		37.4		39.1	
Av. "age" per ship	5.1		3.8		10.0		5.5	
St. Dev.	3.9		3.6		6.7		5.3	

[a]These are, in fact, five-year periods in all cases. No slave ships, however, were listed as having entered Virginia in the years 1730, 1748, or 1757. Also, I have arbitrarily assigned slaves listed as coming any time within a two-year span to the even-numbered years.

[b]A number of ships listed as coming from Virginia actually came from other regions. But since port officials in the interior listed any slave ship which initially stopped at the Lower James district to drop off slaves on their way up-river as being originally from the Lower James, there is a problem of double counting. Six of the 23 ships listed as originating in the Southern Colonies are in this category, while a seventh is doubtful.

[c]Within the Africa category I placed the 4 ships listed as coming from England. Given their tonnage and the number of slaves they carried, these ships belonged in the Africa route.

[d]The total column includes, in scattered periods, 8 ships of unknown origin which transported 965 slaves.

Source: Donnan, *Documents,* IV, 188-234.

But this high volume of shipping and low average number of slaves carried was more a function of the intervention of continental coastwise and West Indian shippers in bringing in slaves than of the nature of the direct Africa slave trade. Actually, the bulk of the slaves came from Africa in relatively few vessels. The Virginia slave trade can thus be conceived of as at least two, if not three, essentially different trades. The Africa-to-Virginia route with its 199 slaves per vessel accounted for only 25 percent of the ships, but 81 percent of the slaves who arrived.[6] This was almost exclusively a slave importation system, with little other commercial activity involved. The British West Indian and coastal North American shippers, on the other hand, were much less specialized slave traders, and probably engaged in the transportation of slaves as just one part of a general import trade involving a whole range of goods, including people. This is clearly reflected in their average numbers of 12 and 22 slaves per voyage respectively. Thus, although the British West Indian traders accounted for 64 percent of the slave ships, they brought in only 12 percent of the slaves delivered to Virginia ports. The coastal shippers, for their part, brought in just 4 percent of the slaves but accounted for 10 percent of the shipping.

Not only were the three trading zones different in total numbers of slaves and in average number carried, but they also differed in average tonnage employed. Here again, the African shippers had both a higher average tonnage and also a much higher ratio of slaves per ton than those in the other two major routes.[7]

[6] The fact that two-thirds of the slaves came directly from Africa challenges those who argued for a heavy colonial preference for West Indian seasoned slaves. It would appear that there was, in fact, some moderate amount of tax discrimination against West Indian as opposed to African slaves in the Continental colonies. Also, despite preferences expressed by some planters and merchants in the Southern colonies for Gold Coast slaves, the flow of slaves from the different regions of Africa to America were determined almost exclusively by African considerations. (Darold D. Wax, "Preferences for Slaves in Colonial America," *Journal of Negro History*, LVIII, no. 4 [October, 1973], pp. 379ff.) This same inability of supposed planter preference to influence the selection of slaves arriving to their shores is also evident in the trade to the French West Indies. (Gabriel Debien, *Les esclaves aux antilles françaises* [xviie-xviiie siècles] [Basse-Terre and Fort-de-France, 1974], p. 41.)

[7] The tonnage figures used throughout this chapter are the so-called "registered tonnage" of the pre-1773 variety. This measure is both smaller (about one-third less) than the pre-1773 "measured tonnage" and also considerably less than the post-1773 tonnage measurement. (For a discussion

Table 6.3
Ratio of Slaves to Tons of Shipping by Region of Provenance of Slaves
Arriving in Virginia
(standard deviations in parentheses)

Region of Provenance	Average Slaves per Ship		Average Tons per Ship		Ratio of Slaves/ Ton		
Northeast & Middle Atlantic	8 ⎱		36.2 ⎱		0.4 ⎱		(1.1)
		22		43.7		0.5	(1.0)
South	47 ⎰		56.7 ⎰		0.7 ⎰		(0.9)
British West Indies	12		51.9		0.2		(0.4)
Africa	199		91.0		2.3		(0.9)
General av.	62		61.2		0.8		(1.1)
No. of ships	644		634		634[a]		

[a]Eight unknown ships included. Excluding Virginia-originated slaves would bring the South's total to 0.5 slaves per ton.

Source: Same as table 6.2.

This sharp difference in average numbers of slaves landed between the direct Africa-to-Virginia and the West Indies-to-Virginia trades seems to be similar to the pattern observed in the Cuban slave trade at the end of the 18th century.[8] Both these trades, which might be termed modified Caribbean systems, contrast sharply with the Brazilian experience, which represents the other extreme. Involved exclusively in an Africa-to-America trade, Brazilian slavers in the early and mid-18th century were landing on average a minimum of 316 slaves per trip, a figure that rose to 440 slaves landed per vessel by the end of the century.[9]

of these various measures, see Christopher J. French, "Eighteenth-Century Shipping Tonnage Measurements," *Journal of Economic History*, XXXIII [1973], 434-443; Frederic C. Lane, "Tonnages, Medieval and Modern," *Economic History Review*, XVII [1964], 213-233.)

[8] In 1790, for example, direct African slavers to Havana averaged 251 slaves landed as compared with 43 slaves landed per voyage for ships coming from Caribbean ports. For Cuba, however, the primary re-export islands were Jamaica and Dominica, whereas Barbados played this vital role for Virginia. (Herbert S. Klein, "North American Competition and the Characteristics of the African Slave Trade to Cuba, 1790 to 1794," *William and Mary Quarterly*, XXVIII [1971], 93.)

[9] The first estimate is based on adults shipped from Luanda in Angola between 1723 and 1771 (see above, Chapter 2). These represented 203,904 slaves shipped in 549 vessels, for an average of 371 Africans shipped per voyage. Assuming a mortality rate of 10-15 percent—by the end of the cen-

Before we deal further with the contrast between the Africa-Virginia and Africa-Brazil trades, it is essential to determine if the Africa-Virginia route was representative of the entire English Atlantic slave trade. From all available evidence it is obvious that the capacity of English slave shipping in the 18th century was far higher than the landed figures for Virginia. Thus, the 103 ships that left the port of Liverpool to engage in the African slave trade in 1771 carried an average of 274 slaves per vessel.[10] Even as early as the beginning of the century, some 45 English ships sailing from England to Africa estimated that they would carry 252 slaves per vessel.[11] But, as Anstey's recent re-estimation of the English slave trade shows, until the end of the 1770s English shipping did not begin to reach its limits. Thus, in the decade of 1761 to 1770, the English slave trade involved an estimated 1,341 ships going to Africa, with an average of 112.3 tons per vessel and landing 209 slaves per voyage in America, figures that closely resemble Virginia's for this period. These magnitudes remained constant in the decade of the 1770s, but then rose dramatically in the following two decades. By the 1780s, the averages were 295 slaves landed from ships of 160 tons. By the 1790s, with the introduction of restrictive British legislation, the corresponding figures were 297 slaves landed from an average ship of 207 tons.[12] Supporting evidence for the pre-1770 period also suggests that the tonnage figures for the Africa-to-Virginia route were consistent with overall English African shipping. Thus, for the 1,338 ships listed as having cleared from Liverpool for Africa between 1730 and 1769, the average tonnage was 100.9 tons per vessel. The overall 91.0 tons for the African ships arriving in Virginia therefore seems close enough to the norm for these ships to be accepted as essentially the same.

Given that the Africa-Virginia route approximates the general pre-1770 England-Africa slave trade norms, it can then be asked: was there a basic difference in tonnage between the English and

---

tury this route had a mortality rate of 9.5 percent—then the landed average is 316-334 adult slaves.

[10] Donnan, *Documents*, ii, 545-546. [11] *Ibid.*, 116-118.

[12] Roger Anstey, "The Volume and Profitability of the Atlantic Slave Trade, 1761-1810," in Stanley L. Engerman and Eugene D. Genovese (eds.), *Race and Slavery in the Western Hemisphere: Quantitative Studies* (Princeton, 1974), pp. 4ff.

Portuguese ships used in the direct Africa trade in the 18th century that accounted for this difference of more than 100 percent in the slaves per ship landed in America? The evidence is still too incomplete to warrant any definitive conclusions. However, if Portuguese legal estimates of 2.5 to 3.5 slaves per ton are accepted as valid, then it would appear that 18th-century Portuguese vessels trading from Angola to Brazil averaged between 120 to 168 registered tons.[13] While direct comparisons are difficult because of differing ways of measuring tonnage cross-nationally, it might be suggested that the region of trade in Africa may have been a significant factor. Thus, the largest vessels in terms of carrying slaves for the Virginia trade were the ships arriving from Angola, which averaged 325 persons per vessel and a ratio of 2.9 slaves per ton. This ratio, it would seem, was quite comparable to the contemporary rates in the Angolan-Brazilian trade.

Within the British continental North American slave-importing zone, Virginia was the second most important market for slaves after South Carolina prior to the American Revolution.[14] In many respects, the two trades were quite similar. From 1735 to 1769, when there are comparable statistics for the two regions, both obtained the bulk of their slaves directly from Africa (86 percent for South Carolina and 83 percent for Virginia). Both also had slaves arriving on a large number of vessels from the British West Indies and from continental North American ports. Thus, in the case of Virginia, the remaining 17 percent of the slaves were carried in 75 percent of the vessels, and in South Carolina the 14 percent of the slaves not coming from Africa were carried by 61 percent of the South Carolina vessels. The only major difference between the two trades, aside from volume (with South Carolina in this period importing 32 percent more slaves than Virginia), was the relatively higher slaves-carried-from-Africa figure for

[13] See above, Chapter 2.

[14] The third major zone, Georgia, was almost exclusively a re-export trade from the British West Indies until the late 1760s. Thus, from March 1755 to November 1757 some 30 ships imported 321 slaves for only an 11 slave-per-voyage average. This figure rose to only 19 slaves per voyage in the period from November 1760 to October 1767, when 123 vessels brought in 2,326 slaves. By 1766, however, the first direct Africa-to-Georgia shipments began, and by 1769-1771 the average number of slaves being brought in rose to 151 per ship as 1,362 slaves arrived aboard 9 ships. (Donnan, *Documents*, IV, 612-625.)

Virginia (some 203 slaves per vessel) compared with the low 155-slaves-per-vessel for the South Carolina trade.[15]

Although the Africa-Virginia route involved full-time slavers carrying slaves as their only item, on the other two routes of the Virginia slave trade, slaves formed only one part of a diverse collection of imports coming to the colony. Though tonnage figures indicate that shipping from the West Indies or coastwise could have easily carried ten times the number of slaves, they did not do so. With its 0.2 slaves per ton and its 51 ton averages (higher than the coastwise trade), the voluminous Caribbean shipping was importing molasses, sugar, and other West Indian products into Virginia along with a few slaves on every voyage.[16] Except for Barbados, which seems to have served as the key slave-exporting zone and which may have been a "seasoning" island for Virginia-bound slaves, the rest of the West Indian trade seems totally non-specialized as to slave labor importations. This seems even more the case for the coastwise trade. If we exclude the double-counted, Virginia-originated slave ships, which I believe were all errors of recording, it is evident that incoming coastwise slave trading was as low as the West Indian trade.[17]

[15] For a more detailed analysis of the South Carolina figures, see Herbert S. Klein, "Slaves and Shipping in Eighteenth Century Virginia," *Journal of Interdisciplinary History*, vol. 5 (winter 1975), pp. 393-94, table 5. The sources for the South Carolina trade are Donnan, *Documents*, IV, 310-633; Peter H. Wood, *Black Majority. Negroes in Colonial South Carolina* (New York, 1974), Appendix C, table x; and W. Robert Higgins, "The Geographical Origins of Negro Slaves in Colonial South Carolina," *South Atlantic Quarterly*, LXX (1971), pp. 34-47.

[16] The basic commodities imported into the upper South from the West Indies in 1768 and 1769 were, in order of importance, rum, sugar, molasses, and coffee. In the previous year these four products accounted for 97 percent of the total value of goods in this trade and 96 percent in the following year. Of these products, rum was the key commodity, accounting for 72 percent and 70 percent respectively in these two years. (Calculated from data presented in James F. Shepherd and Gary M. Walton, *Shipping, Maritime Trade and the Economic Development of Colonial North America* [Cambridge, 1972], 229-230.)

[17] Some ships were incorrectly counted twice by port officials because ships that temporarily landed in the Lower James and then headed inland with part of their slaves were counted as landing with a full complement at both ports. This seems to have been the case with the following ships: *Breda* (40 tons), which arrived in 1740; *Clyde* (70 tons) and *Endeavour* (35 tons), both of which came in 1742; *Fortune* (50 tons), in 1734; *Pretty Betsey* (60 tons), in 1736; and *Vernon* (96 tons), in 1742. In all of the above cases, the same number of slaves were listed as landing in a coastal

In this coastwise trade, the prime imports by the 1760s were not slaves but, interestingly enough, re-exports and processed commodities that came from the West Indies. Rum, molasses, and refined and brown sugar made up 95 percent of the total value of goods imported into Virginia from northern ports in the period from 1760-1769.[18]

Although the West Indian and African routes, which brought in 95 percent of the slaves, differed radically in their pattern of delivering slaves, both were quite similar in their seasonal patterns. As can be seen in table 6.4, there was a sharp peaking of slave imports from these two regions in the summer months, with the Caribbean trade reaching its maximum in June and the African trade in July. Although both trades are almost parallel in their seasonal fluctuation, for the African trade there is the added factor of no imports whatsoever in the three winter months of December, January, and February. This seasonality seems highly correlated with planter demands and cropping season, which made the period from late April through early November the prime time for the demand for slaves.[19]

Just as the time of arrivals of slaves was influenced by American factors, so also the unique features of the Chesapeake Bay area created the unusual situation of several market regions for slaves, with no one port or site controlling the trade. The ability of so many Tidewater plantations to dock oceangoing vessels on their lands meant that the ships tended to move into many different reaches of the Chesapeake River system. The Upper and Lower James River, the York River, and the Rappahannock dis-

---

port as were listed as arriving a few days later inland. Several other cases among the eighteen sailings listed as having originated in Virginia ports involved the dropping off of part of the slaves whom they carried at the coastal port and the rest inland. In this case, it is almost impossible to evaluate the total number of slaves actually shipped from the port of origin. Finally, there is one case of a double-counted entry into one port. This was the *Two Sisters* (50 tons), listed with different masters and owners, but arriving from the same port, with identical tonnage, registration, and construction information, on 25 March 1742.

[18] David C. Klingaman, "The Development of the Coastwise Trade of Virginia in the Late Colonial Period," *Virginia Magazine of History and Biography*, LXXVII (1969), 132.

[19] The Maryland slave trade was also brought to a virtual halt between November and April. (Wax, "Colonial Maryland and the Slave Trade," pp. 16-17.)

Table 6.4
The Number of Slaves Arriving in Virginia by Region of Origin,
by Month and Season of Arrival, 1727-1769
(no. of ships in parentheses)

Month & Season	New England & Middle Colonies	South	British West Indies	Africa	Total[a]	
Winter	22	20	352	. . .	394	(72)
December	6	12	113	. . .	131	(40)
January	5	8	43	. . .	56	(16)
February	11	. . .	196	. . .	207	(16)
Spring	5	3	1,339	4,934	6,281	(138)
March	1	3	155	24	183	(18)
April	1	. . .	367	1,563	1,931	(49)
May	3	. . .	817	3,347	4,167	(71)
Summer	204	605	2,299	17,683	21,613	(237)
June	5	217	1,427	6,216	7,865	(85)
July	. . .	344	482	6,837	8,285	(81)
August	199	44	390	4,630	5,463	(71)
Fall	15	284	462	5,281	6,167	(123)
September	1	283	162	3,088	3,659	(43)
October	8	1	201	2,193	2,403	(46)
November	6	. . .	99	. . .	105	(34)
TOTALS	246	912	4,452	27,898	34,455	(570)

[a]The totals include 947 slaves whose region of origin is unknown.

Source: Same as table 6.2.

tricts were obviously the key zones for landing slaves (see table 6.5). Within this general movement, there appears some important variation, with the larger direct African ships going inland to the York, Upper James, and Rappahannock, while the West Indian and inter-coastal ships were using Hampton in the Lower James as their prime port of call.[20]

Given the unusually detailed recordings of the British colonial naval lists, a whole range of questions can be answered about the nature of the vessels involved in this trade. Because of the provisions of the Navigation Acts, ship's origin and port of registration

[20] This same pattern also can be seen in the period from 25 March 1718-1725 to March 1727. Incomplete returns of Africa-originated slave ships show the York and Rappahannock Rivers to be the prime centers of importation. The former received 8,572 slaves in 59 ships for an average landed of 145 slaves, while the latter imported 2,186 Africans in 14 ships for an average of 156 for each vessel. (Donnan, *Documents*, IV, 183-187.)

Table 6.5

The Number of Slaves Arriving in Virginia Port Districts by Region of Origin, 1727-1769

(number of ships in parentheses)

Virginia Districts	REGION OF ORIGIN			Totals	
	British North America	British West Indies	Africa		
Accomac[a]	110 (3)	15 (2)	· · ·	125 (5)	
South Potomack	25 (1)	86 (2)	949 (7)	1,060 (10)	
Rappahannock	2 (1)	791 (20)	4,431 (28)	5,224 (49)	
York River	7 (5)	987 (37)	14,613 (67)	15,607 (109)	
Lower James River	110 (27)	2,960 (327)	2,487 (16)	5,557 (370)	
Upper James River	1,163 (26)	142 (22)	9,834 (44)	11,139 (92)	
James River	· · ·	2 (1)	· · ·	2 (1)	
TOTALS	1,417 (63)	4,983 (411)	32,314 (162)	38,714 (636)[b]	

[a]These six standard naval districts, arranged here in a north-to-south listing, were sometimes referred to differently in the Donnan citations. Thus the Lower James District was sometimes referred to as Hampton, or just the Lower District. The Upper James District was often referred to as just the Upper District. The one listing for the James River, which was not a separate district, cannot be associated to either district on the James.

[b]There were 8 ships with 965 slaves unknown as to port of origin or arrival.

Source: Same as table 6.2.

were prime items of concern to port officials; thus, detailed information is available on ship construction, ownership, and even age for each of the major trade routes. Along with these facts, the names of ships, their masters, owners, and tonnage provide enough information to construct frequency tables for the sailings of the ships involved in the Virginia trade, giving key data by which the overall specialization of this trade can be compared with other Atlantic routes.

In analyzing the data on construction, as presented in table 6.6, it appears that most of the ships involved in the trade were

Table 6.6
Region of Construction of Slave Ships Arriving in Virginia, 1727-1769
(standard deviations in parentheses)

Region	No. of Ships	Total Gross Tonnage	Average Tons per Ship	Average "Age" per Ship (in years)[a]
New England & Middle Atlantic	110	6,602	60.0 (34.0)	5.9 (4.3)
South	124	8,434	68.0 (38.5)	3.1 (2.6)
British West Indies	47	1,876	39.9 (23.2)	3.8 (2.8)
Plantations[b]	220	9,819	44.6 (27.4)	4.1 (3.5)
England	100	8,948	89.5 (37.8)	11.5 (7.5)
TOTALS[c]	601	35,679	59.4 (36.6)	5.5 (5.3)

[a]The average "age" of the ship was computed by subtracting the year of construction from the year of arrival in Virginia. There were only two cases when the ship's age was unknown.

[b]This was the generic term used for shipping constructed in England's American possessions.

[c]The unknowns as to region of construction include 32 ships with total gross tonnage of 3,104 tons, for an average of 97 tons per vessel. Among these unknowns were the 20 foreign-built prizes captured by the British.

Source: Same as table 6.2.

built in America. The combination of the New England, Middle Atlantic, Southern, and generic "plantations" (meaning New World British colonies) production accounts for over 84 percent of the shipping. This means that American-built ships not only dominated the West Indian and Coastwise trades, where they accounted respectively for 96 percent and 93 percent of the ships, but were even important in the shipping coming directly from Africa. On this route, they accounted for 44 percent of the ships, with English-built ships making up the rest. That the tonnage of these American-built vessels was equal to that of the English-built ships is indicated by the fact that the latter accounted for 56 percent of the total number of ships and 58 percent of the gross tonnage involved in this route. But on the whole, English-built ships, compared with all of the colonial-built vessels, were much larger and, although they accounted for only 16 percent of the total ships built, they made up 28 percent of the gross tonnage, and carried 58 percent of the slaves coming from Africa.[21]

In a comparison of construction with ownership, the dominance of American-built shipping is again impressive. Fully 100 percent of the ships owned by Southern and West Indian merchants, and 93 percent of the Northern and Middle Atlantic colonial-owned ships, were colonial-built. Of the shipping owned by English merchants, 40 percent was American-made.[22]

Although ship construction may have been primarily a colonial affair, ownership was another matter. In those areas where large profits were to be made, or where English imports were involved, English capital predominated. In the overall trade, English capital brought 79 percent of all slaves to Virginia, even though only 28 percent of the ships were English-owned.[23]

Of the total number of ships coming from Africa, English merchants owned 87 percent, and these ships carried 89 percent of the slaves coming from this region. But even the 6 percent that English merchants owned of the shipping that went between the West Indies and Virginia accounted for 29 percent of the slaves coming from that zone, which indicates English specialization in the slave trade in this area as well. In the New England and Middle Atlantic trade to Virginia, English participation was less than 1 percent, though it dominated the Southern-originated shipping. The probable errors in double recordings with the Virginia ships, however, may account for the bulk of that latter ownership. Thus, the English essentially dominated the slave trade,

[21] Herbert S. Klein, "Slaves and Shipping in Eighteenth-Century Virginia," *Journal of Interdisciplinary History*, v, no. 3 (winter, 1975), table 9, p. 401.
[22] *Ibid.*, table 10, p. 402.   [23] *Ibid.*, table 11, p. 403.

if not the overall shipping, that came to Virginia in the 18th century.[24]

Although the English owned the majority of the real slavers, the inter-coastal and West Indian trades were controlled by the British North American merchants. As Pares noted in his study on the Continental-West Indian trades, most of that trade was owned, except for the unique case of Bermuda, by continental merchants.[25] In the case of the ships bringing slaves, this meant that 64 percent of West-Indian-originated traders were owned by North American merchants.

As for the inter-coastal traders, the pattern of ownership markedly favored the port from which the ship sailed. Thus, of the ships that arrived in Virginia from the Northern and Middle Atlantic colonies, 80 percent were directly owned in the exporting ports. Although the sample of ships coming from southern ports is extremely small, it would appear that Southerners also owned the bulk of their own shipping. This is clearly the case when several broken voyages of ships coming from other regions—which stopped in Lower James ports and were then listed as carrying slaves from that district to the Upper James—are eliminated. This reduces the total of Southern-originated slavers to just 11 ships, and raises the Southern ownership rate to 54 percent.

From the above evidence it would appear that colonials were barely keeping pace with the British in this particular trade in slaves. Although 75 percent of the gross tonnage engaged in the slave trade had been built in England's New World possessions, only 57 percent of that tonnage was owned by the colonists. The British metropolitan merchants owned fully 43 percent. The British home merchants controlled the African slave trade, just as they controlled the largest ships and those longest in service. The West Indian merchants, in turn, owned only a minor share (13 percent) of the total trade, even though fully 55 percent of the total tonnage was arriving from their islands. In terms of the Continental Colonies, both their share of construction and of

[24] *Ibid.*, table 12, p. 405. In the Maryland trade, British merchants controlled the slaves until the final moment, simply using local merchants as agents. (Wax, "Colonial Maryland and the Slave Trade," p. 20.) This was most likely the pattern of the trading arrangements in Virginia as well.

[25] Richard Pares, *Yankees and Creoles: The Trade between North America and the West Indies before the American Revolution* (New York, 1968), p. 8.

ownership was relatively high and about equal, that is, 42 percent of the tonnage was owned by them.

By moving from gross overall statistics on shipping to an analysis of the individual ships themselves, we can obtain a better idea as to both the nature of the several trading routes that made up the Virginia slave trade, and its rate of specialization, that is, the long-term commitments through the number of multiple voyages of the slavers in this trade compared with the other Atlantic trades. From table 6.7 we can calculate the mean and median

Table 6.7
Frequency of Voyages of Slave Ships
Arriving in Virginia, 1727-1769

No. of Voyages per Ship	Total No. of Ships by Frequency of Voyages	Total No. of Voyages
1	373	373
2	62	124
3	23	69
4	6	24
5	6	30
7	2	14
9	1	9
TOTALS	473	643[a]

[a]There was one ship unknown as to name and therefore impossible to identify. As for the problem of double-counted Virginia voyages, I have retained the original naval-office listings in the above table since their recording would make no major difference to the overall outcome.

Source: Same as table 6.2.

voyage rates for these 644 ships' arrivals. As the table indicates, the highest multiple voyage in this 42-year period was 1 ship with 9 sailings. The mean was 1.3 voyages per ship and three-quarters of the boats made only one voyage.

Of the ships with the highest multiple voyage, the most typical sailing was that between Virginia and the West Indies. Of the 9 ships that made 5 voyages or more, all but one were directly engaged in the West-Indies-Virginia route. Of these 8 vessels, all but 2 were primarily from Bermuda and the others came from several different Caribbean ports, including Barbados. The ship that completed the most voyages from Africa was the *Liverpool Merchant* out of England. Built in Liverpool, this 80-ton vessel was typical in both its tonnage and slaves-landed figures. In 5 sailings, it carried 130-193 slaves, averaging 166 slaves landed, which was only slightly below the African-originated slavers' mean.

One further item, incidentally revealed by the registration and construction information, is the impact of privateering on the continental West Indian and British merchant shipping. The records show that there were 21 ships (or 4 percent of the total) originally built in foreign countries that had been made prizes by the British and sold to private English and colonial merchants. These 21 ships had made 23 voyages to Virginia in this 42-year period, averaging about 114.0 tons per vessel, and accounted for 4 percent of the voyages. The majority (14) of these vessels came from the French merchant marine.[26]

To place the Virginia slave trade in its broadest context, several major comparisons are in order. First is the relative importance of the Virginia slave trade in the context of the total British North American slave trade. Unfortunately, complete comparative data for North America currently are available only for the later 1760s and early 1770s. But broad comparisons with the South Carolina figures do suggest some relative trends before this period. Although the two were roughly equal as importers in the 1735-1740 period, the relative importance of Virginia declined to the point whereby 1760-1769 South Carolina was importing almost three times as many slaves. It could be argued from this limited data that earlier in the century Virginia weighed more heavily within the total British North American slave trade than it did by the second half of the 18th century. By then, Virginia was only a small part of the trade. In the total British North American estimates recently published by Shepherd and Walton for the period from 1768 to 1772, the upper South imported only 23 percent of the total slaves brought to the continent, compared with 74 percent who arrived in lower southern ports. Considering that the imports for the upper South also contained Maryland's, which may have made up at least half of the total, it could be estimated that by the decades of the 1760s and 1770s, the Virginia slave

[26] The condemnation and sale of these ships go from 1742 to 1768, with the majority occurring in the early 1760s.

trade was entering a period of decline, and accounted for only 10-20 percent of the total number of slaves arriving in the continent.[27] Even in its most expansive stage in the earlier years of the century, Virginia probably never absorbed more than half of the total arrivals, and was most likely in the range of a third of the total numbers of slaves coming into British North America.

If the Virginia slave trade was an important but minor part of the entire continental slave trade, how did it measure against the total merchant shipping coming to Virginia in the 18th century? Here again, we are faced with rather fragmentary and, at times, contradictory evidence. The official *Historical Statistics of the United States* provide data for incoming shipping only for the Lower James port of Hampton, and then just for ten non-consecutive years, between 1727 and 1772. From this quite limited sample, however, it is evident that the slavers (that is, those ships carrying one slave or more) represented an extremely small proportion of the entire merchant shipping coming to Virginia in the 18th century. In its best year in relation to total shipping—1739—some 26 slavers arrived in all 6 naval districts. At the same time, 102 general cargo ships arrived in the port of Hampton alone. Adding the slavers to the Hampton total shows that 20 percent of all ships (with general cargo shipping for the other 5 naval districts unknown) in this year were slavers. But this was the peak year, for in 1727 the figure was 7 percent; in 1731, some 2 percent; in 1733, 15 percent; in 1752, 10 percent; and in the 2-year period of 1768-1769, it dropped to barely 1 percent as the number of slavers declined and general shipping to Hampton experienced a rapid increase.[28]

In the context of England's overseas trade, the slave trade to Virginia formed a part of what was the largest single trading

[27] Shepherd and Walton, *Shipping*, 142, Table 8.2. Comparing Shepherd and Walton with Donnan's Virginia data for 1768 and 1769 shows that Virginia accounted for only 34 percent and 48 percent respectively of the total slave imports for the "Upper South."

[28] U.S. Bureau of the Census, *Historical Statistics of the United States, Colonial Times to 1970* (2 vols., Washington, D.C., 1975), II, 1181; Series Z 266-285. Middleton, *Tobacco Coast*, p. 251, cites the *Virginia Gazette* as his source for saying that 937 ships entered Virginia ports from 1736 to 1766, thus making the slavers 56 percent of the total shipping. But this figure of total shipping would appear much too low, compared to the official naval port figures upon which the fragmentary Hampton data are based, and it can be assumed that the newspaper seriously under-recorded total merchant ships' arrivals.

route: that is, the West Indies and plantation continental American zone. In 1771-1773, for example, of 375,000 tons of English shipping engaged in overseas trade, the largest single route was to the West Indies and America, which absorbed 153,000 tons, or 40 percent of total tonnage.[29] Most of this shipping was involved, of course, in bringing back the sugar, tobacco, and rice that was being exported by the West Indies and Southern colonies respectively. In this trade, the merchants of London were dominant. But in the slave trade, which formed a rather specialized sub-group of this large commerce, the outports of Liverpool and Bristol played a more prominent role. Especially in the early part of the 18th century, Bristol ships dominated the slave trade over London and Liverpool.[30] This is reflected in the Virginia trade. Here, Bristol slavers accounted for 50 percent of the British-owned tonnage, with Liverpool controlling a third, and London only 12 percent.

In sum, three routes brought slaves to Virginia: a direct African trade that involved shipments of native Africans to the New World; a Caribbean route that brought in both Africans and West Indian creoles; and, finally, a coastwise trade that probably brought in a majority of creole slaves. Of these three trades, only the direct African route was exclusively a slave trade. On the other two routes, the general shippers seem to have included greater or lesser numbers of slaves as the opportunity offered, but their primary concern was with general merchandise. This specialization by the African traders, as opposed to non-specialization of the others, meant that the direct African trade accounted for the majority of slave arrivals, though only a minor

[29] Ralph Davis, *The Rise of the English Shipping Industry in the Seventeenth and Eighteenth Centuries* (London, 1962), p. 17.

[30] In the first two decades of the 18th century, London was the predominant slaving port, though Bristol accounted for just over 40% of the total African voyages. By the 1730s Bristol fully dominated the trade, though the rise of Liverpool kept its total share of African sailings to 46%. In the decade of the 1750s a major decline set in, with Bristol ships dropping on average to only 25% of all voyages in the period 1750-1759 and to just 12% in 1771. Its place as the primary port lasted for only the two decades of the 1730s and 1740s, with Liverpool taking over half the trade by the 1750s. D. P. Lamb, "Volume and Tonnage of the Liverpool Slave Trade 1772-1807" in Roger Anstey and P.E.H. Hair, eds., *Liverpool, the African Slave Trade, and Abolition* (Liverpool, 1976), p. 91, table 1. On the role of Bristol in the North American trade, see W. E. Minchinton, "The Slave Trade of Bristol with the British mainland colonies in North America, 1699-1770," *ibid.*, pp. 39-59.

part of total shipping. Also, this was the route totally dominated by metropolitan merchants. Although British North Americans dominated the coastwise and the general West-Indian-to-continental-North-American trade, the English controlled the direct Africa-to-Virginia route. Their ships were the biggest and the oldest and brought in the most slaves. Theirs were also the only ones that so systematically specialized in the slave trade.

Finally, in evaluating the Virginia slave trade in the general context of the Atlantic slave trade, we find that we are dealing with one end of a continuum. For Virginia, with its three slave-producing streams, its relatively low numbers of arriving slaves, and its low average figures of slaves carried directly from Africa, stands in sharp contrast to the Brazilian extreme of high annual imports, direct African trade, and high average-carried numbers. For the majority of large slave plantation societies, their slave trades probably fell between these two extremes, with those of the West Indies variously sharing elements of both.

Chapter Seven

The English Slave Trade
to Jamaica, 1782-1808

From its conquest by the English in 1655 until the end of the slave trade in 1808, Jamaica had been transformed from a primarily subsistence agrarian economy into one of the world's largest plantation commercial crop regimes. In that period over 600,000 Africans were transported to the island and Jamaica had become the largest single importer of African slave laborers in all British America. While the growth of the Jamaican sugar economy had been relatively slow in the first fifty years after its conquest from the Spaniards, by the 1720s it had become the dominant West Indian sugar production center, a fact reflected by its displacement of Barbados as both the largest sugar exporter and slave importer in the British Caribbean. By this period it was importing over 2,000 slaves per annum, a figure that would rise to over 8,000 per annum by the last thirty years of the British slave trade.[1]

While the general growth of this slave trade has been reasonably well known and well studied in terms of total volume since the 18th century, surprisingly little is known about its internal dynamics or how it compares to the other trades both within the British Empire and with the other European powers. Who carried the slaves, on what type of shipping, from which ports in Africa, at what costs in mortality in slaves—all are but a few of the unstudied questions involving this enormous forced migration in human beings. Little is known to date on the age and sex of the arriving slaves, or the conditions of their living or dying. And, despite all the traditional literature, relatively few systematic studies exist on the actual commercial and naval organization of the trade to this island.

Although few of these questions can be fully answered, I have

[1] Philip D. Curtin, *The Atlantic Slave Trade, A Census* (Madison, Wisconsin, 1969), p. 140, table 40. This figure represented close to 50 percent of all British Caribbean slave imports.

gathered together a set of statistical data by which to analyze the Jamaican slave trade in order systematically to compare it to the other major and minor slave trades to the Americas. The source of these statistics is the naval lists kept by the Jamaican officials for arriving vessels reaching the major ports of Jamaica.[2] Unfortunately, these lists are incomplete for many years and only beginning in the 1780s are they available on a large scale and on a reasonably systematic basis in the Public Record Office. Although these records have major lacunae even after this period, these gaps can be partly filled from shipping lists published by Parliament in the late 1790s and early 1800s,[3] and from a unique collection of shipping materials gathered by the House of Lords in the 1790s in order to analyze in detail all aspects of the trade. These records cover the period from 1791 to 1799 for about 38 percent of all ships that left England in order to engage in the slave trade with Africa and America.[4]

Systematizing these diverse sources, one is able to create a set of materials that account for an important part of the shipping that brought slaves to Jamaica between 1782 and 1808. Thus, while the data are not complete, they probably represent a reasonable sample of all aspects of the Jamaican trade at its apogee.

In a comparison of the resulting statistics of the English slave

[2] PRO, Colonial Office, CO 142/19-25.

[3] These include *A&P*, 1801-1802, IV, pp. 452-479, document No. 2 in "Accounts presented to the House of Commons respecting the trade to the Coast of Africa for slaves," 19 May 1802; and *A&P*, 1806, XIII, pp. 798-801, documents No. 6 and 7 in "Accounts . . . relating to the African Slave Trade," 2d and 16th July 1806.

[4] HLRO, *Papers*, "Return to an Order of the Right Honorable House of Lords dated the 10th of July 1799, directing the clerk of the Parliaments to cause to be extracted from the several log books and Journals of Ships employed in the Slave trade in each year 1791 to 1797. . . ," dated 28 July 1800 and with a shelf list no. 5/J/11/2 "Slave Trade Accounts." I am indebted to Professor Roger Anstey for calling my attention to these papers. He calls this source "Lords List A" and has made use of it in his recent studies "The Volume and Profitability of the British Slave Trade, 1761-1807" in Stanley L. Engerman and Eugene D. Genovese (Eds.), *Race and Slavery in the Western Hemisphere: Quantitative Studies* (Princeton 1975) and *The Atlantic Slave Trade and British Abolition, 1760-1810* (London, 1975). This list contained a large number of ships whose African port of destination was not known. This latter information, however, could be found for some of these ships in other documents, and this information was coded in. These supplementary lists will be found in HLRO, *Papers*, 19 June 1799, 25 June 1799 and 9 July 1799; and in Parliamentary Papers, *A&P*, 1795-96, XLII (849).

Table 7.1
Number of Slaves, Crew, and Tonnage of Selected Slave Ships
Arriving in Jamaica, 1782-1808[a]

Period & Year of Arrival	No. of Ships	Average No. of Slaves per Vessel	Average Tons per Vessel	Average Slaves per Ton per Vessel	Average Crew per Vessel
1. 1782-1788	130	396 (158)[b]	172 (79)	2.6 (1.2)	34 [13][c]
1782	11	467	196	2.7	41
1783	11	491	168	3.1	39
1784	38	409	167	2.8	37
1785	30	368	175	2.3	30
1786	16	353	136	2.7	28
1787	16	374	165	2.5	30
1788	8	334	240[d]	1.4	28
2. 1791-1799	268	328 (101)	236 (81)	1.4 (0.2)	31 [10]
1791	11	293	229	1.3	n.a.
1792	32	308	236	1.4	n.a.
1793	58	286	215	1.4	n.a.
1794	19	324	219	1.5	n.a.
1795	19	316	227	1.4	n.a.
1796	24	349	244	1.4	30
1797	30	356	250	1.4	30
1798	31	396	280	1.4	37
1799	44	334	231	1.5	n.a.
3. 1800-1808	283	289 (86)	294 (97)	1.0 (0.2)	31 [11]
1800	56	338	297	1.2	n.a.
1801	25	300	331	0.9	n.a.
1802	34	285	312	0.9	31
1803	25	296	320	0.9	25
1804	21	263	281	1.0	33
1805	17	277	306	0.9	37
1806	30	285	292	1.0	34
1807	59	261	271	1.0	30
1808	16	250	247	1.0	28
TOTALS	681	220,985	168,839		11,485

[a]These are the ships whose records survived in complete form and had information on both tonnage and the number of slaves carried.

[b]All figures in parentheses represent the standard deviation.

[c]While other variables are based on 681 ships, the number of crew was known for only 362 ships. The total number of ships for each period are in brackets.

[d]These 8 ships from the first half of 1788 are clearly atypical of both the period, and even of the years 1788 and 1789. Of the 127 ships (of 21,044 total tonnage) that left England in 1788 and the 116 slave ships (19,266 tons) that left in 1789, the average for both years was 166 tons; A&P, 1790, xxxi (705b), "An Account of the Number of Ships ... which cleared ... to Africa, in 1788 and 1789."

Sources: For the period 1782-1788, 1805-1808, PRO,CO 142/19-25; for 1791-1795, HL RO, Papers, 28 July 1800; for 1799-1801, A&P, 1801-1802, IV, 452-479; a combination of the above three sources for the 1796-1798 period; and, finally, the 1802-1804 ships were collected from A&P, loc. cit, and A&P, 1806, XIII, 798-801.

trade with other 18th-century slave trades, it becomes obvious that the Jamaican trade is of major proportions. It is clearly the largest regional slave trade within the English-American context, and is comparable to the other leading 18th-century trades, the French and the Portuguese. In the pre-1790 period, the English were on a par with the French and the Portuguese. While the most relevant comparative data come from the pre-1780 period, they are close enough in time to be considered reasonable proxies of the activities of the various nationalities in the 1780 period. Whereas in the 1780s the English were averaging some 396 slaves per vessel delivered in the West Indies, the French in the 1770s were bringing in some 341 slaves per vessel.[5] The Portuguese, for their part, were shipping some 377 slaves per vessel from Luanda, Angola, in the 1760s, which probably meant numbers landed on the order of 320-340, depending on the rates of mortality suffered by the slaves.[6] Thus the numbers carried per ship by the English slavers at the peak of the Jamaican trade were somewhat greater than the numbers carried on the ships of the other leading slaving nations of the last quarter of the 18th century.

But while the other traders, above all the Portuguese, steadily increased their ability to carry slaves in the following decades, the ability of the English traders steadily declined. Whereas the average number of slaves carried to Rio de Janeiro kept rising into the upper 400s decade by decade, especially as an increasing share of the trade was coming from East Africa,[7] the opposite was the case with Jamaica. Although the total numbers of slaves coming to Jamaica kept increasing (see table 7.6), the carrying capacity of each arriving slaver kept declining decade after decade in this still preeminent slave importing island. Nor was Jamaica unique, for British slavers participating in the newly opened Cuban slave trade after 1789 also experienced these same lowered levels of carrying capacity.[8]

[5] Calculated from the published lists of Nantes slave ships from 1748 to 1792 in Dieudonné Rinchon, *Le trafic négrier* (Paris, 1938), Tome i, pp. 248-301.

[6] Calculated from data in table 2.2.

[7] For the relevant data, see Herbert S. Klein, "The Trade in African Slaves to Rio de Janeiro, 1795-1811: Estimates of Mortality and Patterns of Voyages," *Journal of African History*, x, No. 4 (1969); and "O trafico de escravos africanos para o porto de Rio de Janeiro, 1825-1830," *Anais de Historia* (Assis, São Paulo), v (1973).

[8] Herbert S. Klein, "The Cuban Slave Trade in a Period of Transition,

The causes for this dramatic decline were the parliamentary slave trade regulating acts of 1788 and 1799. These acts were designed to reduce the number of slaves-per-ton ratio that was considered a major way of relieving what was viewed as the overcrowded conditions, which in turn were assumed to have caused excessive mortality to both slaves and crew in the Middle Passage.[9] Dolben's Act of 1788 reduced capacity by defining slaves-per-ton ratios, while the 1799 act diminished the legal limits even further by using space measurements below decks rather than crude tonnage as the criteria for the numbers to be carried. The net impact of these two acts was to reduce the slaves-per-ton ratio from 2.6 in the pre-reform period to one slave per ton in the last decade of the trade. At the same time, the general changes in ships tonnage measurements that occurred at the end of the 18th century may also have had an impact on reducing the slaves-per-ton figure, since preliminary investigations indicate that on average the new measurements raised ships tonnage figures.[10] Thus the post-1788 rise in average tonnage may be either a change in the size of ships utilized or simply new and higher measurements of tonnage for old ships. These changes, of course, might have diminished the impact of the parliamentary reforms on the slaves-per-ton ratios. But the reduction of average carried from 396 slaves per voyage to just 289 slaves per voyage was unqualifiedly a result of the parliamentary Acts. It seems well

---

1790-1843," *Revue française d'Histoire d'Outre-Mer,* LXII, Nos. 226-227 (1975), pp. 72-73, Table 2.

[9] Dolben's Act of 1788 is reprinted in Elizabeth Donnan, *Documents Illustrative of the History of the Slave Trade to America* (Washington, 1931), Vol. II, pp. 582-589. It would appear that the slaves-per-ton ratio on average dropped 46 percent as a result of the 1788 act and another 28 percent after the 1799 decree (see table 7.1). However, if the adjustment for the change between registered and measured tonnage after 1786 is made; and one were to use the crude formula for estimating how ship's tonnage was increased by the new measuring act, then it could be argued that the 1799 act had a much more important impact on reducing slaves-per-ton ratios than Dolben's Act. (For a more detailed discussion of this issue, see Herbert S. Klein and Stanley L. Engerman, "Slave Mortality on British Ships 1791-1797" in Roger Anstey and P.E.H. Hair, eds., Liverpool, *The African Slave Trade, and Abolition* [Liverpool, 1976], p. 125, n. 27.)

[10] On this issue see Christopher J. French, "Eighteenth-Century Shipping Tonnage Measurements," *Journal of Economic History,* XXXIII (1973), 434-443; and Ralph Davis, *The Rise of the English Shipping Industry in the Seventeenth and Eighteenth Centuries* (London, 1962), p. 7n; and Lamb, "Volume and Tonnage," *loc.cit.*

proved that it was only parliamentary regulation that succeeded in reducing those figures of numbers carried even in the context of an increasing volume of trade.[11]

Thus the pre-1788 Jamaican shipping has characteristics that make it more similar to the early 18th century than to the post-1788 slave trading, at least in terms of the pattern of loading slaves aboard the ships. While Virginia-bound African slavers in the 1727-1769 period were averaging only 199 slaves per voyage as contrasted to 327 slaves per voyage in the pre-reform Jamaican trade, the average per-ton ratio in both African-originated trades was quite similar, indicating similar manners of carrying slaves. The difference in the volume of slaves transported between the two trades was therefore due to the overall size of the shipping employed, for Virginia-bound slavers were averaging only 91 tons, compared to the 172 tons of the Jamaican-bound ships. But the two trades averaged 2.3 and 2.6 slaves per ton respectively, and in the vessels under 100 tons, Virginia-bound slavers were carrying slightly higher slaves-per-ton ratios than the latter Jamaican traders. It was only in the crucial 100-199-ton range (which accounted for 36 percent and 53 percent of the Virginia and Jamaican African slavers respectively) where the Jamaican-bound ships were distinct. Here the pre-reform shippers carried a slave per ton more (3.3 to 2.3 per ton in the 100-149 range and 2.7 to 1.3 in the 150-199 tonnage class) than the Virginia shippers. Thus both the increasing tonnage of the ships, the larger number of ships employed, and a tighter crowding in the middle range of 100-199 tons category accounted for the general increasing volume of the 18th-century trade. But both trades showed the standard pattern of decline in slaves-per-ton ratios as the tonnage of the shipping increased.[12]

In this sense, the British African slave trades to Virginia and Jamaica resembled the 18th-century French slave trade from Africa. All three slave trades show the same higher ratio of slaves per ton for the smaller ships, which progressively declines as tonnage increases.[13] The reasons for this common pattern, typi-

[11] For a more detailed analysis of the impact of the parliamentary regulations on the slave trade, see Klein and Engerman, "Slave Mortality on British Ships," pp. 119ff.

[12] The simple correlations between slaves per ton and tonnage was −.21 for the Africa-Virginia ships and −.45 for the pre-reform Jamaican ships.

[13] The French ratios ran from 2.4 slaves per ton for ships under 100 tons,

fied by the pre- and post-reform Jamaican slave ships (see table
7.2) appear to be largely structural. That is, there appears to
have been a size limitation in terms of available space needs determined by the amount of food, water, and supplies that a slaver
had to carry, which decreased the capacity to carry slaves as the
number of tons of a ship increased.

Table 7.2
Average Ratio of Slaves per Ton for Slave Ships Entering
Jamaican Ports, 1782-1808, by Category of Tonnage
(number of ships in parentheses)

Category of Tonnage	1782-1788	1791-1799	1800-1808	Total
01 - 49	2.0 (2)	1.8 (3)	. . .	1.9 (5)
50 - 99	2.2 (9)	1.6 (4)	1.3 (9)	1.7 (22)
100-149	3.3 (52)	1.5 (28)	1.2 (10)	2.5 (90)
150-199	2.7 (17)	1.5 (68)	1.2 (21)	1.6 (106)
200-249	1.9 (20)	1.5 (49)	1.1 (47)	1.4 (116)
250-299	2.0 (14)	1.4 (61)	1.0 (70)	1.3 (145)
300-349	1.6 (13)	1.3 (32)	1.0 (52)	1.1 (97)
350-399	1.3 (3)	1.3 (18)	0.9 (39)	1.0 (60)
400-449	. . .	1.3 (4)	0.9 (15)	1.0 (19)
450-499	. . .	. . .	0.8 (14)	0.9 (14)
500 & Above	. . .	1.1 (1)	0.8 (6)	0.9 (7)
GENERAL AV.	2.6 (130)	1.4 (268)	1.0 (283)	1.5 (681)

Source: Same as table 7.1.

Just as there were important changes in the size and carrying
capacity of English slave ships during the 18th century, there
were also important changes in their African sources of supply.
In the early 18th century, British slave ships were reasonably active in all the major slave trading zones along the Western coast,
by the last quarter of the century, however, the two zones of most
active concentration were the Bight of Biafra and the Congo-
Angola area. In a special survey of slave shipping in the 1790s
done by the House of Lords, these two zones accounted for 78
percent of the slaves and 75 percent of the ships arriving from
known African ports to Jamaica, a pattern similar to all the other

with a steady decline to 1.3 slaves per ton for ships above 350 tons. (Calculated from data in Rinchon, *Le trafic négrier, loc. cit.*; and from Rinchon's
unpublished collection of recordings of Nantes slave ships for the period
1697-1747 found in CRHFA, Fonds Rinchon, Boîtes 10 à 12. I am indebted
to Dr. Robert Stein for calling my attention to this latter source.)

major New World importing slave societies of the English empire.[14]

This concentration of slave shipping in the Bight of Biafra and along the Congo and Angolan coast reflected general late-18th-century trends in slave-trading activity of most of the major European slave-trading nations. Though Luanda and the ports to the south remained in Portuguese control, the region to the north was open to all traders, who progressively found this Congo or Loango coast a most important region for slaves in the latter part of the century.[15]

In many other respects, the late-18th-century trade to Jamaica also reflected general patterns to be found in all the important trading zones. Thus the age and sex ratios of the slaves arriving on Jamaican shores were similar to those for the Africans transported to the other major regions of America in the 18th century. There is the same dominance of males and of adults, with the majority of slaves being men in their prime years of life. The low ratio of women is reflected in both the adult and the children categories and, at least for the years of the trade covered by the House of Lords register of shipping seems invariant.

Before we examine some of the reasons behind this sexual imbalance, and its implications for the importing slave societies, it is worth taking a more detailed look at the age and sex categories

[14] Whereas the Congo-Angola area was a traditional slave exporting zone, the Biafran ports came into prominence as a major source for slaves only in the 18th century. (Curtin, *The Atlantic Slave Trade,* p. 228.) It is estimated that no slaving was done at Old Calabar, for instance, prior to 1650, and that serious slaving activity began only well into the 18th century. (A.J.H. Lathan, *Old Calabar, 1600-1891. The Impact of the International Economy Upon a Traditional Society* [Oxford, 1973], pp. 17-22.) The Gabon estuary trade just north of Cape Lopez also came into full slave activity only late in the 18th century. K. David Patterson, *The Northern Gabon Coast to 1875* (Oxford, 1975), pp. 33ff. By the 1760s these two zones of Biafra and Congo-Angola accounted for 46 percent of the slaves going to British America, a figure that rose to 72 percent in the last two decades of the British trade. The only other significant region sending slaves was the Gold Coast, which accounted for some 8 percent of the total in this last period. (Michael Craton, *Sinews of Empire, A Short History of British Slavery* [New York, 1974], p. 75, and Anstey, "Volume," p. 13, table 5.)

[15] In an analysis of the slave populations on selected plantations throughout Saint Domingue in the period from the middle years of the 18th century until the 1790s, Debien shows that Congo slaves were consistently the single most important group. (See Gabriel Debien, *Les esclaves aux antilles françaises* [*xviie-xviiie siècles*] [Basse-Terre and Fort-de-France, 1974], chapter ii.)

Table 7.3
The Region of African Provenance of Slaves Arriving in English Slave Ships
in the West Indies, 1791-1798
(number of ships in parentheses)

African Region of Provenance	Jamaica	St. Vincent	Grenada	Total All[a] Ports
Senegambia	190 (1)	355 (2)	409 (2)	1,075 (6)
Sierra Leone	5,544 (21)	795 (4)	851 (4)	9,770 (40)
Windward Coast	3,420 (10)	641 (3)	566 (3)	4,840 (17)
Gold Coast	2,721 (9)	1,968 (9)	. . .	8,573 (30)
Bt. of Benin	315 (1)	209 (1)	. . .	912 (3)
Bt. of Biafra	18,218 (59)	2,740 (9)	4,368 (20)	31,328 (109)
Congo-Angola	12,168 (39)	168 (1)	2,073 (8)	20,038 (67)
Unknown	*13,279 (40)*	*2,194 (9)*	*597 (3)*	*18,427 (60)*
TOTALS	*55,855 (180)*	*9,070 (38)*	*8,864 (40)*	*94,963 (332)*
Av. slaves per ship	310	239	222	286
St. Dev.	102	101	88	105

[a]This total includes arrivals in some 15 other lesser West Indian ports, both British and Foreign.

Source: HLRO, Papers, 28 July 1800.

Table 7.4
Age and Sex Characteristics of Slaves Shipped on
English Slavers to Jamaica, 1791-1798

Year	Men	Women	Boys	Girls	Totals[a]
1791	1,284	822	115	127	2,348
1792	5,085	3,509	459	241	9,294
1793	7,066	4,635	516	326	12,543
1794	3,582	1,941	353	239	6,115
1795	3,762	2,127	315	202	6,406
1796	3,755	2,304	176	116	6,351
1797	2,178	1,372	129	68	3,747
1798	1,964	1,013	66	37	3,080
TOTALS	*28,676*	*17,723*	*2,129*	*1,356*	*49,884*
Mean	192	120	24	16	335
St. Dev.	67	53	20	14	107

[a]This total includes only those slaves for 149 ships whose age and sex were known and is therefore a much smaller sample of the total of slaves who arrived in Jamaica in this period.

Source: Same as table 7.3.

149

of the Africans arriving in Jamaica, and comparing them with a similar age and sex breakdown for the slaves arriving in the port of Havana, Cuba, during this same time period of 1791 to 1798. There is overall a marked similarity between these two sets of slave populations in the dominance of males and adults. But most striking are the differences between these two importing regions. First, there were many more women among the Africans arriving in the ports of Jamaica during this period than were arriving in Cuba.[16] This sharp difference in sexual ratios may in fact be due to differences in supply areas, for, among the African areas supplying slaves to Jamaica, the Bight of Biafra was the single most important importing zone, with the Angola-Congo area a close second. In the former region, females made up almost half of the slaves being shipped from its ports in the 1790s. This certainly helps to account for the much lower imbalance between the sexes.

Table 7.5
The Average Sex Ratio and Percentage of Children
Carried per Ship, Arriving in West Indian Ports,
by Region of African Provenance, 1791-1798
(number of ships in parentheses)

African Region of Provenance	Sex Ratio	Percentage Children
Senegambia	210.3 (5)	10.5 (5)
Sierra Leone	210.5 (29)	22.0 (24)
Windward Coast	207.7 (15)	14.2 (9)
Gold Coast	184.0 (26)	12.4 (21)
Bight of Benin	187.3 (2)	6.0 (1)
Bight of Biafra	137.9 (79)	14.3 (22)
Congo-Angola	216.7 (60)	14.4 (39)
Unknown	*188.1 (56)*	*11.7 (43)*
GENERAL AV.	*183.3 (272)*	*14.3 (164)*
St. Dev.	118.2	11.8

Source: Same as table 7.3.

In all probability, the Cubans were importing the majority of their slaves from the Congo-Angola area, whose sex ratio of 217 was close to the norm for ships carrying over 200 slaves per voyage (i.e., those presumed to be coming directly from Africa).[17]

[16] The former had a sex ratio of 162 males per 100 females, and the latter an overall 230 males per 100 females (with 221 being the ratio for ships assumed to have come from Africa). (See Klein, "The Cuban Slave Trade," p. 83, table 8.)
[17] Unfortunately, the sources for the Cuban slave trade—the naval lists

Another significant difference is in the importance of children in the two trades. While there is probably some overlap into the adult category by the British, which provide only two age categories for the entering slaves, as opposed to the three age categories given by the Spanish customs authorities, there is still little doubt that there were important differences in age as well as in sex balances between the two contemporaneous trades. While the Jamaicans were importing more women than the Cubans, they were clearly importing fewer children. Taking only the under-8 category for the Spaniards and comparing it to the English category of boys and girls (which approximates 10 years and below) still gives the English trade only 7 percent children as opposed to 20 percent for the Spanish trade.[18]

The cause, or causes, for these differences are difficult to ascertain without detailed price and supply information on both the African and American markets. But it would seem from the presently available price data that preferences of the Jamaican and Cuban planters cannot fully explain the sexual imbalance that did exist. This imbalance, therefore, is most likely influenced by the conditions of supply and the relative value of men and women in the internal African labor markets.[19] The fixed transportation costs and the much lower sale prices would seem to explain sufficiently the relative scarcity of children in the trade. Since adult transportation costs were similar to child costs, there was a strong economic incentive to ship the much more profitable adults.

But an explanation of the overall trends in relation to women and children still leaves unanswered why there should be such differences between two Caribbean islands that were importing approximately the same number of slaves during this time period. Clearly one general influence is the existence of an important

---

housed in the Archivo General de Indias, Audiencia de Santo Domingo, legajo 2207—contain no information on the origins of the arriving slave ships.

[18] The standard British formula was to define children as under 4 feet 4 inches in height. This is the approximate height that should have been reached by early teenage. For the Cuban data, see Klein, "The Cuban Slave Trade," table 9, p. 84.

[19] Curtin found in the Senegambia region that, in fact, the price paid for women on the local internal slave markets at the end of the 17th century was twice that paid for men, thus discouraging their removal from Africa. (Philip Curtin, *Economic Change in Precolonial Africa: Senegambia in the Era of the Slave Trade* [2 vols.; Madison, 1974], I, p. 1976.)

stream of re-exported slaves coming into Cuba from the other Caribbean regions. These slaves were more heavily male and more predominately children than were the slaves coming from Africa. But even though this explains a part of the difference between the two islands, the fact remains that the African-originated Cuban shipping still had more children and much fewer women than the slaves arriving from Africa to Jamaica.

Clearly the Cubans must not have been trading as heavily in the Biafran ports as the English suppliers. But even if we accept this, an unexplained difference still exists. Could this be related to the participation of North American and French traders in the Cuban trade who were going to different sources than the Jamaican-bound British? Could it be related to the timing of the newly expanding Cuban trade and the relative price and market conditions on the island? Or, finally, could it be explained by other factors? There are, unfortunately, too many unknown variables left to analyze this problem systematically at this point. But it is obviously important to realize that within the general pattern of the trade that brought adults and males predominantly to American shores, there were important differences among the importing colonies, even during the same time period, and that demand-and-supply factors need to be more clearly delineated to understand these variations. But, whatever the specific causes for these age and sex imbalances, the fact that Africans still represented 36 percent of the slave population twenty years after the closing of the Jamaican slave trade[20] meant that these distortions had a major impact on the growth rates of the island's slave population until well after 1808.[21]

Up to this point, the emphasis has been on the way slaves were carried, their origins in Africa, and the age and sexual balances of the arriving slaves. Data are also available from the 18th-century reports that enable us to make some kind of estimate of how many of the arriving slaves actually remained on the island. So massive was the Jamaican trade, even by the standards of the

[20] Edward Brathwaite, *The Development of Creole Society in Jamaica, 1770-1820* (Oxford, 1971), p. 164.

[21] For negative growth rates, see G. W. Roberts, *The Population of Jamaica* (Cambridge, 1957), and for a detailed analysis of how African migration affected West Indian slave growth rates, see Jack E. Eblen, "On Natural Increase of Slave Populations: The Example of the Cuban Black Population, 1775-1900," in Engerman and Genovese, *Race and Slavery*, pp. 211-248.

Portuguese South Atlantic trade,[22] that the arriving slaves were enough to meet local planter demands, replace the declining slave population, and still provide a surplus of slaves for re-export. In groups that were usually small in number, but that sometimes could go over a hundred in one voyage, both English and foreign shipping took Jamaican slaves to Central America, Northern South America, the French islands, and Cuba, as well as to some of the other English possessions. Usually in shipping that was half of the tonnage that crossed the Atlantic, and with crews of only three or four men—thus indicating a very local shipping—these general cargo ships would carry slaves from Kingston and Montego Bay to the rest of the Caribbean. While the rhythm of the re-export trade varied from year to year, overall it accounted for just under a fourth of the slaves brought to the island in the period from 1739 to 1787, with the 1780s being a peak period. In terms of the direction of that trade, it would appear that in the early 18th century there was a very intensive trade to Cartagena on the northern coast of South America.[22a] This trade is especially relevant in that the available evidence indicates that the English were feeding, acclimatizing, and healing the recently arrived Africans on Jamaica before sending them on to Cartagena. This early-18th-century change in shipping procedures, whereby slaves were first rested in Jamaica and then trans-shipped to the mainland, effectively reduced disease among the arriving slaves in Cartagena, according to royal medical records.[23] The importance of Cartagena lessened during the rest of the century, as available statistics indicate that from 1774 to 1787 the majority or 88 percent of the re-exported slaves went to foreign West Indian ports. But even though the primary direction was for-

[22] In the late 1790s, Jamaican ports were probably the largest single importing region in all the Americas. The largest port in the Brazilian region, Rio de Janeiro, in the five-year period from 1796 to 1800 was importing on average 8,754 slaves per annum; the ports of Jamaica in the same period averaged 12,316 slaves. See Klein, "The Trade in Africa Slaves to Rio," p. 538 and below, table 7.6.

[22a] In the period from 1722 to 1727, for example, 8 English ships carried 3,949 slaves from Jamaica to this South American port in 22 voyages; while between 1730 and 1739 9 English ships carried 5,053 slaves in 30 voyages on the same route. (Jorge Palacios Preciado, *La trata de negros por Cartagena de Indias* [Tunja, Colombia, 1973], pp. 311, 341-342.)

[23] David L. Chandler, "Health Conditions in the Slave Trade of Colonial New Granada," in Robert B. Toplin, ed., *Slavery and Race Relations in Latin America* (Westport, Conn., 1974), pp. 51-88.

eign colonies, principally Spanish, the nature of the trade changed from decade to decade and depended on both local economic conditions and international trade restrictions. Thus while the Jamaican naval lists in the PRO indicate that the Spanish ports of Santo Domingo and mainland Spanish America were the major recipients of Jamaican re-exported slaves in the 1780s, by the early 1790s Havana had become the chief receiving zone, even though English trans-Atlantic slavers were now directly sailing to its shores.[24] Then by the 1796-1801 period Santo Domingo

Table 7.6
The Number of Africans Arriving in Jamaica and
Re-transported off the Island, 1704-1800

Quinquennium	No. of Ships	Arrivals	Re-Shipped Off Island	Percentage Re-Shipped	Percentage Re-Shipped Going to Foreign West Indies
1704-1708	84	21,412	5,252	25	n.a.
1709-1713	85	21,126	8,613	41	n.a.
1714-1718	112	28,326	12,868	45	n.a.
1719-1723	128	29,192	15,523	53	n.a.
1724-1728	162	38,078	13,590	36	n.a.
1729-1733	222	51,647	26,214	51	n.a.
1734-1738	122	30,024	9,883	33	n.a.
1739-1743	135	30,397	3,815	13	n.a.
1744-1748	144	38,629	9,981	26	n.a.
1749-1753	128	29,063	5,502	19	n.a.
1754-1758	200	44,780	5,446	12	n.a.
1759-1763	127	35,623	5,505	15	n.a.
1764-1768	171	38,570	6,177	16	n.a.
1769-1773	132	30,589	3,437	11	n.a.
1774-1778	n.a.	64,248	10,866	17	82
1779-1783	n.a.	29,594	2,962	10	95
1784-1788	n.a.	43,593	17,691	41	92
1796-1800	n.a.	61,580	5,294	9	75
TOTALS[a]		666,471	168,619	25	

[a]There was no information for the period from 1789 to 1795.

Source: For the number of ships, and the period 1704-1738, Richard B. Sheridan, *Sugar and Slavery. An Economic History of the British West Indies, 1623-1775* (Baltimore, 1973), pp. 502-504. For 1739-1787, *A&P*, 1790, XXIX (698), pp. 497-498; *A&P*, 1789, XXIV (622) for the direction of the re-shipped slaves for 1774-1787; for 1796-1800 see *A&P*, 1801-1802, IV, document no. 2, pp. 476, 478-479; and *A&P*, 1790, XXXI (705) for 1788.

[24] PRO,CO 142/20,23. On the English participation in the newly opened Cuban slave trade, see Klein, "The Cuban Slave Trade," p. 72, table 2.

again became the primary port of re-export, taking 2,617 of the 5,294 slaves leaving Jamaica. In this later period the United States had emerged as a major receiver of these Jamaican re-exported slaves, accounting for 23 percent of the total, though the Spanish possessions still took 75 percent of them.[25]

Although Jamaica differed from the other English colonial slave societies in the volume and intensity of its slave trade, it shared many of the same features of the rhythm of the trade. Most pronounced in this respect, was the marked seasonality in the arrival of Jamaican-bound African slaves (see table 7.7). The

Table 7.7

Seasonal Variation in the Arrival of Slaves and Ships to Jamaica, 1782-1808, by Number of Months Slaves Were Known to Have Landed
(out of 25-year period)

Season & Month	Total Known Months	Total Ships	Total Slaves	Average No. of Ships per Month	Average No. of Slaves per Month
1. *Winter*	64	240	78,804	3.8	1,231
December	22	90	31,069	4.0	1,412
January	21	71	23,285	3.4	1,109
February	21	79	24,450	3.8	1,164
2. *Spring*	55	157	50,509	2.9	918
March	18	57	20,046	3.2	1,114
April	19	49	14,343	2.6	755
May	18	51	16,120	2.8	896
3. *Summer*	51	150	46,327	2.9	908
June	19	58	19,086	3.1	1,005
July	17	55	16,039	3.2	944
August	15	37	11,202	2.5	747
4. *Fall*	52	136	45,735	2.6	880
September	17	36	11,495	2.1	676
October	15	33	11,962	2.2	798
November	20	67	22,278	3.4	1,114
TOTALS	222	683	221,375	3.1	997

Source: Same as table 7.1.

key importing period was the late fall, the winter, and the early spring, or the months of November through March. This was the period with highest volume of shipping and the largest number of slaves carried per ship.[26] The causes for this pattern of sea-

[25] *A&P*, 1801-1802, IV, p. 476.
[26] This same seasonality response has also been noted in the 17th-century

sonal variation, noted for the other leading importing ports, have always been difficult to ascertain, but seem to be most closely associated with the following factors: Atlantic wind and current conditions, African crop and weather patterns, and American work demands based on harvest cycles. On all coasts and over all routes, local weather and sailing conditions determined the speed of the Middle Passage and the ease of slaving along the African coast and inland rivers. African weather and crop conditions determined the availability of slaves in any given season, and, finally, American harvesting periods made their impact felt on demand. Though American demand was modified somewhat by the universal practice among all nations of selling slaves on credit (which lessened the impact of seasonal cash flows for planters), nevertheless it seems to have been the primary causal factor influencing seasonal migration in most trades from West Africa.

A unique feature of the House of Lords 1790s survey is the data provided on the overall timing of the trade in relationship to the various "legs" of the slaving voyage. In this respect, it would appear that there were important variations in sailing times from England to the various parts of Africa as well as in the length of time it took to collect African slaves along the coast. Clearly, as is evident in table 7.8, there was some correlation between sailing time from England and location north-south along the coast. What minor variations occurred are probably accounted for by local wind and current conditions. Trading and supply features, however, primarily determined the sharp differences in the time spent by the slave captains in obtaining their slaves on the various African coasts. Thus the boat trading and up-river voyages necessitated by the scattered nature of the slave supply areas in the northern regions (especially Sierra Leone and the Gold and Windward coasts) explain the much longer time required to outfit full complements of slaves than occurred in the Angola-Congo area. Here the centralized nature of trading activities and fixed location arrangements evidently were instrumental in reducing

---

slave trade to Jamaica, when there was a very high volume of slave and ship arrivals in the January-through-June period for the years 1686 to 1691. (W. A. Claypole and D. J. Buisseret, "Trade Patterns in Early English Jamaica," *Journal of Caribbean History*, v [November, 1976], p. 6.)

Table 7.8
The Comparative Sailing Times of All Ships to Africa and
Trading Times along the Coast and of Middle-Passage Time of
Jamaica-Bound Vessels, 1791-1798
(number of ships in parentheses)

African Region	From England (in days)	Stay on Coast (in days)	Trip to Jamaica (in days)
Senegambia	64 (5)	72 (6)	34 (1)
Sierra Leone	74 (41)	158 (41)	52 (21)
Windward Coast	68 (19)	176 (18)	61 (10)
Gold Coast	81 (30)	131 (30)	56 (10)
Bt. of Benin	100 (3)	81 (3)	85 (1)
Bt. of Biafra	75 (111)	100 (113)	68 (63)
Congo-Angola	106 (67)	95 (69)	62 (40)
Unknown	*99 (55)*	*111 (57)*	*57 (41)*
Av. no. days per ship	*85 (331)*	*114 (337)*	*61 (187)*
St. Dev.	40	70	22

Source: Same as table 7.3.

coastal time to a minimum.[27] Finally, while the various West Indian ports differed in their distance from the regions of Africa, the times given for the Africa-to-Jamaica run show a fair degree of similarity in time from the ports of the Windward Coast south, with only those to the north experiencing a lower average sailing time.

While comparative time data are relatively scarce, both early 18th-century Dutch and French slave-trade data indicate that there was a substantial reduction in the length of time spent trading for slaves along the African coast by the end of the century. Thus, while in the 1790s English slavers spent on average 114 days cruising along the coast or operating in fixed trading camps, the Dutch in the late 17th and early 18th centuries needed 228 days to carry out their African trading,[28] and the French

[27] Compare, for example, the trading experiences in the 1750s and 1760s of Captain John Newton along the Sierra Leone coast and those of Captain Pierre Van Alstein at Cabinda, which typify these two contrasting patterns. (See *The Journal of A Slave Trader* [John Newton], 1750-1754, eds. B. Martin and M. Spurrell [London, 1962], pp. 11ff., and Dieudonné Rinchon, *Pierre-Igance-Liévin Van Alstein, Captaine négrier* [Dakar: Memoires de IFAN, no. 71, 1964], pp. 107ff.)

[28] Johannes Postma, "Mortality in the Dutch Slave Trade, 1675-1795," paper presented at the MSSB Symposium on the Economic History of the Trans-Atlantic Slave Trade, August 1975.

slavers from Nantes prior to 1777 averaged 154 days in Africa.[29] Since mortality and diseases in general increased the longer it took to assemble and ship the slaves, the reduction in African trading time must have had an impact on lowering Middle Passage mortality rates in the late 18th and early 19th centuries.

The cause for this improved time schedule can only be surmised. Enough comparative data do not exist at the present time to resolve this fully; nevertheless, it would seem obvious that both European and African factors that increased the speed and efficiency of the trade were important. The use of more specialized ships,[30] along with the higher number of vessels and the better coverage of all markets, was matched by a more reliable and more rapidly accumulated supply of slaves.

In terms of shipping, it was not so much the increase in individual ships tonnage that may have accounted for shipping efficiency, but rather the concentration of ships in a middle-range category of 100-200 tons, which seemed the most appropriate for British trading needs. In fact, average tonnage of slave shipping had changed little in the Atlantic slave trade between 1680 and 1780. The Royal African Company, for example, reported having dispatched 249 ships in the 1680s to Africa to engage in the slave trade, with their tonnage reaching 147 tons per vessel, while in the war period—1691-1713—it embarked 184 vessels averaging 186 tons. Thus for the 122 Jamaican-bound slave ships between 1782 and 1787 the average tonnage was just 167 tons. But these averages mask fundamental changes. For the dispersion around the mean tonnage had changed in important ways. Whereas the Royal African Company had 28 percent and 20 percent respectively of their ships in these two earlier periods coming in at less than 100 tons, and another 4 percent and 7 percent respectively being of 400 tons or above, the figures for the 1780s were quite distinct. Here only 8 percent of the ships were listed as less than 100 tons, and none appeared in the above 400 category. What

[29] These calculations are based on an analysis of 475 Nantes slave ships trading to Africa from 1713 to 1777 and found in ADLA, Serie B, 4577-78, 4583-84.

[30] The slave trade was unique among English merchant trades in its early and extraordinarily extensive adoption of the new and costly invention of copper sheathing. (See Gareth Rees, "Copper Sheathing, An Example of Technological Diffusion in the English Merchant Fleet," *Journal of Transport History*, New Series, i, No. 2 [September 1971], pp. 85-94.)

Table 7.9
The Comparative Tonnage of English Slave Ships in
Four Different Periods, 1680-1788

Tonnage	Royal Africa Co. Ships 1680-1688	RAC Ships, 1691-1713	Africa-Virginia, 1728-1769	Africa-Jamaica, 1782-1788
Under 50	11	9	6	2
50- 99	58	28	89	9
100-149	85	60	56	52
150-199	34	16	6	17
200-249	31	17	3	20
250-299	11	12	...	14
300-349	6	22	1	13
350-399	3	8	...	3
400 & Over	10	12	...	...
TOTALS	249	184	161	130

Sources: For Royal African Company ships, see K. G. Davies, *The Royal African Company* (London, 1957), p. 192; the Virginia trade calculated from Donnan, *Documents*, IV, 175-182; and the Jamaican data, same as table 7.1.

had occurred, obviously, was that an optimal size ship had now come to dominate the trade, with 54 percent of the ships being in the 100-199-ton range. It would thus appear that a much more specialized vessel had emerged in the English slave trade than a century earlier.[31] This would mean that a vessel in the 100-149 ton range made the ideal transport for slaves across the Atlantic. That the British could have employed larger tonnage is obvious when we look at both the Royal African Company ships of a century before and the contemporaneous West Indiamen, which averaged at least 100 tons more per vessel than the slavers. That the British did not employ this larger tonnage, at least prior to 1800, would seem to suggest that coastal and upriver African trading required the use of smaller ships, and the optimal carrying capacity for slave ships was in this lower range. That all analyses of the relationship of slaves carried per ton show a steady decline in the ratio of slaves per ton carried as tonnage increases, would also suggest that a simple increase in tonnage offered no great increase in ability to carry slaves. Thus because

[31] That slave ships were totally specialized in their role of carrying slaves, and engaged in no other trade, has been shown in a study of Liverpool slave ships in the last decade of trade undertaken by D. M. Williams, "Abolition and the Re-Deployment of the Slave Fleet, 1807-11," *Journal of Transport History*, New Series, No. 2 (September 1973), pp. 103-105.

of water, food, and equipment storage needs, a basic minimum space was required to carry a maximum supply of slaves without running risks of major mortality losses.[32]

Changes in British trading practices may also have been important in diminishing mortality. Clearly the change in British merchant practices, from fixed fort and monopoly company control to a free competition and boat trading, was an important factor in making British slavers more responsive to changing African slave supply patterns. Thus the rise of new African traders and the development of new trade routes met an immediate response from individual ships' captains, who could move their floating markets to the new sources of supply. Also, the relative increase or decrease of supplies of slaves would find a rapid response among the slave trade merchants in England and the slave captains along the coast. In any case, it was most likely a combination of all these factors which reduced the element of time in the trade, and thus ultimately had an impact on reducing mortality itself over the long term.[33]

One of the distinguishing features, in fact, about the mortality data available for the late-18th-century Jamaican slave trade is their relatively lower ratio compared to earlier-18th-century trades. Excluding ships that reported no mortality, the 301 remaining ships listed in the House of Lords register for all shipping going to the West Indies in the 1790s, the death toll in the Middle Passage was 56 deaths for every 1,000 persons on board. While this figure was high even by epidemic standards of nonmigrating 18th-century peasant populations, and is even understated because it is a short-time period rate for an unusually

[32] It was reported by one slave captain that it was a general custom to fill the puncheons and casks that carried supplies to Africa to trade for slaves with water and provisions on the Middle Passage, and "when the Cargo is disposed of, and converted into Negroes, those casks, with the firewood and Provisions, completely fill it [the Hold] again." (Testimony of Mr. Norris, *A&P*, 1789, xxiv [633], p. 17.) Equally the custom, as measured on a half dozen ships, was to carry at minimum a double supply of water. Thus the slave ship the *Brooks* carried in the late 1780s 34,000 gallons of water for its 600 slaves and 45 sailors for a Middle Passage lasting 49 days, despite the fact that contemporaries agreed that slaves were given just 3 pints of water per day, which would have meant carrying just under 12,000 gallons. (*A&P*, 1788, xxii [565], pp. 1-3.)

[33] For an analysis of the development of such new trading groups on the Gold Coast, see Kwame Yeboa Daaku, *Trade and Politics on the Gold Coast, 1600 to 1720* (Oxford, 1970).

healthy part of the total populations (persons 15-40), it nevertheless represents a considerable improvement over the mortality suffered in the early part of the century. Thus slaves carried by the Dutch West India slave ships in the period from 1680 to 1749 suffered a mortality in the Middle Passage of 168 deaths for every 1,000 leaving the African coast.[34] Equally, slavers from the French port of Nantes between 1713 and 1777 suffered a mortality among the slaves they carried of 120 per 1,000, while some 35 Danish slavers between 1777 and 1788 suffered a rate of mortality among its slaves of 149 per 1,000.[35]

Comparable to the English decline was the Portuguese decline in slave mortality, with Middle Passage mortality for arriving Africans to Rio de Janeiro in the period 1795 to 1799 being 77 per thousand.[36] While this mortality is higher than the British, I would hesitate to say that the English slavers experienced any unusually low rates. Such a position is difficult to maintain, first of all because of the extreme random quality of mortality by year; secondly, the time period covered by the House of Lords survey is too short. Thus, in selected years, even the Portuguese trade experienced mortality rates in the low 30s comparable to the British figures. Nevertheless, there seems sufficient general evidence from enough of the various European trades to say that, overall, mortality in the Middle Passage was slowly declining in the 18th century.

In attempting to disaggregate the mortality data and analyze them by African region of origin, we find it immediately evident that the Bight of Biafra region, already unusual for the high number of women who were shipped from its ports, experienced the highest rates of mortality for slaves crossing in the Middle Passage. The cause for this differential mortality might be due to the higher incidence of women and their higher rates of mortality. But when we check mortality by sex and age, it is evident that adult males and females experienced almost identical rates of mortality from the same ports.[37] Alternatively, it might be

[34] Postma, "Mortality," table 1.

[35] See above n. 29; and Sv. E. Green-Pedersen, *Om forholdene på danske slaveskibe med soerlig henblik på dødeligheden 1777-89* (Elsinore, 1973), p. 70, table 1.

[36] Klein, "The Trade in African Slaves," table 1, p. 538.

[37] Overall adult mortality was 61 per 1,000 for women and 54 per 1,000 for men, with mortality for Bight of Biafra slaves being 111 for women and

Table 7.10
Average Mortality per Ship of Jamaican- and
New-World-Bound Slaves by
African Region of Provenance, 1791-1798
(number of ships in parentheses)[a]

African Region of Provenance	Jamaica	All American Ports
Senegambia	16 (1)	29 (5)
Sierra Leone	28 (21)	37 (37)
Windward Coast	27 (9)	36 (15)
Gold Coast	19 (9)	27 (26)
Bight of Benin	6 (1)	43 (3)
Bight of Biafra	111 (57)	106 (105)
Congo-Angola	31 (36)	37 (63)
Unknown	*15 (32)*	*16 (47)*
Av. mortality per ship	*54 (166)*	*56 (301)*
St. Dev.	75	72

[a]Mortality is expressed as deaths per thousand.

Source: Same as table 7.3.

argued that differential mortality out of the exporting ports was in fact based on African conditions. If it is accepted that the relative participation of women was controlled by African traders, then the consequent increase of women in the Biafra area could in turn be due to generally poorer economic conditions, which made it impossible for Africans to prevent women from entering the international slave-trade market. This in turn might mean that a generally failing economy or society provided a group of persons who were less physically able to endure the rigors of the Middle Passage than slaves emerging from the other African ports.

These speculations are still in the very tentative stage of analysis, but what is worth stressing about the available data is the sharp regional differentiations in the mortality experienced in the

103 for men. While there is a difference, it is not significant enough to account for the quite sharp regional variation. Interestingly enough, however, child mortality was uniformly high from all regions, 159 per 1,000 for boys and 225 per 1,000 for girls. But their participation was limited for all regions and there appeared little regional variation in their mortality rates. For reasons that are not readily apparent, the high rate of child mortality in the English trade contrasts sharply with the lower than adult rates experienced by children in the Portuguese slave trade.

English slave-trade ships. This same largely unexplained pattern of regional variation in mortality could also be found in both the Portuguese and French slave trades of the 18th and 19th century. While current and wind conditions explain some of the variation, and sailing time from the East African coast explains all the variation in that differential mortality, most of the differences in the West African rates are difficult to explain. When sailing times differ by only a few days, the slave mortality should seemingly not be too different—as, for example, in the rates experienced by Brazilian-bound slaves from Benguela and Luanda. Yet sharp mortality differences do occur. This would seem to suggest, then, that local crop and disease conditions both along the coast and in the cachement areas for slaves strongly influenced the ultimate mortality pattern experienced in the Middle Passage, and possibly even in comparatively different rates of what has been called "seasoning" mortality or early adjustment to local epidemiological conditions in America. Local crop failures could conceivably have a dramatic impact on small defined areas, without affecting relatively nearby ports or regions, because of the difficulties of internal transportation. Given the quality of information on the economic conditions in the interior or even the coast areas in 18th and early 19th century Africa at the present time, it is difficult to define more precisely the connection between local African conditions and mortality in the Middle Passage.

While we have been primarily concerned with the movement of slave shipping and the numbers, mortality, and characteristics of the Africans brought to Jamaica over time and by port of origin, it is also worth noting some of the unique characteristics of the slave ships themselves within the total context of both American and European merchant shipping in the 18th century.

First of all, as has been recently commented upon at great length by other scholars, the magnitude of the triangle trade between Great Britain, Africa, and the West Indies has been greatly exaggerated.[38] Such were the demands and timing of the slave

[38] One of the first critiques of the traditional view of the triangular trade was by R. B. Sheridan, "The Commercial and Financial Organization of the British Slave Trade, 1750-1807," *Economic History Review*, Second Series, xi, no. 2 (1958), pp. 249-263. This critique was carried further by J. E. Merritt, "The Triangular Trade," *Business History*, iii, no. 1 (December, 1960), pp. 1-7; and Gilman Ostrander, "The Making of the Triangular Trade Myth," *William and Mary Quarterly*, 3rd Series, xxx (1973), pp.

trade and of the West Indian export trade that in fact there was a totally separate West Indian fleet that arose to service just the trade between England and the British West Indies. These ships were on average much larger than the slave ships, and carried a much lower ratio of crewmen per ship and by tonnage. Although slavers did bring back sugar and other West Indian products on their return to England, they often went back in ballast and made only a relatively small part of their total profits from this part of the trade. The bulk of the sugar and other tropical colonial products exported to England went out in the West Indiamen, ships that rarely if ever left this direct two-way trade between colonies and mother country. This same pattern of a specialized slave fleet and a West Indian cargo fleet for the direct (or *droiture*) trade characterized the French West Indian trade as well.

Most striking in comparing these two specialized fleets of slavers and West Indiamen, is the difference in tonnage and in number of crew carried. While 2,470 West-India-bound ships leaving British ports averaged 214 tons in the five-year period 1783 to 1787, the 628 ships leaving for Africa averaged only 150 tons. This same pattern can be discerned as well in the shipping from Nantes in the 18th century. In the five-year period from 1779 to 1783, for example, ships engaged in the "Droiture" or direct West Indian trade were 52 percent greater in tonnage than the slave ships leaving for Africa.[39]

At the same time, the number of crewmen was smaller in the direct trade. Thus, the crew per ton ratio of some 252 ships that left Liverpool outbound for Africa between 1785 and 1787 was

635-644. The more extreme statements of the critiques have recently been challenged by Walter E. Minchinton, "The Triangular Trade Revisited," MSSB paper presented at Colby College, 1975; and B. K. Drake, "Continuity and Flexibility in Liverpool's Trade with Africa and the Caribbean," *Business History*, xviii, no. 1 (January, 1976), pp. 85-97. The general consensus now would be to acknowledge that the dominant share of the West Indian and North American staple trades were shipped directly to Europe by North Atlantic merchantmen, but that the slavers to a very limited extent and for relatively brief times did engage somewhat in the direct staple trade on their return to England. Also, Minchinton has properly pointed out that both the slave trade and West India trade were usually controlled by the same metropolitan port commercial houses.

[39] Calculated from data given in Jean Meyer, *L'armement nantais dans le deuxieme moitié du XVIIIe siècle* (Paris, 1969), pp. 83-86.

Table 7.11

The Comparative Tonnage and the Value of Exports to the Regions for English Ships
Leaving for Africa and the British West Indies, 1763-1787

Quinquenium	Ships	Tons	Average Tonnage	Total Value of Exports	Average Value per Ship
1. Africa					
1763-1767	781	87,959	112.6	£2,452,581[a]	£3,140
1768-1772	803	83,742	104.3	3,367,507	4,193
1773-1777	629	68,980	109.7	3,030,800	4,818
1778-1782	268	35,187	131.3	1,173,766	4,379
1783-1787	628	94,270	150.1	3,455,737	5,502
2. British West Indies					
1763-1767	2,047	350,549	171.3	£5,365,994	£2,621
1768-1772	2,199	385,411	175.3	6,561,652	2,984
1773-1777	2,344	430,282	183.6	7,316,012	3,121
1778-1782	2,366	435,344	184.0	6,274,952	2,652
1783-1787	2,470	529,235	214.3	6,988,809	2,829

[a]All pounds sterling were rounded.

Source: A&P, 1789, xxvi (646), part IV, table no. 10, "A General Abstract of the Number of Ships, with their
tonnage, that have cleared out and entered inwards, between Great Britain and Africa and the British West
Indies ... ."

0.17 crewmen per ton, whereas the 249 ships leaving for the West Indies from this same port carried 0.09 crewmen per ton. Except for privateers, and warships (which averaged 0.77 crewmen per ton in Nantes), the slave trade used the largest crew of any trade in the merchant marine. This need for sailors was, of course, related to both the demands of trading and the need to guard the captured slaves. Especially among the boat traders, there was a large demand for sailors to purchase and oversee the slaves. But even among the fixed fort or fixed coastal traders, there was a need for a large number of sailors to control the slaves. In the 18th-century French data in fact, the average crew size on slave ships was greater even than on British slave ships of the same period.[40]

Despite the declines in tonnage and even more significantly in the numbers of slaves carried after the Parliamentary regulatory acts there is, interestingly, no decline in the number of slaver crewmen (see table 7.1). Yet it was evident in the British parliamentary hearings on the slave trade, that these crewmen were rather costly supernumeraries in the normal running of the ships. One of the major findings of the parliamentary commissions, in fact, was that slavers fairly regularly discharged an important number of their crewmen in the Caribbean and paid them off in devalued colonial sterling.[41] Yet, despite their cost, their numbers per ship do not decline over time along with that of the slaves. One might tentatively suggest here that both the general need of African trading, and even more the question of security, meant that while numbers of slaves carried might decline, captains considered a minimum number of crew absolutely essential for survival and safety.

Nor were these needs unique to the British trade. For in all slave trades where the data are available on crews, tons, and slaves, there is the same high correlation between the numbers of slaves carried and the number of sailors manning the ships.[42]

[40] Thus, Nantes slavers between 1785 and 1789 averaged 38 sailors per voyage in 178 sailings, *ibid.*, p. 86.

[41] See the testimony of John Knox, in *A&P*, 1789, xxv (635), pp. 96ff. This ill treatment of sailors, in fact, was one of the most important issues used by the abolitionist to discredit the slave trade; see F. E. Sanderson, "The Liverpool Delegates and Sir William Dolben's Bill," *Transactions of the Historical Society of Lancashire and Cheshire*, cxxiv (1972), pp. 68-69.

[42] In the Nantes slave trade, the simple correlation between the number

Table 7.12

Outbound British Shipping from Liverpool, Exclusive of Coastal Traders, 1785-1787

Year	AFRICA			BWI			IRELAND			TOTAL		
	Ships	Tons	Crew	Ships	Tons	Crew	Ships	Tons	Crew	Ships	Tons	Crew
1785	79	10,982	1,900	86	13,409	1,521	855	43,357	4,408	1,446	123,095	11,641
1786	92	13,971	2,240	76	15,325	1,261	754	39,351	3,900	1,338	128,859	11,494
1787	81	14,012	2,300	87	17,463	1,380	816	50,339	4,460	1,476	160,366	12,795
TOTALS	252	38,965	6,440	249	46,197	4,162	2,425	133,047	12,768	4,260	412,320	35,930
Mean		154.6	25.5		185.5	16.7		54.9	5.3		96.8	8.4

Source: *A&P*, 1789, XXVI (646), Part iv, no. 3, "Mr. Norris's Supplements to the Account of the Trade of Liverpool... ."

That this was not simply a function of increasing tonnage is evident when we compare crew and ton ratios on West Indiamen and slavers. The West Indiamen averaged one crewman for 11.1 tons. The slavers, on the other hand, averaged almost double that figure, or one crewman for every 6.1 tons. That the West Indiamen were the norm can be seen in the fact that the Irish traders averaged 10.4 tons per sailor, and overall in the three-year period from 1785 to 1787 all ships leaving Liverpool averaged 11.5 tons per crewman (see table 7.12). Clearly, ships of the same tonnage or larger than the slavers did not need one crewman for every 6 tons simply to man the ships. Half that number was sufficient. Equally, crew-per-ton ratios on slavers behave exactly like slave-per-ton ratios, both diminishing sharply as the tonnage of ships increases—further proof of the lack of ship's size, as expressed in tonnage, from being the primary factor influencing the number of sailors needed to man the slave ships.[43]

In comparing the African slave trade shipping with other merchant shipping of Great Britain, we find several other points worth noting. First, a study of the relative value of British exports to the West Indies and Africa confirms many individual studies of the commercial organization of the slave trade. As many scholars have noted, the most important cost to Europeans in the African slave trade were the goods sent from Europe to purchase the slaves. These goods consisted of European manufactured implements, bar iron, and high-cost East Indian textiles imported from India. These costs, in fact, far outweighed the cost of the ship itself and most determined the ultimate losses and

---

of slaves carried and the number of crewmen for 130 ships was +.64. This same patttern could even be discerned for some 12 ships engaged in the slave trade to the Spanish Indies in 1637, where the simple correlation between crew and slaves was +.77. [Colin Palmer, *Slaves of the White God, Blacks in Mexico, 1570-1650* (Cambridge, Mass., 1976), table 5, p.18.] While this latter sample is quite small, it is interesting to note that the average of 7.7 slaves per sailor for these 17th-century Spanish-America-bound ships was quite close to the 8.7 slaves per sailor found in the 18th-century Nantes slave-trade vessels. In the Jamaica slave trade, for the 362 ships that contained the relevant data, the correlation between the number of sailors and slaves was +.52, compared in this case to a relatively low correlation of +.34 between numbers of sailors and tonnage of ship.

[43] The simple correlation coefficient between crew per ton and tonnage was −.62, which is quite similar to the −.57 figure between slaves per ton and tonnage.

profits of the trade.[44] This high cost of a slave ship's "outfitted," or *mise hors*, cargo can be seen in the figures for the British overseas commerce in which the value of African goods can be compared with all other outbound cargoes. In the estimates for the British trade to Africa and the West Indies in the 1783-1787 period, for example, the values of exports to the former averaged out at £36.6 per ton, compared to just £13.2 per ton on the West-India-bound vessels.[45]

The late-18th-century British shipping data also shows the relative unimportance of the African trade in terms of overall shipping. While slavers and West Indiamen together accounted for some 500 ships leaving Liverpool in 1785-1787 period, they still represented only 12 percent of the total non-coastwise shipping leaving that port. Taken alone, the African-bound ships accounted for only 6 percent of the ships, 9 percent of the tonnage, and 18 percent of the sailors leaving England's premier slave trading port. Thus, even within the context of Liverpool shipping, the slave trade represented only a small part of total shipping activity even when combined with the West Indies trade. This is not to say that this trade did not involve a large percentage of Liverpool merchants or that it did not exercise an important impact on the local merchant community, but it should be stressed that only a small percentage of British merchant ships actually engaged in this highly specialized trade.

[44] Among the numerous studies on the subject of profitability, two recent works on the English trade are worth noting. These are Roger Anstey's major analysis of most of the available data in "Volume," pp. 13ff., and David Richardson, "Profitability in the Bristol-Liverpool Slave Trade," *Revue française d'Histoire d'Outre-Mer*, LXII, nos. 226-227 (1975). For studies on French slave-trade profitability, see below, Chapter 8.

[45] *A&P*, 1789, XXVI (646), Part IV, no. 3, "Mr Norris Supplements to the Account of the Trade of Liverpool. . . ." In 1790, it was reported that Liverpool merchants were currently outfitting 139 ships for the slave trade. These ships totaled 24,907 tons, carried 3,853 sailors and were worth £361,608. The value of their outbound cargoes to Africa were double the value of the ships themselves, and totaled £730,938. This meant that the ships averaged £15 per ton, the African bound cargo £29 and the combined total ship and cargo at £44. *A&P*, 1790, XXIX (698), pp. 500-509. Using alternative data, Anstey found that 65% of the final outfitting cost of slave ships was made up by the value of the African bound cargo, a figure almost identical to the 1790 official results. Roger Anstey, *The Atlantic Slave Trade and British Abolition, 1760-1810* (London, 1975), appendices 3, 4.

Not only was the number of slavers small in comparison to overall English merchant shipping, but there had also been major shifts in the participation of London and the Outports in the slave trade in the 18th century. Whereas Bristol had been the dominant slave-trading port in the first half of the century, Liverpool after the 1750s rapidly began to challenge its supremacy.[46] Thus, while Bristol accounted for the majority of Virginia's African originated slave-trade vessels,[47] by the 1780s Liverpool was dominant, accounting for over 74 percent of the slaves and 72 percent of the ships arriving in Jamaican ports.[48] Also, Bristol's secondary position was now being challenged by London, which had moved into second place as Jamaica's leading supplier of slaves. If anything, these figures from a sample of the Jamaican slave trade even underestimate the dominance of the Liverpool slavers. Of the 1,283 slave ships (with a total of 380,893 tons) that left the three ports to engage in the slave trade in the ten-year period between 1795 and 1804, Liverpool accounted for 86 percent of the ships and 85 percent of the total tonnage involved.[49]

This same dominance of Liverpool was true also of the ports of construction of the slave ships. Of the 161 slavers built in England, 61 or 38 percent were built in the Liverpool dockyards, making Liverpool the single largest English construction site for slave ships. But while English and colonial built ships made up 55 percent of all the slavers listed in the PRO Jamaican sample, there had been major changes in terms of the regions of construction of the English slave ships. Whereas the thirteen colonies of British North America had been the major supplier of slave ships in the early-18th-century Virginia trade, even for those owned in England, this shipbuilding zone had entirely disappeared as a supplier to the slave-trade fleet. Instead, England itself was now the single largest supplier, followed by ships built in foreign

[46] For the rapid rise in Liverpool slave shipping, see Gomer Williams, *History of the Liverpool Privateers and . . . the Liverpool Slave Trade* (London and Liverpool, 1897), table VIII, p. 678.

[47] Bristol dominated the Virginia trade, accounting for 59 percent of the slaves and 55 percent of the ships, with Liverpool and London dividing the rest. (Klein, "Slaves and Shipping in Eighteenth Century Virginia," Table 11, pp. 403-404.)

[48] There were 380 Liverpool-owned ships that carried 124,215 slaves to Jamaica in this period, compared to London's 90 ships and 29,146 slaves and Bristol's 47 ships and 13,358 slaves.

[49] Williams, *History of Liverpool*, p. 680, table XI.

colonies (mostly French and to a lesser extent Spanish possessions) and seized as prizes. Thus while Prize vessels had made up only 4 percent of the early-18th-century Virginia slave ships, the figure had risen to 45 percent in the 1782-1808 period. This surprisingly large contribution of foreign-built ships was obviously due to the impact of the major series of colonial wars that marked the second half of the 18th century.

In analyzing the English merchants' participation in the slave trade, we find the dominance of Liverpool evident, as well as a high degree of specialization in the slave trade. Of the total number of shipments, less than one-third were the sole voyage of a merchant, over two-thirds were by merchants who were involved in two or more shipments.[50]

Table 7.13
Number of Merchants of England Who Participated in the
Jamaican Slave Trade, 1782-1809, by Number of Shipments

No. of Slave Shipments	No. of Merchants Shipping Slaves	Total No. of Shipments
1	117	117
2	36	72
3	11	33
4	9	36
5	4	20
6	2	12
7	3	21
8	2	16
11	3	33
TOTALS	187	360[a]

[a]There were five shipments of slaves for whom the merchant was unknown.

Source: Same as table 7.1.

In terms of concentration of ownership of the ships and the arriving slaves, the English merchants seem quite comparable to other slave traders. Thus taking just the leading 5 percent and 10 percent of the participating slave-trade merchants gives figures

[50] This compares to a 2.4 shipment average for Liverpool merchants shipping between 1783 and 1793; see "A Circumstancial Account of the True Causes of the Liverpool African Slave Trade, By An Eyewitness-Liverpool, 1797," reprinted in *Liverpool and Slavery: An Historical Account of the Liverpool-African Slave Trade*, by a Genuine "Dicky Sam" (Liverpool, 1884), p. 113.

of concentration of holdings among the imported slaves of 23 percent for the first group and 36 percent for the second.[51] This compares to a 40 percent figure for the top 10 percent of importing merchants in Rio de Janeiro in the 1825-1830 period.[52]

Table 7.14
The Leading Merchants (Top 10 Percent)
Who Imported Slaves into Jamaica, 1782-1809

Name of Merchant	No. of Vessels	No. of Slaves Imported
T. Leyland & Co.	11	3,489
W. Thompson & Co.	11	3,389
A. Calvert & Co.	11	3,343
W. Boats & Co.	8	4,313
T. Clarke & Co.	8	3,192
J. Gregson & Co.	7	3,246
B. Hammond & Co.	7	1,945
W. Dickson & Co.	7	1,931
W. Aspinall & Co.	6	1,961
J. Aspinall & Co.	6	1,927
R. Taylor & Co.	5	1,461
T. Earle & Co.	5	1,452
G. Case & Co.	5	1,148
C. Butler & Co.	4	2,608
R. Kitchin	4	1,640
J. Margetson	4	1,331
T. Hinde & Co.	4	1,299
J. Shaw & Co.	4	1,235
G. James & Co.	4	1,072

Source: Same as table 7.1.

Along with the concentration of slaves and ships in a few merchant hands, there is also the superiority of Liverpool shippers in the leading merchants category. Of the 19 merchant houses that accounted for the top 10 percent of participating slave traders, all but 3 were located in Liverpool. This would seem to suggest that the participation of non-Liverpool merchants was probably more random than the specialized slave trader participation evident in Liverpool.[53]

[51] While this figure would obviously change, should all the missing data from the PRO shipping records be found, I do not believe that it would alter in the direction of greater participation and lesser concentration, especially since contemporary observers stressed the concentration of power in a few Liverpool slave trading houses.

[52] Klein, "O trafico de escarvos," pp. 94-95.

[53] While Liverpool represented 84 percent of the major merchants, their shipping represented only 72 percent of the Jamaica slave trade.

This concentration of ownership among the Liverpool merchants trading to Jamaica was also reflected in contemporary analyses of the nature of the Liverpool slave-trading community itself. Thus a 1797 report found that in the 10 years between 1783 and 1793, roughly 10 merchant houses dominated the local slave trade. Although there were on average 35 merchant houses participating in the trade in any given year, these 10 leaders accounted for over half of the ships leaving for Africa and almost two-thirds of the number of slaves permitted to be carried.[54]

Thus by the end of the English slave trade certain basic features can be discerned. The first is the evident dominance of Liverpool in a trade that it had entered in a serious way only in the late 1730s. The second is the continuing role that Jamaica played to the end as the leading slave receiving port, a place it had taken from Barbados in the 1720s and had never relinquished. While British Guyana emerged in the last decades as a major new region of importation, it still remained secondary to Jamaica. Equally in terms of volume, Jamaica remained one of the primary centers of slave importation in America up to the time of Abolition.

But the volume and direction of the trade masked certain important shifts in the origin of the slaves and the tonnage and carrying capacity of the slave ships themselves. Whereas the regions north of the Niger River had predominated in supplying slaves to English ships in the early 18th century, by the last half of the century and the first decade of the new century, the Congo-Angola area and the Bight of Biafra had emerged as the dominant centers. The growth of Biafra as a key region introduced new aspects in the pattern of sexual divisions among the slaves and the rates of mortality in the Middle Passage. The relatively heavier flow of women out of Biafran ports meant that the dominance of males in the arriving slave ships of Jamaica was less than other major trades, such as those to Cuba and Brazil in the same period. At the same time, the higher incidence of mortality among Biafran-originated slaves may have also reflected basic problems within the Biafran region, whereby local groups suffered from

[54] "A Circumstancial Account," p. 113. In a listing of all the Liverpool merchants engaging in the slave trade in 1790, of the 39 merchant houses listed, those who outfitted 4 or more ships (9 houses), accounted for 59 percent of the ships and 60 percent of the gross tonnage. *A&P*, 1790, XXIX (698), pp. 500-509.

such deprivations that they were unable to keep local women off the international slave market. Or, conversely, it could be related to different economic and social use of women in the area. But, whatever the causal connection between these two phenomena, the differences shown by Biafra stress the importance of distinguishing among the differing out-migration regions in determining the basic trends within the slave trade over time.

Although the Biafran rates of mortality were extremely high, it is undoubtedly true that over the whole of the 18th century, mortality in the Middle Passage was on the decline. The evidence of the increasing speed of African purchase, the introduction of innoculation and other primitive health measures, and the development of more specialized middle-range-tonnage ships with their copper sheathing, may all have combined to reduce time, hunger, and the incidence of epidemics among the Africans, and thus directly to reduce overall mortality in that part of the slave trade which consisted of the seaborne voyage from Africa to America. Even at these reduced rates, of course, the slaves suffered what would have been a mortality crisis among sedentary peasant populations in the 18th century. It is also apparent that while the parliamentary regulatory acts reduced both the average number of slaves carried and the slaves per ton ratio in a dramatic manner, these efforts had little major impact in reducing the mortality of the Middle Passage. Although most of the material is still quite fragmentary, the studies of the English, French, and Portuguese trades agree in that they all show no significant correlation between slave mortality and the number of slaves carried.[55] Finally, all the materials on the merchants who owned the slave ships and the ships themselves point to a high degree of specialization in the hands of a few leading merchant houses, along with a clearly defined slave trade routing, with its own unique pattern of tonnage, crews, and cargoes that distinguished the slave trade from all other major English mercantile trades in the 18th century.

[55] The simple correlations between slaves carried and mortality was −.15 in the Jamaican trade in the trade in the 1790s, +.07 in the French slave trade from Nantes (1713-1777) and less than +.01 in the Portuguese slave trade to Rio de Janeiro in the 1795-1811 period.

Chapter Eight

The French Slave Trade in the 18th Century

France was the third largest European slave trading nation in the 18th century, and probably accounted for just over a fifth of the African slaves transported to America. Following the English and Portuguese examples, the French participation in the Atlantic slave trade was intimately tied to the growth of its own American plantation empire. This explains why France began to participate in the trade only late in the 17th century and ended its role as a major supplier at the end of the 18th, with the impact of the French and Haitian Revolutions.

While French interlopers had involved themselves in the Atlantic slave trade from early in the 16th century, serious French participation began only with the development of the monopoly trading companies in the second half of the 17th century.[1] It was the *Compagnie des Indies Occidentales* that undertook the first major systematic scheduling of ships in the Atlantic trade after 1664. This venture was followed by several other monopoly companies who controlled the trade until well into the 1720s, when free traders finally succeeded in definitively breaking their control over trading.[2] The use of both monopoly companies and later free traders was part of the French government's efforts to promote viable plantation economies in the West Indies, and followed a pattern similar to the English.

Colonizing the islands of the Lesser Antilles in the first half of the 17th century, the French, with the aid of Dutch technology, capital, credit, slaves, and markets, began to develop a thriving sugar export economy by the second half of the century. With the succesful development of Guadeloupe, the French sugar empire in the Caribbean received a major impetus and from then on

---

[1] Marcel Chailley, *Histoire de l'Afrique Occidentale Française*, 1638-1959 (Paris, 1968), p. 85ff.

[2] Abdoulaye Ly, *La Compagnie du Sénégal* (Paris, 1958), p. 93ff.

never ceased its growth and expansion. From Guadeloupe, sugar expanded to the virgin fields of the island of Martinique, which by the early 18th century became the leader of the American French sugar zone. Martinique, in turn, finally lost its preeminence to Saint Domingue by the 1740s as this newly developed French possession became the single most productive sugar and coffee plantation economy in all of the West Indies.[3]

But whereas the rapid initial growth of the French trade paralleled that of the English, the context of international imperial struggle was to prove a more decisive element in the development of the French slave trade. In the conflicts over empire in America, Africa, and Asia between England and France, the superior naval power of England led to the constant interruption of French slave-trade activities, and the subsequent breakthrough of illegal traders, both in slaves and in colonial products, into the closed French imperial commercial system. While the French were more than able to compete as free traders in the African markets, and were even assumed by contemporaries to be the most efficient of traders, British naval supremacy meant that English interlopers could totally capture the French markets in times of war.[4] It also meant that sustained growth of trading activities was constantly hampered by the necessity to rebuild shattered trading markets after each imperial conflict, a phenomenon that lasted to the era of Napoleon. The French were also required to rebuild a major part of their slave fleet after major conflicts. But, despite these factors, the trade continued to grow until late in the 18th century.

This exogenous factor of international conflict, however, finally led to conditions of crisis in the French slaving industry by the 1780s, at least in terms of supplying the French plantation islands. Thus in 1784 the Crown abolished the last of the monopoly company rights over trade, which had led to a private tax on all slaves exported by the free traders from Africa, and switched to a direct government subsidy to encourage slave trading to the French islands. The collapse of St. Domingue in slave revolts in the 1790s and the final English wars proved too devastating to overcome,

[3] Gaston-Martin, *Histoire de l'esclavage dans les colonies françaises* (Paris, 1948), p. 95ff.

[4] On the beginnings of the Anglo-French rivalry in this area, see Gaston-Martin, *Nantes au xviiie siècle. L'ère des négriers (1714-1774)* (Paris, 1931), pp. 220ff.

even despite this new development, and the French slave trade collapsed by the late 1790s.[5] While French slave traders continued to operate after the fall of Napoleon in the 19th century, and formed a substantial part of the illegal international slave trade to the Caribbean, their participation in the 1800s would never match the scale of their activities in the pre-1790s period.[6]

In this 130-year period, the French established relatively few permanent establishments on the African coast, with those at the Senegal River and Wydah (Juda) on the Gold Coast being the most important.[7] Otherwise, the French Atlantic port free traders essentially operated out of seasonal or quite temporary locations all along the coast from Senegal to the Congo, and were even extraordinarily active along the East African coast. In fact, the French were the only serious competitors to the Portuguese in the Mozambique region and carried on a thriving slave trade from East Africa throughout the 18th and into the 19th centuries. Unlike the Portuguese, however, the French East African traders did not carry their slaves to America, but rather to a series of islands off the African coast (Bourbon, Isle de France), where they developed thriving sugar and slave plantation colonies.[8]

The development of the French trade was also matched by a growing concentration of activities in one port. While La Rochelle and Le Havre had been major slaving ports in the 17th century, by the beginning of the 18th century Nantes rose to be the primary port, much as Liverpool would be later in the 18th century. Also, like Liverpool, its dominant position would be closely tied to its vital role in Europe's East Indian trade, for the Indian textiles were to be the primary staple in Europe's trade with Africa.[9]

[5] Jean Meyer, *L'armement nantais dans la deuxième moitié du xviie siècle* (Paris, 1969), pp. 81-83.

[6] Jean Meyer, "Le commerce négrier nantais (1774-1792)," *Annales, E.S.C.*, No. 15 (1960), pp. 120-129. See also the study by Serge Daget, "Catalogue des navires . . . de participation au trafic négrier atlantique entre 1814 et 1833," Abidjan, Dec. 1973 mimeo. Also, see his study "L'abolition de la traite des noirs en France de 1814 à 1831," *Cahiers d'études africaines*, xi (1971).

[7] Chailley, *Histoire, loc.cit.*; and Simone Berbain, *Études sur la traite des noirs au golfe de Guinée, Le comptoir Français de Juda au xviie siècle* (Paris, Mémoires de IFAN, No. 3, 1942).

[8] Edward A. Alpers, "The French Slave Trade in East Africa (1721-1810)," *Cahiers d'études africaines*, x, no. 2 (1970).

[9] In five selected years (1767, 1769, 1771, 1774, and 1776) slave ships from the port of Rouen shipped a total of 3.9 million *livres tournois* worth

Unlike Liverpool, however, Nantes also enjoyed several other advantages that encouraged its very early and active involvement in the slave trade. It was already one of France's leading ports in the 17th century, and had developed exceedingly close ties with the Dutch and other Northern European capital markets. This promoted its general interest in Asia as well as the New World trade, even before Africa was opened to its merchants. Finally, Nantes enjoyed special tariff arrangements that gave the Nantes merchants further advantage over their competitor ports.[10] Because of all these factors, Nantes established majority control over the French slave trade as soon as that trade was opened up to free traders in 1716,[11] and while competition grew in the latter

of goods to Africa. Of this figure, 1.4 million livres consisted of Indian textiles. Not only were the Indian cloths the single most valuable commodity being shipped—representing 36 percent of the total value of all trade goods, but it also represented 63 percent of the value of all cloths, European and East Indian combined (with the total textile value coming to 56 percent of the 3.9 million figure). (Pierre Dardel, *Navires et marchandises dans les ports de Rouen et Du Havre au XVIIIe siècle* [Paris, 1963], p. 141.) The reason for this great demand for East Indian textiles had to do not only with the brilliance and quality of the colors, but also with the durability of these colored cloths and their ability to hold their color through numerous washings and in hot climates, at least according to a French commercial analysis in the 18th century. (See M. Chambon, *Traité général du commerce de l'Amérique pour Marseilles* [2 vols.; Amsterdam & Marseilles, 1783], II, 389.) The trade also was an important stimulus to the textile industry within France itself. (See Pierre H. Boulle, "Marchandises de traite et développment industriel dans la France et l'Angleterre du xviiie siècle," *Revue française d'Histoire d'Outre-Mer*, LXII, nos. 226-227 [1975], pp. 316ff.)

[10] Meyer, *L'armement nantais*, p. 53ff; and Pierre H. Boulle, "Slave Trade, Commercial Organization and Industrial Growth in Eighteenth-Century Nantes," *Revue française d'Histoire d'Outre-Mer*, LIX, no. 214 (1972), pp. 76ff.

[11] "The "free trade" law of 1716 was a complex act, which both taxed and encouraged a select group of ports to enter actively and legally into the African trade. Only Rouen, La Rochelle, Bordeaux, Nantes, and, under certain restrictions, St. Malo were permitted access to trade along the coasts of Western Africa. The slave merchants using these ports were required to pay a tax of 20 livres on every slave delivered in the French Antilles, and had to return to these five home ports. However, the Crown permitted a 50 percent exemption to these free traders on all goods imported, including the West Indian sugar, and gave them the privilege of importing foreign textiles and merchandise needed in the slave trade. This law is reprinted in Chambon, *Traité général du commerce*, II, pp. 314-19. By 1741, all other French ports trading with the French Antilles were also given free access to the trade, which brought in, among other new ports, the key ports of Le Havre, Honfleur, and Marseilles (*ibid.*, pp. 320ff).

part of the century, it remained the primary slave trade port in the 1790s.[12]

In terms of the periodization of the Nantes slave trade in the pre-Revolutionary period of the 18th century, roughly four major periods can be discerned, which can be described both in changing structural and historical terms. The first era lasted until the mid 1720s, when the trade virtually stopped for a three-year period.[13] The cause for this crisis seems related to the revival of the Compagnie des Indies and its temporary monopoly over the Guinea trade in 1723-1725.[14] The next period lasted from the revival of the free trade through the Seven Years War (1756-1763), which saw the full-scale development of the trade in terms of volume and the overwhelming dominance of Nantes in the total trade. The profound crisis of the Seven Years War, which saw the destruction of the major portion of the slave fleet, was followed by an even greater growth in the trade and basic changes in both

[12] Prior to 1745, Nantes slavers accounted for 70 percent of all French slave-trading activity, which progressively declined to 62 percent of all voyages in 1748 to 1755; to 55 percent in the postwar period of 1763 to 1778 and to just 47 percent in the last boom-era of 1783 to 1792. Even when it was in the minority, Nantes was still the single most important port. Up to 1755 La Rochelle and Bordeaux were its prime competitors, whereas Le Havre and Bordeaux were the challengers afterwards. These figures calculated from data provided in Perry Viles, "The Slaving Interest in the Atlantic Ports, 1763-1792," *French Historical Studies* (Fall, 1972), pp. 530-531, n. 2; and Jean Mettas, "Honfleur et la traite des noirs au xviiie siecle," *Revue française d'Histoire d'Outre-Mer*, LX, No. 218 (1973), p. 10.

[13] All authors agree on a total stoppage of Nantes slave-trade activity in the mid-1720s. Calculating dates of return, Gaston-Martin (*L'ère des négriers*, p. 115) lists no ships returning in 1725 and 1726. Using dates of departure, Dieudonné Rinchon, in his pre-1748 manuscript listing (found in CRHFA, Fonds Rinchon, Boîtes 10 à 12, "statistique"), lists none leaving in 1723 and 1725.

[14] Gaston-Martin, *L'ère des négriers*, p. 15; also in his as yet unpublished study, Jean Mettas lists 1723 to 1725 as the period of greatest activity of the Compagnie des Indes, in which they equipped respectively 8, 14, and 18 ships from the port of Lorient. (Jean Mettas, *Repetoire des expéditions négriers français au xviiie siècle* [Paris, L'Société Française d'Histoire d'Outre-Mer, forthcoming]. Using alternative documents, Nardin listed 44 company ships that carried 15,928 slaves from Africa in this three-year period. For 36 of the company ships, the tonnage is known, with the mean tonnage being 286 (standard deviation 114), which was almost double the mean tonnage of the free-trade ships in the same period (see table 8.1). (Jean-Claude Nardin, "Encore des chiffres: La traite négriere française pendant la première moitié du xviiie siècle," *Revue française d'Histoire d'Outre-Mer*, LVII, no. 209 [1970], pp. 442-444.)

volume of slaves carried and tonnage of the ships employed. This final growth period was seriously contained during the Wars of American Independence (1778-1783), which in turn was followed by the last and greatest boom in the Nantes trade. Legal changes in tonnage regulations and subsidies for shipping slaves (replacing traditional taxes) ushered in this new period in the 1780s, and by the early 1790s the crisis of the Revolution brought an end to major participation by France in the Atlantic Slave Trade.

To date, only the period to 1777 has sufficiently complete data to make it possible to systematically analyze the relevant variables. The basic source is the survey of the 18th-century Nantes slave trade compiled by Dieudonné Rinchon in both published and manuscript form. This is a listing of over 1,300 French slave ships that sailed from Nantes between 1697 and 1793, of which 783 have complete data available for only the period from 1711 to 1777.[15] Because Rinchon made errors of designation in his listing of African ports, and failed as well to include any information on arrival and departure times on all the sectors of the voyage, his data have been supplemented by using an alternative dataset provided by Robert Stein from the same listing of ships in the Archives Départemental de la Loire Atlantique.[16] While the Stein dataset covers the years 1713 to 1777 for only 501 ships, there are complete time listings for almost all of these ships. Thus the latter source, which agrees in numbers shipped and mortality at sea with the two Rinchon datasets, has been used for computing sailing and trading time and for the analysis of the impact of time and African port on slave and crew mortality.

A preliminary analysis of the basic variables of the number of

[15] The published lists of Nantes slave ships from 1748 to 1792 are found in Dieudonne Rinchon, *Le Trafic Négrier* (Paris, 1938), tome I, pp. 248-301. I am indebted to Professor Philip Curtin for the use of his codebook and punched dataset of these materials. The unpublished collection of recordings of Nantes slave ships that Rinchon made for the 1697-1748 period are to be found in CRHFA, Fonds Rinchon, Boîtes 10 à 12. The Rinchon manuscript listing contains some 400 voyages, from which 45 were eliminated either because of incomplete recordings or because the figures gave zero mortality rates. The printed list starts in 1748 and contains 910 ships, of which, for the same reasons, only 428 were retained. Also, in dealing with crew mortality, we must make a further reduction because of the frequent lack of such data.

[16] Found in series B, 4577-4578, 4583-4584, and 4589-4596.

slaves shipped, the ship's tonnage, and the number of crew carried would seem to suggest that there was a more fundamental break between the pre-1723 period and those which came later. From viewing just these aggregate averages we find it evident that the earlier period saw a slave fleet carrying fewer slaves and more crew than it did in the later years. Overall slaves per ton ratios changed little, and there was only a moderate increase in average tonnage. But these general statistics mask more fundamental changes, which did occur within the trade, particularly in relationship to the types of ships being employed.

Table 8.1

Number of Slaves, Crew, Ships, and Tonnage of Selected[a] Slave Ships
Leaving Nantes, 1711-1777

Period	No. of Ships	Average No. of Slaves per Vessel	Average No. of Tons per Vessel	Average Slaves per Ton per Vessel	Average Crew Size per Vessel
1711-1722	113	283 (134)[b]	149 (82)	2.0 (0.7)	51 (24)
1726-1755	400	340 (143)	158 (81)	2.3 (0.7)	37 (13)
1763-1777	270	341 (140)	170 (68)	2.1 (0.6)	37 (9)
TOTALS	*783*	*332 (142)*	*161 (77)*	*2.2 (0.7)*	*39 (15)*

[a]Excluded from this analysis were ships that had zero or unknown figures for slave mortality, as well as those which were incomplete on either the number of slaves sold in America or purchased in Africa. The tonnage categories are based on only 764 ships (113, 397, and 254 by respective periods) and crew data was available for only 730 ships (89, 395, and 246 respectively by periods).

[b]All figures in parentheses represent the standard deviations.

Source: The pre-1748 ships were taken from Rinchon's manuscript recordings in Le Centre de recherches sur l'histoire de la France atlantique (Nantes), Fonds Rinchon, Boîtes 10 à 12 (statistique); and those from 1748-1777 come from his published study. See Dieudonné Rinchon, *Le trafic négrier, l'organisation commerciale de la traite des noirs* (Bruxelles, etc., 1938), tome I, pp. 247-302. I am grateful to Robert Stein for calling my attention to the Rinchon manuscript, and to Philip D. Curtin for making available his punched dataset taken from the Rinchon book.

Taking tonnage figures first, by using the average figures we miss an important change in the distribution of the ships by tonnage class. For in the French slave trade of the 18th century, just as for the English trade, there is a progressive concentration of ships in the middle tonnage range. This concentration clearly reflects the emergence in both trades of highly specialized ships exclusively engaging in the slave trade. As can be seen in table

8.2, there is a wide spread of ships around the mean tonnage figure in the pre-1723 period, a spread that decreases considerably in the second period (to 1758) and that is reduced even further in the period after the Seven Years War.

Table 8.2
The Distribution of Nantes Slave Ships According to
Categories of Tonnage, by Period, 1711-1777

Tonnage	1711-1722	1726-1755	1763-1777	Total
1- 49	. . .	5	1	6
50- 99	37	96	34	167
100-149	27	79	51	157
150-199	14	89	77	180
200-249	18	56	54	128
250-299	3	46	26	75
300-349	11	14	5	30
350-399	1	4	3	8
400-449	2	5	2	9
450-499	. . .	. . .	1	1
500 & over	. . .	3	. . .	3
TOTALS	113	397	254	764
Mean tons	149	158	170	161
St. Dev.	82	81	68	77

Source: Same as table 8.1.

While the English and French tonnage figures are not quite the same measure, they can be compared *grosso modo*, especially in these broader tonnage categories. In so doing, we find it evident that the early French ships exhibit a strikingly similar pattern of distribution as that shown by the Royal African Company ships trading for slaves from England in the 1691-1713 period. Of the 113 slavers that sailed from Nantes in this earlier period, only 55 percent were in the mean tonnage range of 100-299 tons. Of the 184 comparable English ships, only 57 percent were in this category.[17] The only major difference between the two was the fact that the smaller vessels of under 100 tons were more heavily represented among the French traders than among the contemporaneous English traders.

Clearly, such a dispersion of ships tonnage proved a detriment to efficient trading, for both the English and French trades of the 18th century showed a remarkably similar movement toward the

[17] K. G. Davies, *The Royal African Company* (London, 1957), p. 192.

concentration of ships in the mean tonnage range of 100-299 tons. Thus the French ships in the middle period increased their share of these ships to 68 percent, a figure that jumped to 82 percent in the post-1763 period. This later figure is, in fact, almost identical to the British tonnage distribution of 130 slavers that traded to Jamaica in the 1782-1808 period, which registered 80 percent in this tonnage category.[18]

That a modal type of ship was emerging in the trade of the 18th century is especially evident when we compare slave tonnage to that of the tonnage of other trades. Just as average slave tonnage in the Liverpool trade of the 18th century was quite low compared, for example, to the average tonnage of the West Indian merchantmen, so too, the same pattern was evident among the Nantes slave ships with their equivalent West Indian merchant ships. Thus, in the period from 1749 through 1783, some 2,266 West Indiamen sailed for America from Nantes and averaged 261 tons. The 575 slave ships that left Nantes in this period, and whose tonnage is preserved, averaged only 157 tons, a full hundred tons less. Nor was the average tonnage of the *négriers*, as the slave trade vessels were called, appreciably above the average tonnage engaged in the coastal (or *cabotage*) trade, whose 1,046 ships during this same period averaged 127 tons.[19] Thus, like the English, the Nantes merchant fleet clearly differentiated between the smaller *négrier* and the larger *droiture* or West Indiamen vessel.

Where the two differed markedly from the English experience was in the average number of crewmen that they carried. The French West Indiamen on average carried much larger crews than did the English West Indiamen. In the period from 1784 to 1788, when comparable data exist, 529 *droiture* ships carried 29 crewmen, compared to the 17 average for the British vessels; and the *négriers* averaged 35 crewmen to 26 for the British.[20] While the relative disparities between these two trades were comparable in this period, over the longer period from 1749 to 1793, there was relatively little difference to be noted between the French West Indiamen and the French slavers in terms of average crew. The former had 32 slaves for the 3,200 *droiture* ships, and the

[18] See above, Chapter 7.
[19] Calculated from data provided in Meyer, *L'armement nantais*, pp. 83-86.
[20] See above, Chapter 7.

slavers carried on average 33 crewmen in their 835 vessels.[21] In this respect, it would seem that there were important differences between the French and British trades. Why there was a higher average crew size is difficult to ascertain. Since there was also a 50 percent higher average crew size with the French in their coastal merchantmen compared to the Liverpool traders, then it may be surmised that the French in all their merchant naval trades simply had a different and possibly more inefficient organization of crews for sailing their ships.[22]

Though the French were possibly inefficient compared to contemporary English practice of the late 18th century, the longer time series of the French slavers do show a decline in crew size on the *négriers* through the course of the 18th century. That the mean crew size in the pre-1723 period was 51, with some vessels carrying over 100 sailors, clearly indicates an inefficient use of crewmen. This may be due to the need for much more extensive trading along the coast necessitated by trade at this early stage, when the French may have been forced to use many men to develop new contacts and markets. There may also have been needs for self-defense that required that these early French slavers defend themselves, not only against slave revolts, but also against foreign interlopers who were intent on stealing their cargoes or their slaves. Thus, the crew size might not indicate inefficient trading practices, so much as early and intensive competition and inexperience in trading. Whatever the cause, the indices of high numbers of crewmen would seem to be associated with the early

[21] In terms of the coastal trade, some 1,762 vessels using Nantes listed an average crew of 10 men, while the 100 fishing vessels averaged 17 crewmen per vessel.

[22] This latter hypothesis does find some support in the literature. Throughout the late 17th and early 18th centuries, the English had succeeded in reducing the number of seamen needed to man their ships. By 1766 this increased efficiency meant that London's West India trade ships were operating with one sailor per 14 tons, compared to only about 11 tons per sailor in 1751, and just 9 tons per sailor in 1726. (Ralph Davis, *The Rise of the English Shipping Industry in the 17th and 18th Centuries* [London, 1962], pp. 71-73.) While the tonnage data are not quite comparable, the decline of crew size and increase of ton per crewmen ratios was much less dramatic in the direct Nantes-West India trade. In the 1740s, for example, this trade had one crewman per six tons of ships; this rose to 8 tons per crewman in the 1760s and only 9 tons per crewman in the 1770s. (Meyer, *L'armement nantais*, pp. 83-84). To move from measures of crew per ton to relative rates of efficiency, as is done by Davis, is to assume a certain pattern of relative wage rates, which presently are unavailable.

period of major slave trading in a European nation's experience with the slave trade, and the decline of the average crew size could be an important index, along with tonnage changes, in the increasing maturity and dominance of a nation's participation in the trade.

Finally, in terms of the distribution of crew per ton, the French slavers exhibit the same pattern as shown in almost all the other trades. That is, the larger the vessel, the less would be the crew per ton ratio; and, the smaller the vessel's tonnage, the higher the ratio of sailors to ton is discovered.[23] This almost universal pattern suggests basic size limitations and carrying capacity of slave ships in all trades, due possibly to the minimum needs for space for provisions for maintenance of slave and crew life in the Middle Passage. The fact that the larger ships progressively disappear from the trade strongly suggests that contemporaries were well aware of these limitations and began to design and build ships in the optimal range for carrying the maximal number of slaves possible in an efficient manner.

In the carrying of slaves, there were also important changes in the French trade in the course of the century. First of all, it is evident that there was a major rise in the number of slaves carried, on the order of 17 percent from the earlier to the later period of the trade. But these gross statistics mask an even more steeply changing curve. Looking at the data by decades, we find that the 320-350 range of average number of slaves shipped, which was the norm from the 1730s to the 1760s, jumped to 376 slaves shipped from Africa for the 104 ships leaving in the 1770s. This later figure is comparable to that of the Angolan trade of the Portuguese in the period from 1723 to 1771 which averaged only 5 percent higher. Equally, it was similar to the figures for the number of slaves being carried by the British slavers at the same time.

A comparison of the ratio of slaves carried per ton in the pre-1784 French slave trade data yields results similar to those for the pre-1790 English slave-trade materials. Though the tonnage measurements are not quite comparable, both French and English slavers were carrying on average between 2.0 and 2.5 slaves per ton. Also, both trades exhibited the same pattern of declining slaves per ton ratio as overall ship's tonnage increased. Just as

[23] The simple correlation between crew per ton and tonnage is −.55.

the ratio of crew per ton declined, the bigger the vessel became; so too did the slaves per ton ratio, which exhibited an almost identical pattern. What is impressive about this statistic, is that despite the relative differences in ship's tonnage measurements, this pattern holds for all the 18th-century trades, and the correlations are almost identical.[24] This clearly defined pattern, and the same tendency of declining ratios of sailors per ton with increasing tonnage, give substantiation to the argument maintaining that basic space limitations due to the storage needs of food and equipment kept a maximum level on the ability to carry slaves successfully across the Atlantic.

Table 8.3
Slaves per Ton Ratios by Categories of Tonnage in
Nantes Slave Ships, by Period, 1711-1777
(standard deviations in parentheses)

Tonnage	1711-1722	1726-1755	1763-1777	Total
1- 49	. . .	1.7	1.5	1.6 (0.9)
50- 99	2.1	2.6	2.1	2.4 (0.8)
100-149	2.4	2.6	2.2	2.4 (0.7)
150-199	2.0	2.4	2.3	2.3 (0.6)
200-249	2.0	2.2	2.1	2.1 (0.4)
250-299	1.4	1.8	2.0	1.8 (0.5)
300-349	1.4	1.6	1.5	1.5 (0.4)
350-399	1.1	1.5	1.2	1.3 (0.6)
400-449	1.5	1.5	1.1	1.4 (0.3)
450-499	. . .	. . .	0.7	0.7 . . .
500 & over	. . .	1.1	. . .	1.1 (0.1)
TOTALS	2.0 (0.7)	2.3 (0.7)	2.1 (0.6)	2.2 (0.7)
No. of ships	113	397	254	764

Source: Same as table 8.1.

In obtaining their slaves on the African coast, the French relied on much the same markets as the primary 18th-century traders, the British. Their ships about equally worked along the rivers and coastline of the Upper Guinea coast, fully exploited the Gold and Slave Coasts, and finally dealt extensively along the Loango and Angola coasts. These coastal designations were quite broad, and since often the port registers listed just these general terms, it is difficult to determine the different smaller regional changes

[24] The simple correlation between slave per ton and tonnage is −.38. For comparable results from other trades, see Chapter 7, n. 12.

in the supply of slaves.[25] But as we view the movement of slaves by decade, it is evident that the three major zones were active sources from the beginning. As was evident with both the English and Portuguese traders, the French consistently took their largest average number of slaves per vessel from Angola and their smallest number from the Guinea coast.[26] Nevertheless, through

Table 8.4
Number of Africans Shipped on Nantes Slave Ships
from Africa, 1711-1777
(number of ships in parentheses)

| Period | AFRICAN REGIONS | | | Total[a] |
	Guinée	Gold Coast	Angola	
1711-1722	263 (3)	2,361 (7)	1,447 (3)	4,071 (13)
1726-1755	18,323 (67)	35,963 (108)	23,815 (57)	78,261 (233)
1763-1777	40,552 (121)	19,231 (51)	21,103 (55)	83,818 (235)
TOTALS	*59,138 (191)*	*57,555 (166)*	*46,365 (115)*	*166,150 (481)*
Av. slaves per ship	310	347	403	345
St. Dev.	142	127	129	138

[a]This total includes 9 ships unknown as to African port.

Source: ADLA, Série B, 4577-4578, 4583-4584. I am indebted to Robert Stein for making this series available to me. I have decided to use this smaller sample set of data because of its more precise definitions of African ports than was available from the larger Rinchon listings.

[25] It is worth noting that there is some variation in the 18th-century French designations of the Guinea and Gold Coast. Some 18th-century maps bring the Guinea Coast up to Cape Mount and thus include only the areas which the British called Senegambia and Sierra Leone. Others bring the Guinée designation down to the Cape of Three Points (adding the Grain, Ivory and part of the Gold Coasts). All charts agree on defining Cape Lopez as the border between the Gold Coast and Angola. Thus even in its limited sense, the Gold Coast of 18th-century French designations includes what the British called the Gold Coast and the areas of Benin and Biafra. Since the use of either Guinée designation involves only 8 ships that have little impact on the overall statistics, I have adopted the limited Cape Mount boundary given in a 1756 listing of French trading ports in Africa (reprinted in Cailley, *Histoire de l'Afrique occidentale française*, pp. 88-91). I am indebted to Serge Daget for his help in identifying 18th-century French place names.

[26] The difference in average number of slaves carried between Angola and the combined figures for the Gold and Guinea Coast in the Rinchon dataset can be explained by the fact that the ships going to Angola had a slightly higher tonnage (on average around 11 percent per vessel) and a higher slave per ton ratio (also around 11 percent per ship).

the 1770s, the Guinea area kept a steady flow of slaves going to America. Also, like the British, the French did a great deal of coasting off the African shoreline. They often stopped in the Senegambia ports to pick up African foodstuffs for the Middle Passage, did some moderate purchasing, and then moved southward to concentrate more fully on slave trading itself.

The destination of the French slave traders in the New World changed over time. The flow of migrant slave labor tended to follow the fortunes of the plantation economy in the West Indies and was intimately associated with American sugar production. In the earlier part of the century, Martinique was heavily represented in the flow of slaves, while by mid century, Saint Do-

Table 8.5
African Slave Arrivals on Nantes Slave Ships
in West Indian Ports, 1711-1777

| Period | AMERICAN PORTS | | | Total |
	St. Domingue	Martinique	Others[a]	
1711-1722	13,004 (56)	11,096 (49)	1,983 (8)	26,083 (113)
1726-1758	80,415 (267)	29,942 (114)	1,210 (9)	111,567 (390)
1763-1777	70,583 (231)	1,693 (12)	6,393 (24)	78,669 (267)
TOTALS	164,002 (554)	42,731 (175)	9,586 (41)	216,319 (770)
Av. slaves per ship	296	244	234	281
St. Dev.	129	117	134	129

[a]Of these 41 ships, 16 went to Grenada, 14 to Cayenne, and 11 to Cuba and Puerto Rico. It should be stressed that this is an incomplete listing, due to the large number of ships excluded because of unknown variables. Also, the Rinchon listings seem to have missed several vessels, since archival sources for this same period list at least 12 ships going to Guadeloupe.

Source: Same as table 8.1.

mingue was the dominant zone and accounted for 72 percent of the arriving slaves. This dependence on Saint Domingue further increased during the 1770s, to 90 percent, and probably remained at or near that level in the following decade. Thus the impact of the Haitian revolution on the French slave trade was even more profound than had it occurred a century before, for by now the ports of Saint Domingue absorbed all but a small fraction of the total French effort in the Atlantic Slave Trade.[27]

[27] Of the 229 slave ships that arrived in America between 1783 and 1791,

Up to this point, the general patterns of trade have been analyzed on the basis of the summary statistics gathered by Rinchon. Fortunately, there exist complete data for these same ships in the Nantes departmental archives that give detailed information on the timing of trade. This information permits the reconstruction of the pattern of sailing times in the legs of the voyage, the time spent crusing the African coast trading for slaves, and the impact of seasonality on the movement of slaves and ships. What seems readily apparent is that the trade, despite some early observations by Gaston-Martin to the contrary,[28] did experience some marked seasonality in terms of the movement of ships from the port of Nantes. The peak months were May and June, with the winter months (December-February) being relatively slack periods. The actual sailing times from France to the African coast were little influenced by season, and the primary factor influencing the days at sea was the distance of the region from Europe. Thus, the sailing times to Guinea and the Gold Coast were approximately the same, though local wind and current conditions on the Guinea coast probably cut the advantage of distance somewhat, thus making it equivalent to the farther Gold Coast shores. But, both were quite different from Angola, which required thirty days more sailing time.

When viewed over the course of the sixty-six years of the trade covered here, the sailing times to the Guinea Coast reveal certain variations. Sailing to the former region, especially after the Seven Years War, now took, surprisingly, thirty days longer on average than before the war. The decrease of Angola sailing time seems more plausible, especially as the spread of sailing times around the mean times are much more bunched than in the case of Guinea.[29] There is also not sufficient internal port designation within the broader Angolan category to establish precise comparative sailing times.

As there seem to be no clear trends and easily explained

---

of whose port of arrival is known, 225 of them arrived in Saint Domingue. (J. Everaert, "Les fluctuations du trafic négrier nantais [1763-1792]," *Les Cahiers de Tunisie*, Tome xi, No. 43 [1963], p. 61.)

[28] Gaston-Martin, *L'ère des négriers*, p. 64.

[29] To give some sense of the comparative spreads of observations around the mean sailing time, one can calculate the coefficient of variation. This statistic gives a high of .52 for Guinea, .47 for the Gold Coast, and a much lower .37 for Angola, which indicates a far more tightly clustered grouping of ships around the mean sailing time.

Table 8.6
Average Sailing Time (in Days) from Nantes to
African Regions
(no. of ships in parentheses)

Period	AFRICAN REGIONS		
	Guinée	*Gold Coast*	*Angola*
1711-1722	46 (3)	61 (6)	120 (2)
1726-1758	68 (70)	81 (108)	120 (57)
1763-1777	91 (122)	83 (50)	100 (55)
General Av.	82 (195)	81 (164)	111 (114)
St. Dev.	43	38	42

Source: Same as table 8.4.

changes in sailing times over this period from France to Africa, there are also some unexplained changes in actual trading times along the African coasts during this same era. Trading time on the coast actually increased during the course of the century for all three major regions. I would have assumed that growing familiarity with the local markets would have increased the efficiency of the French traders and thereby reduced their costly time on the coast. Given the high mortality of crewmen on the coast—which was the most risky leg of the entire voyage for the seamen—[30] and the potential for increased problems with disease for the slaves, it might be supposed that trading time would have gone down. Certainly when viewed from the perspective of the trades of the late-17th- and early-18th-century Dutch (who averaged 228 days on the coast) and the late-18th-century English (who completed their trading in just 114 days on average), the French were about midway in the time they had to employ in African trading. Since the Dutch were earlier and the English were later, I had assumed that the French were moving toward the English pattern, but this in fact may not have been the case.

Another curious phenomenon in the African data is the time of departure, where seasonal variations suddenly emerge as a serious factor. In all three coastal trades, the period from May through September consistently proved to be a low point in the

[30] Of the five major legs of the voyage, the two most dangerous for the seamen were the coastal trading period in Africa, which accounted for 53 percent of the 2,107 known crew deaths among the Nantes slave ships (another 862 crewmen died, but their place of death was unknown) and the Middle Passage, during which 35 percent of the deaths occurred.

Table 8.7
Average Time Spent Trading on the African Coast (in Days)
by Region and Period
(no. of ships in parentheses)

| Period | AFRICAN REGIONS | | | Total |
	Guinée	Gold Coast	Angola	
1711-1722	60 (3)	139 (6)	165 (3)	126 (12)
1726-1758	145 (69)	133 (105)	158 (56)	143 (230)
1763-1777	165 (119)	168 (50)	173 (55)	168 (224)
General Av.	*156 (191)*	*144 (161)*	*165 (114)*	*154 (466)*
St. Dev.	89	94	76	88

Source: Same as table 8.4.

number of slaves shipped. But this pattern of seasonal movement from Africa is also a complex issue. In this low season there seems to be no increase in mortality that would force the traders to avoid these months as a risk period. Also, one would expect that if captains would wish to leave the coast for any reason before the low period of May through September, they would rush through their trading in the months preceding May and be more leisurely in the period afterward, but there occurs no significant correlation between month of arrival in Africa and time spent on the coast.[31] Equally, there is little correlation between sailing time and month of departure in terms of the low migration season correlating with longer sailing times.[32] Finally, there is no variation in the average number of slaves carried per vessel between the peak or low seasons, the volume differences being explained exclusively on the basis of more or fewer ships employed in the trade.

The fact that the peak period for slave arrivals in America was January through June would seem to argue that it was American demand factors that explain this seasonal change in volume. For, this six-month period between January and June was the peak of the harvesting season in the West Indies, when the planters had their greatest need for labor on the plantations.[33] The fact that

[31] The simple correlation between the month of arrival and time spent on the coast is +.055.

[32] The simple correlation between the length of the voyage of the Middle Passage and the month of departure from Africa is +.037.

[33] Michael Craton, *Sinews of Empire: A Short History of British Slavery* (New York, 1974), pp. 127ff.

this seasonal variation appeared in the migrations from all three major African regions of different geographical zones, climates, and markets would seem to further support the thesis that African supply problems were not the major factor in accounting for the seasonal variation in the movement of slaves. Moreover, this same seasonal variation can be found at other times and in other trades, all closely linked to American sugar harvesting periods.[34]

Aside from seasonality, were there any variations over time in the all important Middle Passage crossing? Unfortunately, the most complete data on this come from only one of the New World

Table 8.8
Middle Passage Time (in Days) of Slave Ships
from Nantes from Africa to Saint Domingue
(no. of ships in parentheses)

Period	AFRICAN REGIONS		
	Guinée	Gold Coast	Angola
1711-1722	59 (1)		115 (1)
1726-1758	84 (34)	120 (74)	72 (45)
1763-1777	87 (98)	101 (45)	68 (51)
Average trip	*86 (133)*	*113 (119)*	*71 (97)*
St. Dev.	38	33	20

Source: Same as table 8.4.

islands, that of Saint Domingue. There was for the ports of this island a noticeable decline in the average sailing time in the course of the century. Sailing times were affected by wind and current conditions, not just by nautical miles. Thus the ports of the Congo and Angola are much closer in sailing time to the West Indies than the physically much closer ports of the Gold and Guinea coasts.

While not as precisely marked as the seasonality, there also appeared to be a definite shift downward in the sailing times in the Middle Passage during the course of the century in two out of the three major African regions. The average sailing time from the Gold Coast considerably dropped between the second quarter and third quarter of the century, while the ships sailing the Angola to Saint Domingue route showed a consistent decline in

[34] For example, in the nine years in which complete monthly reports are available, there is a sharp rise in slave imports into Cuba in the sugar harvesting months (see below, Chapter 9).

all three periods. Only in the Guinea route was there no clearly defined decline in sailing time. Moreover, though the available time data is unfortunately limited to only the island of Saint Domingue, this sample would seem to support the idea that most ships tended to make the trips in relatively well-known and therefore anticipated lengths of time. The fact that in each case two thirds of the ships made the trip in no more than 20 to some 37 days beyond the average sailing, depending on the region, meant that a captain could securely provision his boat in expectation of making an Atlantic crossing in approximately the same time as he and his fellow captains had done before.

Finally, in examining the turn-around time of the traders in the Caribbean island, we find that the few complete records indicate that, on average, slavers took three months to unload their slave passengers and take on a return cargo to Europe.[35] Given the fact that slave ship arrivals did not always coincide with harvesting of the sugar crop, and that the average slavers were relatively small vessels, most slavers tended to go with mixed cargoes that were readily available, including sugar. But in the French West Indies, as in the British, the Caribbean-European sugar trade was principally in the hands of the larger West Indiamen vessels engaged in the so-called "direct" or *droiture* trade.

The new archival sources now available on the Nantes slave trade also provide an unusual amount of information on the pattern of slave and crew mortality. Such information can be used to evaluate the role of several frequently discussed factors affecting the mortality on slave ships. Of particular concern are measures of crowding (such as numbers of slaves per ton), the African sources of supply, the carrying capacity of vessels, the length of time slaves spent in internal transit to African ports, the time between arrival at port and ship's departure (the time on the coast) and the length of the voyage from Africa to the New World. The Nantes data provide information on all but the internal African transit time, and thus are a uniquely valuable source for the analyses of these issues.

The annual average mortality experience of ships that departed from Nantes in the period between 1712 and 1777 shows a sharp

---

[35] There were only 29 ships that had complete data on arrival and departure time. These were all grouped in the 1763-1764 period and had a mean Caribbean port stay of 94 days (with a standard deviation of 33 days).

year-to-year fluctuation as well as a mild downward trend over the century.[36] The 1772-1777 period had an average mortality below that of previous periods, only 5 of the previous 47 years having a mortality rate below that of the highest in this six-year period. This reduction was not due to shifts in African ports of departure, nor to marked variation in ship's tonnage, carrying rates, or sailing time. Rather, the decline characterized all African regions, and cannot be explained in terms of any of the expected variables. A long-term decline similarly characterized the mortality rates of the crews, and the determinants of this decline remain an issue for further examination.[37] The distribution of mortality by ships, indicates both the wide range of experience in the trade as well as the occurrence, although infrequent, of the very high mortality that has been frequently pointed to in the literature. Certainly some slave ships experienced high mortality, but this was not typical of the Middle Passage.

In trying to analyze the possible determinants of this mortality pattern, we constructed an index of overcrowding by determining the number of slaves shipped per ton of vessel. It was anticipated, given the debates on so-called "tight packing," that mortality would be highest where the number of slaves per ton was greatest. As seen in table 8.9, such a pattern did not occur. Rather, the mortality rate seems to have been independent of the number shipped per ton.[38] Although slave ships obviously carried more individuals per ton than did other 18th-century vessels, within the range carried, the degree of crowding did not seem to affect mortality.

There is, however, some difficulty raised by the relationship between the measured slaves per ton and the degree of crowding suggested by the material in table 8.10. For it seems that the numbers of slaves per ton was highest on vessels of 100 to 149 tons, falling quite markedly on ships of greater tonnage. Yet these

[36] The particularly high mortality suffered by slaves in the year 1730 was largely due to the fact that 4 of the 12 ships had death rates of 60 percent and over.

[37] Average crew mortality on 439 ships that had data for both crew and slave mortality was 18.3 percent. When the large sample of ships that had crew mortality data (with or without slave mortality information) was analyzed, the crew mortality was slightly lower than this figure, but still higher than the slave mortality rate.

[38] The simple correlation between slaves per ton and slave mortality is −.01.

Table 8.9
Average Slave Mortality per Ship,
by Slaves per Ton per Ship

Range of Slaves per Ton	Average[a] Mortality	No. of Ships
Less than 0.88	192	16
.88-1.389	151	70
1.39-1.639	168	51
1.64-1.889	133	98
1.89-2.139	157	120
2.14-2.389	151	117
2.39-2.639	126	98
2.64-2.889	136	83
2.89-3.139	174	45
3.14-3.389	170	38
Above 3.39	156	27
TOTALS	149	763

[a]Mortality is calculated as the number who died for 1,000 persons shipped.

Source: Same as table 8.1.

smaller vessels had a mortality experience similar to those of the larger ships.[39] Given this relationship, the most appropriate test of the crowding argument and its impact on slave mortality would be to examine the relationship, within a given tonnage group, between the number of slaves per ton and mortality rate. This comparison, however, indicates that the extent of crowding on ships of a given size did not appear to affect mortality.[40] Thus, the best

[39] The correlation of slaves per ton with tonnage is $-.37$; and of slave mortality with tonnage is $-.01$.

[40] This argument is more fully developed in Herbert S. Klein and Stanley Engerman, "Facteurs de mortalité dans le trafic français d'esclaves au xviiie siècle," *Annales, economies, sociétés des civilisations,* Année 31, no. 6 (1976).

While the discussion of crowding aboard slave ships has been based on a slaves-per-ton ratio, it should be stressed that tonnage is a weight and not a volume factor. When tonnage doubles, for example, the interior space available for slaves increases only by a factor of twenty-five percent. To take this difference into consideration, an internal area index was generated as follows:

$$A = T^{2/3}$$

Using this to estimate an index of slaves per area, the relationship to mortality was estimated. Not surprisingly, the results are quite similar to those for the index of slaves per ton, with no significant correlation indicated between slaves per area and mortality rates. For a more detailed analysis of space provided on slave ships, see Herbert S. Klein and Charles Garland,

Table 8.10
Average Slaves per Ton and Average Slave Mortality
per Ship, by Ship's Tonnage

Tonnage	Average Slaves per Ton	Average[a] Mortality	No. of Ships
Less than 100	2.36	145	173
100-149	2.43	137	157
150-199	2.31	172	180
200-249	2.11	137	128
250-299	1.84	146	75
300-349	1.50	186	29
Above 350	1.30	121	21
TOTALS	2.21	149	763

[a]Mortality is calculated as the number who died for 1,000 persons shipped.

Source: Same as table 8.1.

indication at present is that the degree of crowding in itself did not significantly affect mortality within the range observed. Most ships carried between 1.39 and 2.88 slaves per ton, a range that includes the maximum allowed by both English and Portuguese regulations.[41] The relatively narrow range, and the limited effect upon mortality, suggest that economic considerations may have been the important determinant of the degree of crowding, and these considerations no doubt were then reflected in the codes regulating the trade.[42]

"The Allotment of Space Aboard 18th century Slave Ships." Unpublished ms.

[41] For the Portuguese data, which indicated a variation from between 2 to 3 slaves per ton depending on construction, see Herbert S. Klein, "The Portuguese Slave Trade from Angola in the Eighteenth Century," *Journal of Economic History*, 33 (1972), p. 902 n. For the British, see Klein and Engerman, "Slave Mortality."

[42] While it is correct that the expected mortality experience in transit would affect the prices paid for slaves in Africa, after purchase it was economically desirable for captains to achieve a low mortality rate. Thus, as discussed below, "excessive" crowding need not have been a profitable arrangement.

Regression analysis of the 763 ships similarly points to this interpretation. The correlations are poor, neither tonnage nor slaves per ton by themselves accounting for even one percent of the variation in mortality rates. Moreover, as shown by the following multiple regression, where M is mortality rate, T is tonnage, and SPT slaves per ton, both together still fail to account for one percent of the variation (standard errors in parentheses).

It is important to note, also, that ships with the highest slave mortality were also ships with the heaviest mortality of the crew.[43] The data indicate as well that, overall, the mortality of the crew exceeded that of the slaves, although on the Middle Passage itself that of slaves exceeded crew mortality.[44] But the positive relationship between slave mortality during voyage and crew deaths suggests the possible importance of similar factors in mortality. Apparently, the determinants of slave mortality, as

Table 8.11
Average Crew Mortality per Ship,
by Slave Mortality per Ship

Range of Slave Mortality (rate per 1,000)	Average Crew Mortality (rate per 1,000)	No. of Ships
1- 19	133	47
20- 39	117	55
40- 59	137	51
60- 79	167	39
80- 99	180	42
100-119	196	28
120-139	174	24
140-159	208	19
160-199	193	32
200-299	268	49
300-399	199	22
400-499	289	19
Greater than 500	325	12
TOTALS	183	439

Source: Same as table 8.1.

$M = 1625 \quad -.0024T \quad -.4253SPT \quad R^2 = .00039$
$\qquad\qquad (.0071) \qquad (.8060)$

The explanatory power of the regression is increased somewhat (but R^2 remains below .01) when allowance is made for differences in African ports of departure, there being apparent some differences in mortality from different African ports.

[43] The correlation between slave mortality and crew mortality is +.37.
[44] The regression is crew mort = 13.18 + .3718M $\quad R^2 = .1421$
$\qquad\qquad\qquad\qquad\qquad (.0437)$

Strictly interpreted, this suggests that about 70 percent $(\frac{13.2}{18.3})$ of the mortality of the crew occurred at times other than the Middle Passage. Direct data for a number of ships, which give crew deaths at various stages of the voyage, indicate that 34 percent of the deaths occurred in the Middle Passage, while more than half occurred while the vessel was on the coast.

affected by disease and by provisioning, had a similar impact upon the sailors in the crew.

Aside from measuring crowding and its impact on mortality, the new archival materials enable us to measure the impact of sailing time on mortality. It is to be expected that sailing time would have an important effect on mortality. In the simplest case, of course, the longer the voyage, the greater the period of risk and the higher the number of deaths expected. However, there are more important aspects to the relationship between mortality and voyage length. Given the finite capacity of ships, there would be limitations upon the amount of provisions of food and water to be carried. The longer the time at sea, therefore, the more likely that shortage of provisions might occur. Similarly, given the possibilities for spoilage of water and food, as well as the incubation period for diseases, the longer the voyage, the greater would be the expected death rate.[45]

There was a clear positive relationship between slave mortality rates and the length of the Middle Passage.[46] However, the regression indicates that, overall, only about 6 percent of the variation in mortality is explained by the length of the voyage. As noted, there was a great variation from voyage to voyage for any given sailing time below a specified level, which accounts for the relatively low correlation overall. The relationship between time at sea and mortality rates (see table 8.12) was heavily influenced by the difference between average sailing time from an African port, and the actual duration of a specific voyage. For not only was there some increased average mortality with sailing time, but the rates generally rose markedly for voyages that were atypically long. These patterns indicate the great importance of unexpectedly long sailing times on mortality, suggesting the role of provisioning rules and practices in explaining mortality.

In this period, the differences in slave mortality between ships from various African ports did not differ significantly, once allow-

[45] See the discussion in Herbert S. Klein and Stanley Engerman, "Shipping Patterns and Mortality in the African Trade to Rio de Janeiro," *Cahiers d'études africaines*, xv, no. 59 (1975).

[46] The regression is:

$$M = 5.30 + .0874MP, \qquad R^2 = .057$$
$$(.0170)$$

where *MP* is the length of the Middle Passage.

Table 8.12
Slave Mortality Rates in Middle Passage in the 18th-Century French Slave Trade
(number of ships in parentheses)

Time at Sea in Days	Guinée	Gold Coast	Angola	Unknown	Total
ess than 40	8.2 (15)	21.5 (2)	2.1 (4)		8.3 (21)
41- 60	11.1 (28)	12.5 (8)	10.2 (34)	16.7 (2)	11.0 (72)
61- 80	10.4 (44)	21.4 (15)	10.3 (43)	10.3 (2)	12.0 (104)
81-100	10.6 (32)	13.0 (42)	14.4 (13)	10.1 (2)	12.3 (89)
101-120	13.1 (31)	12.1 (39)	11.9 (6)	11.6 (2)	12.5 (78)
121-140	20.7 (13)	16.7 (30)	56.1 (1)	12.5 (1)	18.6 (45)
Over 141	18.8 (12)	22.8 (20)			21.3 (32)
JTALS	*12.2 (175)*	*15.6 (156)*	*11.0 (101)*	*12.2 (9)*	*13.1 (441)*

Source: Same as table 8.4.

ance is made for differences in sailing time. The moderately higher mortality on ships from the Gold Coast is explained, for the most part, by the longer sailing time in the Middle Passage. Such results differ from those for the Portuguese and the English in the 18th-century African slave trades, who, as we have seen, experienced significant differences in slave mortality for the different African export areas. This raises questions as to the nature of the disease environment in African supplying areas, the distance travelled to reach the coast, and the health conditions on the coast. The seeming absence of these distinctions in this 18th-century sample of the French slave trade is difficult to explain.

While challenging the hypothesis of "tight packing" and mortality postulated in the traditional literature, we find still major difficulties in determining exactly what factors did influence the trends in slave mortality, and in establishing why an overcrowding or tight packing pattern might not have been used. Slave ships, it should be stressed, did carry more people than did other vessels, but within the observed range of variation there seemed no relationship between slaves carried per ton and mortality. The reasons for the relatively limited variation in slaves carried per ton might be explained by economic considerations, which precluded the desirability of excessive crowding that might have led to substantial increases in mortality. In that case, where excessive crowding would have led to higher mortality, profits might be less than in ships with a smaller number of slaves and a lower mortality experience. Thus, to show that within a range there was no effect of crowding upon mortality does not necessarily mean either that there were no economic limits on the number of slaves carried or that there was an obvious correlation between profitability and crowding.[47]

Another possible constraint on slaves carried is suggested by the effect that sailing time had on mortality. For, based on expected voyage length, the provisions carried would occupy a substantial part of the capacity of the ship. Given that certain minimal daily needs of food and water were required to maintain slave health and to reduce susceptibility to disease, there were clearly demands for space for this purpose. Any increase in the number of the slaves taken aboard would be at the expense of provisioning and storage space. The constraint here, it should be noted, was on space, and not on costs, for the bulk of the foodstuffs consumed by the Africans in the crossing were purchased on the African coast, with rice and yams serving as staples in the diet. The costs for these foods and for the water represented less than 5 percent of the total costs of outfitting the vessels, and therefore offered little financial restraint on adding extra food.[48]

In analyzing the causes of death in the 18th-century French slave trade, and examining also the evidence of the British slave trade at the end of the century, we find that the primary killers were dysentery, yellow fever, and other unexplained "fevers,"

[47] That Europeans in the earlier years of the trade might have tried to overcrowd their vessels to the point where it affected mortality is suggested in a letter by the Royal Agent in Angola to the King of Portugal in 1638. He reported that slave ships that were currently arriving in Luanda were not content to take the usual 400 or so slaves per voyage, but were trying, in fact, to take 700 to 800 persons per ship. He asked the Crown to prevent this, on the grounds that it seriously retarded ship's departures in the port (i.e., their turn-around time) and "at sea it causes the death of many hundreds of them [slaves] because of the excessive crowding and lack of water." (Diogo Lopes de Faria to the King, Loanda, 16 March 1638, in Padre Antonio Brasio, ed., *Monumenta Missionaria Africana* [9 vols. to date; Lisbon, 1952-   ], vIII, p. 395.)

[48] The Nantes slave ship *Reine de France*, of 150 tons and a 47-man crew, transported 404 slaves from Guinea to Saint Domingue in 1744. For this trip it purchased on the African coast 13,000 lbs. of fresh foods, including rice, chickens, and goats, for the approximate cost in trading goods of 2,500 livres. This represented the approximate purchase cost of 9 slaves in Africa. This same 2,500-livres figure represented under 2 percent of the total value of goods carried by the *Reine* from France to purchase slaves and ivory on the coast. (See Dieudonne Rinchon, *Pierre Ignace Lieven Van Alstein, Capitain Negrier* [Dakar: Mémoires de IFAN, no. 71, 1964], pp. 84-85.)

followed by such communicable diseases as measles and small pox.[49] Given the relationship between food consumption and health conditions and the importance of amoebic dysentery as a cause of slave deaths, problems of sanitation and the maintenance of clean food and water were central to the reduction of mortality at sea. The importance of provisioning rules based upon expected sailing time is seen by the varying patterns shown by the different African ports of exit. For example, if the rate of spoilage of water was simply based upon time at sea, then all slave vesesls should have suffered correspondingly similar rates of mortality after a common length of time at sea. But this was not the case. Equally, it is difficult to comprehend the relationship between food spoilage and the increasing incidence of slave mortality. What does appear certain is that long voyages usually ended with both slaves and crew going on reduced rations, with subsequent increases in scurvy and related dietary diseases. This would seem to support the idea that similar rules of provisioning operated in all trades, with captains provisioning for expected sailing times, plus some allow-

[49] The few published ships' logs constantly cite the "flux" or dysentery, as the single greatest malady suffered. In calculating the cause of death of the slaves shipped by Captain John Newton from Sierra Leone to Antigua in 1751 to 1752, we find that 17 of 24 deaths were listed as due to the "flux," with two more listed as "fever and flux." Some of the flux deaths occurred several weeks after initial contagion, while the bouts of dysentery seemed to come in cycles. (B. Martin and M. Spurrell, eds., *Journal of a Slave Trader, John Newton 1750-1754* [London, 1962], pp. 29ff.; also see Alexander Falconbridge, *An Account of the Slave Trade on the Coast of Africa* [London, 1788], p. 25.) The captain of the French slave ship *L'Economie* reported an outbreak of dysentery among his 217 slaves on his trip from the Congo to St. Domingue in 1753 after two weeks at sea. He reported that the majority of slaves who were buried at sea were killed by dysentery (Rinchon, *Van Alstein*, p. 42). This is the same pattern discovered in several recent surveys of disease and mortality in the Middle Passage. (See David L. Chandler, "Health and Slavery: A Study of Health Conditions Among Negro Slaves in the Viceroyalty of New Granada and Its Associated Slave Trade, 1600-1810" [Ph.D. thesis, Department of History, Tulane University, 1972], pp. 29-41; and Tommy Todd Hamm, "The American Slave Trade with Africa, 1620-1807" [Ph.D. thesis, Department of History, Indiana University, 1975], pp. 222-232.) There were, of course, numerous other epidemic diseases, such as yaws, opthalmia, as well as skin ulceration, which, while crippling and maiming, usually did not lead to death. The trade played a vital part in the transmission of these and other diseases endemic to Africa to the Americas. (Henry Harold Scott, *A History of Tropical Medicine* [2 vols.; London, 1939], II, 982-1010.)

ance for the possibility of longer voyages. But, beyond some added allowance for increased time at sea, provisioning would absorb too much space, and it was when this allowed time was exceeded that the increasing risk of spoilage and unhealthy sanitary conditions meant sharply increased death rates for the slaves and the crew. The sudden appearance of communicable disease distorted this problem, causing death to occur even when adequate supplies were available. Many of these diseases did not lead inevitably to death, though the one that seems to have been extremely difficult to control and that caused a large number of deaths was measles. The incidence of small pox should have been declining over the period, since French and British captains were already routinely innoculating their slaves by the second half of the 18th century.[50]

This sense of randomness of high slave mortality is further reinforced when the experiences of individual slave captains are analyzed. In an examination of the mortality history of twelve French captains who made four or more successful slaving voyages, the generally random quality of high mortality is clearly evident. The most typical pattern was for relatively low rates of slave mortality experienced on several voyages, followed by one unusually high incidence of death. This pattern would seem to suggest that within limits the individual performances of multiple-voyage captains had little impact on slave mortality. Those successful traders who were employed on more than one voyage seem to have experienced the general mortality rates of the trade, or even below general rates on most voyages, with the exceptional high mortality rate occurring infrequently. This would suggest that experience and skill could not in itself prevent catastrophic mortality rates. Equally, it strongly supports the above contentions that these rates were the most likely results of epidemic diseases and/or an unusually lengthy voyage and its concomitant problems of food supply.[51]

[50] See, e.g., *A&P*, 1970, xxix (698), pp. 493-495; and Rinchon, *Van Alstein*, p. 188.
[51] This same pattern occurred as well when the same ship made many voyages and carried comparable numbers of slaves each time. The Portuguese curveta *Santo Antonio Portilhão* undertook 10 consecutive voyages and experienced a random pattern of mortality rates that went from as low as 1.3 percent deaths to 17 percent deaths of all transported slaves on the Middle Passage. See above, table 3.5.

Table 8.13
The Sequential Slave Mortality Experienced by
Nantes Slave Trade Captains Making Four or More Voyages
in the 18th Century[a]

Captain	SEQUENCE OF VOYAGES					
	First	Second	Third	Fourth	Fifth	Sixth
	%	%	%	%	%	%
F. de Beauman	17.8	14.2	3.7	9.3		
G. Denis	35.7	13.7	2.6	7.5		
E. Devigne	19.6	8.5	7.0	1.0	42.8	4.9
R. J. Durocher	5.0	3.3	4.8	3.3		
J. B. F. Gaugy	54.0	3.3	4.1	2.1	5.8	
J. Guyot	3.5	13.3	9.2	10.7	unk.	22.9
P. LeRay	4.6	39.5	8.8	0.0	1.0	15.5
L. Monnier	2.6	4.5	4.1	6.4		
J. Perron	3.1	8.0	8.4	28.2	5.7	
J. Proust	4.3	13.1	22.9	0.2	4.3	
L. Quatreville	4.5	2.8	2.8	5.3		
A. Vandendriesche	3.7	6.2	5.8	16.4	6.6	

[a]This is not an exhaustive list of all captains who made more than 3
voyages, but is only the list for which complete slave mortality in the
Middle Passage could be calculated.

Source: Rinchon, *Le trafic negrier*, pp. 248-302, 307-324.

Up to this point, the analysis of the French slave trade materials has concentrated on the ships and the slaves they carried.
One final area of concern involves the mechanisms of control in
this trade. Through the information provided on the ownership
of the slave ships, one can measure the relative rates of concentration of slave shipping from the port of Nantes in the 18th century. Using the lists constructed by Rinchon, I have calculated
tonnage figures for those voyages (around 90 percent) for which
information was available. The resulting calculations show a very
high concentration of shipping in the hands of a few leading merchant houses. Thus the leading 5 percent of the merchants, in
terms of the number of voyages they financed, controlled 30 percent of the tonnage of the slave shipping employed in 18th-cen-
tury Nantes. The top 10 percent of the merchants accounted for
an even higher 46 percent, and, overall, those who financed four
voyages or more accounted for 69 percent of the total shipping
involved in the trade but only 28 percent of the total number of
merchants. This extraordinarily high concentration of wealth in
the slave trade was unusual even by the standards of the day.

Table 8.14
Distribution of Voyages, Ships, and Tonnage by
Nantes Merchants in the 18th Century[a]

No. of Shipments	No. of Merchants	No. of Ships	Total Tonnage
1	189	189	36,714
2	40	80	14,834
3	31	93	22,058
4	35	140	27,889
5	13	65	14,821
6	6	36	5,970
7	10	70	15,631
8	9	72	15,067
9	5	45	10,511
10	6	60	15,115
11	3	33	10,228
12	1	12	2,330
13	3	39	9,595
14	2	28	5,120
15	1	15	2,410
20	1	20	4,741
21	1	21	4,464
23	1	23	3,050
28	1	28	6,115
29	1	29	5,870
30	1	30	5,930
48	1	48	10,315
TOTALS	*361*	*1,176*	*248,778*

[a]All ships with unknown tonnage were excluded from the calculations.

Source: Rinchon, *Le trafic negrier*, pp. 248-302, 325-339.

In 1725 the government compiled a list of the fortunes of the merchants of Nantes. The top 5 percent of the merchant families controlled only 22 percent of the total merchant wealth of the town, while the top 10 percent of the merchants controlled less than 36 percent.[52]

These very high concentration figures for the French slave traders are similar to those found for the British and Portuguese trades and reinforce the general impression that the high costs of the slave trade created high rates of merchant concentration. While the incidence of single voyage owners (some 52 percent of all owners) indicates that many merchants entered the

[52] Meyer, *L'armement nantais*, pp. 257-261. In this elite of the merchant class were numerous slave traders.

competition for the wealth in black slaves, few were able to sustain a major effort and those few controlled the trade. This concentration, as revealed in the naval recordings, is primarily due to the extremely high costs involved in outfitting a slave vessel and providing the credit needed by the American planters to purchase the slaves that the traders were selling.

The high costs of entrance into the trade were clearly evident in the funds needed to outfit a slave ship. A slave ship cost, on average, three times as much to outfit as a ship in the direct West Indian trade (see table 8.15). This comparative difference in cost

Table 8.15
Comparative Value of an Outfitted Vessel per Ton of
Nantes Ships Engaged in the *Droiture* and Slave Trades, 1763-1777
(in *livres*)

Period	DROITURE		SLAVE TRADE	
	Ships	Value per Ton	Ships	Value per Ton
1763-1771	5	163	29	938
1772-1777	23	160	14	1,050
TOTALS	28	161	43	977
Av. value per ship	64,987		194,625	

Source: Meyer, *L'armement nantais*, pp. 299-301.

was not due primarily to the ships themselves, which were quite comparable in price between the West Indian and slave trades,[53] but to the comparative difference in the costs of the cargo. To outfit a slaver, the cargo accounted for two-thirds of the total costs, and the ship and its equipment a mere one third.[54] Given the relatively cheap costs of the small cargoes being taken to the West Indies, their total impact on the final outfitting (*mise-hors*) costs was only about one third of the total. This explains why the average value of the outfitted slaver per ton was six times the average value per ton of the much larger direct trade ships.

[53] In an evaluation of the ships captured by the English in the Seven Years War, 8 ships in the *droiture* trade were worth 144 livres per ton, compared to 137 livres per ton for the 9 slave ships captured during this same period of 1755-1766. (See Meyer *L'armement nantais*, pp. 380-81.)

[54] There was some variation depending on whether or not the ship was newly built, but, in general, the cargo costs were between 55-65 percent of the total outfitting expenses. (*Ibid.*, pp. 161-163.)

Another high cost factor, of course, was the need to provide loans to the planters in order to enable them to pay for their slaves. Few planters ever paid full cash value on a slave. The common pattern was for a down payment plus promissory notes to pay at given intervals. On average, a consignment of slaves might not be fully paid off for six years, which meant that the slave trade merchant had to have extensive resources to maintain his business enterprise.[55]

These high cost factors encouraged concentration of capital in the slave trade and led to the predominance of merchants who controlled several ships. Given the nature of the trade, multiple-ship ownership offered special advantages over a single-ship ownership. Van Alstein, the Nantes slave captain, for example, records how that advantage operated when he worked for the gigantic firm of Guillaume Grou, which outfitted some 43 vessels between 1748 and 1765.[56] So frequent and coordinated were the sailings of Grou's fleet that he could use his captains in a cooperative purchasing effort. Thus, when Van Alstein first arrived on the coast in his ship *Télémaque*, he was immediately required to sell most of his first week's purchases of slaves to the captain of Grou's ship *Mentor*, so that the latter could quickly terminate his purchases on the coast and leave with a full complement of slaves.[57] Also, this captain was probably able to inform Van Alstein of the latest trading news, while Van Alstein could equally give him the latest West Indian market information. Finally, the sequential movement of his ships allowed Grou a constant flow of cash, which enabled him to continue in full operation the year round, rather than having to suspend most of his activities until the return of his one ship, as would have been necessary for a single vessel owner.[58] Given these advantages and the high costs

[55] Robert Stein, "The Profitability of the Nantes Slave Trade, 1783-1792," *Journal of Economic History*, xxxv, No. 4 (December, 1975), pp. 779-793. Apparently, the period in which the debts were paid off was shorter in the British trade, being about two years at the end of the 18th century. (Roger Anstey, "The Volume and Profitability of the British Slave Trade, 1761-1807," in Stanley L. Engerman and Eugene Genovese, eds., *Race and Slavery in the Western Hemisphere: Quantitative Studies* [Princeton, 1975], p. 16.)

[56] Rinchon, *Van Alstein*, p. 137.   [57] *Ibid.*, pp. 108-109.

[58] This meant that the multiple-ship slave trader had the advantage of being able to stagger his income and obviate the need to obtain high interest loans to reenter the trade when his ships returned, which on average took between 12 and 18 months to complete the triangle voyage (the aver-

of admission, it is therefore no surprise that the trade was a highly concentrated one in terms of the number of merchants who accounted for the majority of the trade.

In reviewing the findings of the Nantes materials in comparison with the preceding studies of the Portuguese and English trades, we note certain basic features to be evident. The manner of carrying slaves, the tonnage of the ships involved, and the mortality experience of the slaves and crew all seem to conform to the same norm of behavior. The nature of the slave trade was such that, despite nationality, regional trading pattern differences, and relative control over African and American markets, there was a basically similar trading experience for all of Europe's major slave traders. All the trades averaged approximately the same tonnage; and all, up to the end of the 18th century, suffered approximately the same rates of mortality for the same reasons. There was the same significant negative correlation between slaves carried and tonnage, with the smaller vessels carrying higher rates of slaves per ton than the larger vessels. This same phenomenon was observed among the crewmen and their ratio of crew per ton to increasing tonnage. Equally, all trades, despite somewhat different manners of estimating tonnage, were carrying 1.5 to 2.5 slaves per ton and averaging at the height of their trades between 350 and 450 slaves per voyage, meaning that the average ships were in the 150-to-250 tonnage range.

Finally, while the French seem to have concentrated on fixed location trading, especially at Juda and on the Loango coast, they also engaged in boat trading, like the British in the Senegambia and Sierra Leone areas. Also like the English, they delivered primarily East Indian textiles, iron and finished metal products, alcohol (in this case brandy), and firearms as the basis of their trade for slaves, and in turn they purchased the bulk of their food supplies for the slaves in the Middle Passage from African sources, using as well the standard trade diet of rice and yams as the staple foodstuffs for the voyage.

The fortunes of war were to affect the French slave trade probably to a greater extent than even the Portuguese, the English, or

---

ages were 88 days for the outward trip from France, 154 trading days on the coast, 90 days sailing in the Middle Passage, 94 days unloading in the West Indies and taking on a return cargo, and 70 days sailing from the Caribbean to Nantes, for a total average of around 496 days or 16 months).

the Cuban traders. The closing of Atlantic commerce by the British, especially in the disastrous Seven Years War, combined with the crisis of the French Revolution, the collapse of Saint Domingue, and the blockade of the Napoleonic period, all destroyed the vital position of French slave merchants in their home markets. As will be seen from the free trade era in Cuba, it also prevented them from successfully competing in the international slave trade of other nations.

Chapter Nine

The Cuban Slave Trade in a Period of Transition, 1790-1843

The last trade to be analyzed is among the oldest and most varied to America—the African slave trade to Cuba. Originating in the earliest days of the settlement of the island in the 16th century, the movement of African slaves to Cuba lasted longer than any other major American slave trade and was not effectively terminated until the mid-1860s. During this 350-year period the trade underwent constant change, reflecting the fundamental shifts in the basis of the Cuban economy. It also experienced all the various phases of both a minor trade, like Virginia, as well as those of a major importing zone, like Rio de Janeiro, Saint Domingue, and Jamaica.

Until Cuba emerged as a major plantation export economy at the end of the 18th and the beginning of the 19th century, it was essentially a marginal economy within the American empire of Spain. In the first fifty years after the Spanish Conquest of 1511, placer gold mining was the primary industry, and the Amerindian population of Cuba and the surrounding islands was the prime source of labor. But the gold deposits were soon exhausted and the Amerindian population decimated, so that the economy drifted into a general cattle and mixed farming enterprise. It was only its choice location as a major entrepôt for New World shipping and a key defensive center in the Caribbean empire of Spain that revitalized the Cuban economy from the mid-17th to the 18th century.

The creation of a major garrison port at Havana and the use of the city as a provisioning site for outbound shipping provided the island's interior with important markets for its food. At the same time, the slow growth of a small freeholders tobacco economy and a thriving lumber industry added to the general economic growth of the island. Although African slaves were constantly brought to the island, the economy as a whole did not

209

produce a surplus sufficient to finance the major importation of slave labor, and the prime labor pool remained free persons of color and whites. Black slave laborers could be found everywhere on the island, but they were primarily concentrated in the large urban centers of Havana and Santiago de Cuba, employed either as skilled artisans or domestics. The only major use of slave labor outside these areas was in the construction and shipbuilding industries, which were kept busy especially in the 18th century, turning Havana into one of the key shipping and fortress centers of the New World.

Reflecting this essentially marginal economy—at least in terms of the European markets—was the type of slave trade going to the island. Throughout this period, Cuba was a minor market in the general Caribbean trade, receiving only part of its African slaves in direct shipments from Africa. An important part of its slave laborers were either *bozales* (recent African arrivals) coming from Africa via the other West Indian islands, or *ladino* (Christian or acculturated) slaves brought in small lots by general merchants who engaged in the slave trade only as a minor activity. Equally, this largely intra-Caribbean trade and even the minor Africa-to-Cuba slave trade was in the hands of foreign nationals. First the Flemish and Dutch in the 16th and early 17th centuries dominated the Cuban slave trade. They were followed by the French and English, with the Cubans and Spaniards playing only a minor role.

But the nature of this relatively small slave trade changed dramatically at the end of the 18th century. For at this point in time Cuba changed from a relatively mixed agrarian economy, with a minor export trade in tobacco and lumber, to one of the world's great plantation regions. The combined impact of Bourbon economic reforms and subsidization, along with the decline of the British islands and the destruction of Saint Domingue, led to the growth of a coffee and sugar export economy of major proportions. To further that growth, the government deliberately encouraged the expansion of the African slave trade to Cuba. Aside from providing tax incentives to Cuban planters and mill owners, the Bourbon monarchy finally ended the monopoly contract, or *asiento* system, and permitted unlimited free access of all foreign nationals into the Spanish American slave trade.[1]

[1] The standard surveys of the colonial economy are by Julio Le Riverend

The declaration of the principle of free trade in slaves in 1789 had its origins in the basic restructuring of the national and imperial economies of Spain. This originated with the Bourbon takeover of the Spanish crown at the beginning of the century. Starting in the decade of the 1740s, Madrid had progressively reduced the severe restrictions on internal imperial trade to the point of allowing total free trade within its empire by the 1780s.[2] But the Spanish government was still unsatisfied with the pace of colonial growth. It was especially interested in increasing the productive capacities of its hitherto neglected plantation centers and it decided actively to encourage these areas, to compete with the French and British plantation islands. Along with these general considerations, the Crown was also severely shaken by the temporary loss of Havana to the British in the early 1760s and was determined to strengthen the island militarily and economically.[3] The most obvious approach was to increase the supply and lower the cost of imported slave labor, and to do this meant that the trade had to be freed from restrictions. Thus the old *asiento* system, as well as the Spanish exclusionist policy, were replaced in February 1789 by the declaration of free trade in slaves.[4]

Brusone. See his *Los origenes de la economia cubana* (*1510-1600*) (Mexico, 1945); and *Historia economica de Cuba* (2nd. ed., Havana, 1965).

[2] On the reforms in imperial trade, see C. H. Haring, *The Spanish Empire in America* (New York, 1947), Chap. xvii. The very rapid growth of Cuban commerce, with all the newly opened Spanish ports at this time, is well illustrated in the statistics provided by Manuel Nunes Dias, "Le mouvement des 'navires de registre' entre La Havana et les ports d'Espagne à l'époque du 'commerce libre' (1787-1789)," *Revue d'histoire économique et sociale*, xlv (1967), 87-104.

[3] On the post-English reform developments in Cuba, see Ramiro Guerra y Sanchez *et al.*, *Historia de la nación cubana* (Havana, 1952), ii, 51ff., 235.

[4] Hubert H. S. Aimes, *A History of Slavery in Cuba, 1511-1868* (New York, 1907), Chap. ii; and James F. King, "Evolution of the Free Slave Trade Principle in Spanish Colonial Administration," *Hispanic American Historical Review*, xxii (1942), 34-56. This position was adopted after the unsuccessful attempts in the late 18th century to promote direct Spanish involvement in the *asiento*, attempts that demonstrated that the Spanish merchants were unable to successfully compete in the direct shipment of slaves. (For a detailed analysis of these unsuccessful "Spanish" *asientos*, see Bibiano Torres Ramirez, *La compañía gaditana de negros* [Sevilla, 1973]. On the pre-1715 history of the *asiento*, see the classic study by George Scelle, *Histoire politique de la traite négrier aux Indes de Castille* [2 vols.; Paris, 1906], and the recent works by Jorge Palacios Preciado, *La trata de negros por Cartegena de Indias* [Tunja, Colombia, 1973]; Enriqueta Vila Vilar, "Los asientos portugueses y el contrabando de negros," *Anuario*

The Free Slave Trade Law of 1789 was to prove a vital factor in aiding the massive entry of black slaves into the Cuban economy. It was also because of this law that the royal naval officials of the port of Havana began collecting the shipping statistics upon which the major portion of this survey of the Cuban slave trade is based. Beginning in late 1789, but especially in the early months of 1790, the Cuban port officials collected information on the age and sex of all slaves entering the port of Havana, as well as the names and nationalities of all ships engaging in the trade. Fortunately, the bulk of these monthly reports have been preserved in the Archivo General de Indias in Spain, and from this source we are able to glimpse both the pre-plantation development slave trade, as well as the full-scale massive trade that dominated the 19th century.

Before we analyze these slave trade figures, it is worth commenting on the pre-existent published statistics. The traditional source for the pre-1821 slave trade statistics come from Alexander von Humboldt. Since Humboldt seems to have had direct access to the same lists that were eventually forwarded to Spain and that now reside in the Archivo General de Indias, it is not surprising that the trends in the two lists are identical, with the difference of only a few hundred occurring in any given year. I would stress that where the AGI totals are less than Humboldt's, this is due invariably to missing months in the collection of port registers for that year. At the same time, when the numbers are slightly higher than Humboldt's this may be due to late additions in the registers sent to Spain that were not listed in the original Havana registers.

In attempting to discern a general trend in the thirty years of the slave trade revealed by these port registers, it is evident that the Cuban slave trade experienced almost constant growth from 1790 to 1820. Although the trade for the first five years began slowly, especially in relation to the exportation of sugar, by the period of world peace in 1800 to 1803, it moved into a period of growth even more rapid than that of sugar. This would suggest, discounting for the moment the crises of the Napoleonic Wars, that in the years prior to 1800 there was a slave labor sup-

---

de Estudios Americanos, xxx [1973]; and the forthcoming dissertation by the Peruvian German Peralta Riveira, "Les mécanismes du commerce esclavagiste [1595-1640]," [Paris: Ecole Pratique des Hautes Etudes].)

ply on the island that could be shifted into the expanding coffee and sugar plantations. But once the output of these plantation crops was expanding continuously, they produced a seemingly insatiable demand for slaves that was frustrated only by non-economic factors such as war and international diplomacy. That the foreign traders recognized the potentialities of this new market is indicated by the fact that all the major world slave-trading nations (except Portugal in these first years) almost immediately entered the Cuban slave market and rapidly began to expand their participation in the trade.

In analyzing the participation of these foreign and national merchants in the Cuban slave trade over time one of the salient features is the enormous impact non-economic and external factors had on the course of the trade. The impact of the Napoleonic Wars are evident in the history of the English and French participation in the Cuban slave trade. The disruption of their shipping because of war and its renewal in the short periods of peace are starkly revealed in the annual importation figures. Equally, the normal participation of even the neutral traders, who were immune to most of the fighting in Europe and America, was seriously affected by the British drive to abolish the Atlantic slave trade. The North American legal participation ends with the Constitutional prohibitions of 1808, while the Danish and English terminate their involvement just a few years prior to the end of the European wars.

Thus by 1808, and even sometime before, the Cuban slave trade became an almost exclusively Iberian trade, predominantly Spanish and with as yet a minor participation of the Portuguese. Also, it is evident that by the Peace of Amiens (1802) long-term structural changes had begun. At this time the trade can be considered to have become the modern 19th-century trade in terms of increased carrying capacities of slave ships. It was only the impact of the last stages of the European wars that prevented this trend from fully developing. Only from 1809, when Great Britain can be said to have effectively dominated the sea lanes, did this secular increase in average numbers of slaves carried appear again in response to normal market conditions.[5]

[5] The evidence for this trend is the increased volume of slave arrivals, accompanied by both a decrease in the number of ships (because of the increase in average number carried) and by a decrease in the ratio of slave ships to total shipping arriving in the port of Havana. Because of this in-

Table 9.1
Sugar Exports from the Port of Havana
and Estimates of Slave Arrivals, 1786-1823

Year	Sugar Exports (boxes of sugar)[a]	Slave Arrivals According to A. Humboldt
1786	63,274	
1787	61,245	
1788	69,221	
1789	69,125	
1790	77,896	2,534
1791	85,014	8,498
1792	72,854	8,528
1793	87,970	3,777
1794	103,629	4,164
1795	70,437	5,832
1796	120,374	5,711
1797	118,066	4,452
1798	134,872	2,001
1799	165,602	4,919
1800	142,097	4,145
1801	159,841	1,659
1802	204,404	13,832
1803	158,073	9,671
1804	193,955	8,923
1805	174,555	4,999
1806	156,510	4,395
1807	181,272	2,565
1808	125,875	1,607
1809	238,842	1,162
1810	186,672	6,672
1811	est. 206,487	6,349
1812	est. 206,487	6,081
1813	est. 206,487	4,770
1814	est. 206,487	4,321
1815	214,111	9,111
1816	200,487	17,737
1817	217,076	25,841
1818	207,378	19,902
1819	192,743	17,194
1820	215,593	15,147
1821	236,669	6,415
1822	261,795	
1823	300,211	

[a]One box (or *caja*) of sugar weighed 16 *arrobas*, or just over 183 kilos. Humboldt, *Ensayo politico*, p. 208, n. 2.

Source: For the sugar statistics and slave imports to 1819, see Alexander von Humboldt, *Ensayo politico sobre la isla de Cuba* (Havana, 1960 ed.), pp. 205-206. For the slave imports for 1820-1821, I have used Hubert H. S. Aimes, *A History of Slavery in Cuba* (New York, 1907), p. 269. I assume that in this listing Aimes accidentally reversed the figures for 1819 and 1820, since in all other respects his figures up to that date are identical to Humboldt. The archival data for the Havana slave trade will be found in AGI, Audiencia de Santo Domingo, legajo 2207.

Table 9.2

The Number of Africans Carried by Nationality of Slave Ships Arriving in Havana, 1790-1820

(number of ships in parentheses)

Quinquennium	Spain	U.S.A.	England	Denmark	France	Portugal	Total[a] All Nations
1790-1794	6,647 (120)	6,854 (155)	6,831 (78)	395 (6)	4,974 (32)	...	28,652 (419)
1795-1799	3,742 (48)	9,344 (291)	3,410 (17)	3,385 (82)	...	339 (2)	20,628 (444)
1800-1804	1,877 (27)	8,201 (216)	16,642 (91)	7,458 (91)	662 (5)	...	35,768 (442)
1805-1809	904 (6)	10,840 (187)	...	1,263 (12)	...	...	13,493 (209)
1810-1814	16,919 (96)	234 (4)	...	...	...	2,578 (12)	20,162 (119)
1815-1819	62,664 (241)	...	...	...	320 (1)	1,054 (5)	64,099 (248)
1820	372 (2)	...	...	...	...	...	536 (3)
TOTALS	93,125 (540)	35,473 (853)	26,883 (186)	12,501 (191)	5,956 (38)	3,971 (19)	183,338 (1884)
Av. slaves per ship	172	42	145	65	157	209	97
St. Dev.	134	56	146	65	145	105	116

[a] The final all nation total includes 57 ships carrying 5,429 slaves. Of these, 16 ships were unknown as to nationality and the rest came from 5 other nations, ranging from 20 ships belonging to Sweden, to 1 ship for the port of Bremen.

Source: AGI, Audiencia de Santo Domingo, legajo 2207.

Equally evident from an analysis of this general trade data is the changing participation of the different nations in the slave trade. Given the fact that the Cuban trade evolved from a complex intra-Caribbean as well as a direct African movement, to an almost exclusively African trade, it was inevitable that the major supplying nations would also change their participation in the trade. Thus in the shipping of Denmark, England, and Spain, there was a move from small shipments of African slaves to ever larger numbers carried as the trade moved into the first decade of the 19th century. There were, of course, nations like France and Portugal that from the beginnings of their participation in the trade seemed to have concentrated on large and apparently direct importations of slaves from Africa. At the opposite end of the spectrum were the North Americans, who from the earliest period until the end of their participation concentrated primarily on smaller shipments of slaves largely within the context of a general Caribbean and American commerce.[6]

The impression of the existence of these trends is re-enforced when we proceed to break down the participation of these nationals in terms of the number of slaves they carried per ship. Fully 70 percent of United States ships carried 50 slaves or less, as compared to only 5 percent for Portugal at the other extreme (see table 9.3). Given its relative inexperience in the slave trade, it is surprising to find that Spain had even fewer vessels in this 50-slaves-or-less category than did France, making it the second

creased trade accompanying the growth of plantation crop exports, slave ships declined from a high of 28 percent (out of 427 ship arrivals—though the 86 foreign slavers accounted for 89 percent of all incoming foreign shipping, as opposed to 10 percent of the incoming Spaniards being slavers—in 1792, to a low of 4 percent in 1816 (out of 1,114 arrivals, of which slavers made up 2 percent of entering foreigners and 6 percent of entering Spanish vessels). (The general Havana shipping statistics are contained in AGI, Audiencia de Santo Domingo, *legajo*, 1835, "Estado en que se manifiesta el numero de embarcaciones mercantes nacionales e extrangeros . . . que han entrado en el Puerto de Havana desde el año 1788 hasta el proximo pasado de 1815 . . ." [1816].)

[6] Much of my previous findings on the intra-Caribbean trade are summarized in Herbert S. Klein, "Slaves and Shipping in 18th Century Virginia," *Journal of Interdisciplinary History*, vol. 3 (Winter, 1975), pp. 383-411, and "North American Competition and the Characteristics of the African Slave Trade to Cuba, 1790-1794," *William and Mary Quarterly*, 3rd Series, xxviii, no. 1 (Jan. 1970).

highest in overall numbers carried. Prior to 1809, however, its average number of slaves carried per voyage was quite low and its interest in its own national trade was still relatively limited. After 1809, this changed greatly, and Spain achieved both major participation in the trade and became oriented primarily toward African shipments.

In equating large numbers carried with primarily African shipments and small numbers carried with an intra-Caribbean trade, I am making several assumptions. The first is that the shipping used in both these routes was quite similar and could have been used to bring in larger or smaller numbers of slaves, as the case might be. In analyzing the ships involved in the slave trade to Havana between 1790 and 1820, it appears that only four types of vessels predominated: the brig (*bergantin*), the sloop (*balandra*), the schooner (*goleta*), and the frigate (*fragata*). Together these ships accounted for 97 percent of the total shipping involved. Each of these types of ships can be found participating in all trades, carrying from the smallest to the largest number of slaves. Since these designations concern the number of masts, the design of sails, and the types of riggings, they can be, and often were, combined with quite different ranges of tonnage per vessel. In this particular period most brigs and frigates were concentrated in the African trade, with sloops most concerned with the intra-Caribbean route. But each of these types of vessels could be found in all routes. Thus the fact that fewer slaves were carried for a particular vessel had little to do with its carrying capacity, and was related more to the type of trade in which it was engaged.

Another part of the argument supporting the idea of distinctive routes within the slave trade to Cuba is the evidence of a limited sample of the trade in 1790, where, for the only time in these reports, the port of origin was given. It is apparent from this sample (see table 9.4) that there is strong evidence for all three routes, each clearly differentiated by the origins and average number of slaves carried per vessel. The example of Dominica, I would propose, strongly supports the idea of a mixed or intermediate trade, using either an island as an entrepôt, or of vessels coming directly from Africa with one stop at Dominica before proceeding on to Havana. Finally, all the current evidence from

Table 9.3

Number of Slave Ships by Number of Slaves Carried and Nationality

(percentage in parentheses)

No. of Africans Carried	NATIONS												Total All Nations	
	Spain		U.S.A.		England		Denmark		France		Portugal			
	n	%	n	%	n	%	n	%	n	%	n	%	n	%
01- 25	74	(14)	515	(60)	63	(34)	55	(29)	7	(18)	...		730	(39)
26- 50	30	(6)	88	(10)	22	(12)	48	(25)	4	(10)	1	(5)	201	(10)
51- 75	55	(11)	73	(9)	10	(5)	24	(13)	4	(10)	1	(5)	174	(9)
76-100	44	(8)	73	(9)	5	(3)	27	(14)	5	(13)	2	(10)	163	(9)
101-125	40	(7)	37	(4)	3	(2)	13	(7)	4	(10)	...		100	(5)
126-150	33	(6)	24	(3)	6	(3)	9	(5)	...		2	(10)	77	(4)
151-175	31	(6)	17	(2)	4	(2)	5	(3)	...		1	(5)	64	(3)
176-200	25	(5)	9	(1)	4	(2)	1	(...)	2	(5)	3	(16)	46	(2)
201-300	113	(21)	10	(1)	36	(19)	7	(4)	4	(10)	4	(21)	175	(9)
301-400	62	(12)	6	(1)	25	(13)	1	(...)a	5	(13)	4	(21)	105	(6)
401-800	32	(6)	1	(...)	8	(4)	1	(...)	3	(8)	1	(5)	48	(2)
801 & above	1	(...)	...		...		...		...		...		1	(...)
TOTALS	540	(100)	853	(100)	186	(100)	191	(100)	38	(100)	19	(100)	1,884	(100)

aDots within parentheses indicate that the figure is less than .01 percent.

Source: Same as table 9.2.

Table 9.4
Ports of Origin of Slave Vessels Arriving in Havana
between January and June of 1790

Port of Origin	No. of Slaves	No. of Ships[a]	Average No. of Slaves Carried per Ship
Guinea	2,015	8	251
Dominica	464	4	116[b]
Jamaica	247	10	24
(New) Providence	39 } 832	3 } 19	13 } 43
Charlestown	1	1	1
St. Eustatius	81	1	81
TOTALS	2,847	27	105

[a]As to types of vessels, in the trade to Guinea there were 5 frigates and 3 brigs. As for the intra-Caribbean trade there were 4 brigs, 9 sloops and 6 schooners.

[b]There is the possibility that Dominica here is operating as an entrepôt and shipping recently arrived African slaves to Cuba.

Source: AGI, Santo Domingo, leg. 2207, ''Estado que comprende el embarcaciones ...'' dated July 1, 1790.

the other trans-Atlantic slave trades in the 18th and 19th centuries shows few African-originated slavers carrying on average fewer than 200 slaves per voyage.[7]

While it is evident from the 1790 sample that there was a sharp differentiation between the intra-Caribbean and direct African trades, the overall Cuban statistics present a rather curious middle ground. That some 16 percent of the ships were bringing in between 100 and 199 slaves would seem to indicate that possibly a third variant route of the trade existed, that is, a type of mixed venture. Most likely these were ships that were arriving from Africa with the intention of supplying several island markets, or were inter-island traders specializing in transporting large numbers of slaves. The fact that 65 percent of these 293 middle-range ships (carrying between 100 and 199 slaves) arrived before 1809, when the trade was still open with the British and French islands, seems to support the thesis that these middle-rank ships were involved in some manner in supplying several islands. Either these were direct African shippers who supplied slaves to several

[7] As will be recalled, 18th-century Portuguese shippers from Angola were averaging 396 slaves per vessel; while shipments into Rio de Janeiro at the end of the century were reaching over 480 slaves per vessel.

islands at once, or, more likely, they were local traders who distributed the newly arrived African slaves from one entrepôt island to other Caribbean locations. Several of the British islands seem to have served this purpose, and in the 1790s even Jamaica reported intra-Caribbean shipping to Havana that sometimes carried over 100 slaves per voyage.[8] Whichever the actual pattern of operation (either directly arriving African slave ships or island entrepôts and the use of local shipping), I would argue that the "mixed trade" involved a predominantly newly arrived African slave contingent, as opposed to the exclusively intra-Caribbean trade, which handled predominantly seasoned and/or creole-born slaves.

Of the three broadly defined routes, clearly the direct African shippers (carrying over 200 slaves) predominated in the long run over both other types of shippers. This predominance might have occurred earlier had it not been for the war. For it was the African route that suffered most from the impact of the Atlantic battles. While the mixed trade route was also affected by the fortunes of war, the impact was less. As for the intra-Caribbean traders, these suffered the least from the European conflicts. Thus the early growth of the African trade, clearly revealed in the period of the Peace of Amiens, was stymied and it was not until after the Battle of Trafalgar, and especially after final peace in 1815, that the weight of the African route was fully felt.

Just as there seem to be important distinctions in the Cuban trade between routes and over time and by national participation, there is also a clear seasonal pattern that is evident in the arrival of slaves. This variation seems to be highly correlated with the sugar harvest, which runs from approximately January through June. In all three sectors of the trade (intra-Caribbean, "mixed," and direct African) the *tiempo muerto* (dead season) after the harvest, or approximately from the end of July through the end of December, is the time of fewest arrivals of slaves. Thus the very marked seasonality that has been noted in all the major Atlantic slave trades also occurs in the trade to Cuba. In these three different trade routes, there was the same response to planter preference for increased labor in harvest times.

While all three routes may have responded to planter demand

[8] See, e.g., the Feb.-March 1796 listings of Jamaican exports of slaves on British and Spanish vessels to Havana in PRO, Colonial Office 140/23.

Table 9.5
Number of Slave Ships Arriving in Havana
by Type of Route, 1790-1820

Year of Arrival	ROUTES		
	Caribbean (under 100 slaves carried)	Mixed (100-199)	African (over 200 slaves carried)
1790	47	5	6
1791	74	9	12
1792	89	19	10
1793	58	5	2
1794	71	9	3
1795	73	5	9
1796	79	10	4
1797	125	10	2
1798	48	4	...
1799	63	10	2
1800	43	2	...
1801	20	4	...
1802	100	24	28
1803	66	18	18
1804	88	15	16
1805	59	17	4
1806	35	12	3
1807	49	9	...
1808	10	4	...
1809	3	2	2
1810	10	15	13
1811	7	12	11
1812	9	7	6
1813	4	5	7
1814	6	4	3
1815	2	13	16
1816	7	18	49
1817	6	18	63
1818	5	8	37
1819	...	3	3
1820	1	1	1
Total ships	*1,257*	*297*	*330*
Av. slaves per ship	31	141	311
St. Dev.	29	30	93
Total slaves	38,653	41,981	102,704

Source: Same as table 9.2.

Table 9.6
The Number of Slaves and Slave Ships Arriving in Havana,
for Nine Years in Which All Months Were Complete
(no. of ships in parentheses)

| Months | ROUTES | | | Total |
	Caribbean	Mixed	African	
January	1,182 (44)	2,004 (15)	3,769 (12)	6,955 (71)
February	1,717 (51)	1,587 (11)	4,060 (13)	7,364 (75)
March	2,307 (68)	1,874 (12)	3,814 (13)	7,995 (93)
April	2,360 (67)	2,397 (16)	2,509 (9)	7,266 (92)
May	1,761 (53)	2,504 (16)	5,403 (16)	9,668 (85)
June	1,156 (37)	1,589 (10)	4,602 (17)	7,347 (64)
July	1,378 (54)	1,437 (10)	4,539 (16)	7,354 (80)
August	876 (37)	1,358 (10)	2,092 (7)	4,326 (54)
September	957 (40)	655 (5)	3,695 (12)	5,307 (57)
October	675 (31)	1,197 (9)	3,553 (11)	5,425 (51)
November	706 (30)	854 (6)	4,403 (15)	5,963 (51)
December	1,250 (44)	1,622 (12)	3,961 (14)	6,833 (70)
TOTALS	16,325 (556)	19,078 (132)	46,400 (155)	81,803 (843)
Av. slaves per ship	29	145	299	97
St. Dev.	28	30	77	113

Source: Same as table 9.2.

in a similar fashion, the age and sexual characteristics of the slaves they brought to Havana were not the same. In terms of the numbers of males present and the number of children, the African route, along with the mixed route, differs markedly from the Caribbean-originated slaves.[9] The fact that there was a larger number of children among the total of arriving female slaves as opposed to the total number of males, explains the similar trend exhibited by these two age and sex variables. In addition to the previous arguments advanced about the paucity of women in the trade, it may be that the very much lower incidence of their participation in the intra-Caribbean trade reflects West Indian planters refusal to export their small share of women.

When viewed over the course of the Spanish documented trade, the increasing number of children and of females reflects the increasing dominance of the direct African trade. In the case of

[9] The routes had the following age and sex breakdowns: the Caribbean was 72 percent male and 68 percent adult; the mixed trade was 70 percent male and 60 percent adult; and the African trade was 69 percent male and just 57 percent adult.

Table 9.7

Age and Sex Characteristics of the Africans Arriving in Havana, 1790-1820

Quinquennium	MALES			FEMALES		
	Adults[a]	Teens[b]	Youths[c]	Adults[a]	Teens[b]	Youths[c]
1790-1794	14,985	1,587	3,885	3,531	1,173	2,062
1795-1799	11,789	1,537	2,846	2,662	763	1,031
1800-1804	18,344	2,548	4,320	6,218	2,004	2,334
1805-1809	6,727	1,172	2,405	1,738	520	931
1810-1814	8,712	2,133	3,711	2,494	1,289	1,823
1815-1819	22,606	7,910	12,558	9,171	5,251	6,603
1820	69	127	73	57	105	105
TOTALS	83,232	17,014	29,798	25,871	11,105	14,889
No. of ships	1,809	1,228	1,296	1,250	945	1,002
Av. per ship	46	14	23	21	12	15
St. Dev.	54	19	27	23	14	14

[a]Adults were listed as *piezas*, meaning *piezas de indias*, which was the standard slave-trade term for adults of both sexes. Though the definition often changes, most authorities agree that it defined adults of ca. 18 years or above.

[b]Teenagers, or *mulecónes* (f. *mulécas*), were defined as being imported Negroes of from 11 to 17 years of age.

[c]Youths, or *muléques* (f. *mulecónas*), are defined as imported or *bozal* Negroes from ca. 7 to 10 years. For these rough definitions see: Constantino Suarez, *Vocabulario cubano* (Havana, 1921), p. 372; and Delfin Donadíu y Puignau, *Diccionario de la lengua castellana* ... (4 vols.; Barcelona, 1890-1895), III. Hubert Aimes defined these last two categories in slightly lower age groups, with *muleque* being 6 or 8 to 12 or 14 years, and *mulecón* from 12 or 14 to 17 or 18 years of age. Aimes, *History*, p. 47n.

Source: Same as table 9.2.

women, non-adults actually outnumber adults in the peak years of 1816 to 1818. Why there is increasing participation of persons under 18, and among them of persons in the youngest age categories, is a difficult problem to assess. It may be that for females, Africans were more willing to part with small children and pre-pubescent females, than with more important adults. Why this same phenomenon should occur with the males is difficult to determine. Clearly this was a new trend of major importance within the history of the Atlantic slave trade. In almost all 18th-century slave trades, children were a distinct minority, usually averaging less than 10 percent of the total slaves carried. The increasing incidence of children therefore reflects basic changes within the trade, most likely due to changes within the African trading zones. It would appear, given their similar costs of transportation and their lower selling prices in America, that children were always less desired by the slave traders than adults. The fact more children were being taken, therefore, may reflect inelasticities in the supply of adults, possibly due to the opening up of new slave trade zones that were reluctant to supply them, or else to continued slaving from areas that had a reduced potential supply of adults. At the same time, the arrival of so many children and women also had their impact on the native population, in terms of promoting a more rapid growth of the slave population and a more balanced sexual breakdown. In fact, large-scale immigration among the whites in the mid-19th century, combined with the changes in the age and sexual makeup of the mid-19th century arriving African slaves, may have been the cause for the unusual patterns exhibited in the census of 1861, which showed the black slave population to have a more balanced sexual division than the whites.[10]

The basic trends established in the Cuban slave trade by 1820 were closely followed in the post-1820 trade. While the post-1820 data currently available are based on the reports of British consuls in Cuba and are far less complete or as reliable as the previous Spanish recorded data, they nevertheless provide enough

[10] By the special slave census of 1857 there were 148 slave males per 100 females, and by the 1861 census the sex ratio for both slaves and whites was 144 males per 100 females. For the 1857 census see *AHN*, Sección de Ultramar, *legajo* 3533, *expediente* 167, no. 98. For the 1861 data see U.S., War Department, Office Director Census of Cuba, *Report on the Census of Cuba, 1899*, Washington, D.C., 1900, p. 81.

material to evaluate the general trends. What emerges from a study of the trade to all Cuban ports from 1819 to 1843 is that the Cuban domination of the trade remains intact and that the African route predominates. Up to 1835, in fact, Spanish flagships dominate the trade, and it has been estimated that over two-thirds of the arriving slave ships originated their expeditions to Africa in Cuban ports.[11] With the signing of the Anglo-Spanish slave treaty in June of 1835, however, it became illegal for Cubans to carry on the trade, and most slavers adopted the Portuguese nationality as a flag of convenience.[12] These restrictions had little other impact on the trade, for the late 1830s was one of the most intensive slaving periods in the 19th-century trade to Cuba.[13] Equally, despite prohibitions to the contrary, Cuban slavers seemed successfully to obtain their slaves from all the major regions along the African coast for most of the period after 1835.

While the number of vessels that sailed from unknown African ports is high, and the number of ships arriving of whose slaves there is no record is even greater, it appears that the known ships carrying slaves were representative of long-term trends. The only change would appear to be the progressive decline of slaves from the Bight of Biafra, which was compensated for by the much heavier participation of Angolan, Congo, and East African slaves in the period after 1835.[14] Aside from this change in direction, the numbers carried from each of the major regions confirms the trends established at the beginning of the century, with East Africa being consistently higher than all other regions, and with the Congo-Angola region coming in with its usual large number of slaves per voyage. What seems distinctive is the unusually high numbers of slaves per vessel that were coming from the ports of the Bight of Benin.

While active slaving continued in Cuba until 1867, available

[11] It would appear that Havana and Santiago de Cuba merchants were the primary financiers of this trade, and accounted for well over two-thirds of the voyages of the trade. (Personal communication of David Eltis, September 3, 1976.)

[12] Aimes, *A History of Slavery*, pp. 126-128; and Leslie Bethell, *The Abolition of the Brazilian Slave Trade* (Cambridge, 1970), pp. 103, 125-126.

[13] David Eltis, "The Direction and Fluctuation of the Transatlantic Slave Trade 1821-43: A Revision of the 1845 Parliamentary Paper," paper presented at the MSSB Conference, Colby, Maine, 1975, diagram 4.

[14] David Eltis, "The Export of Slaves from Africa 1821-43," unpublished ms., table 4.

Table 9.8

The Number of Slaves Arriving in All Cuban Ports, by Region of Origin, 1819-1843
(number of ships in parentheses)

Quinquennium	Guinea through Gold Coast	Bight of Benin	Bight of Biafra	Congo-Angola	East Africa	Total[a]
1819-1823	110 (2)	9 (1)	527 (4)	176 (1)	...	5,036 (22)
1824-1828	841 (6)	3,063 (9)	2,351 (12)	...	...	22,761 (81)
1829-1833	2,412 (11)	3,440 (9)	6,600 (26)	3,846 (10)	...	21,340 (68)
1834-1838	2,655 (9)	5,285 (17)	12,421 (40)	2,672 (10)	805 (2)	38,192 (126)
1839-1843	3,473 (12)	1,724 (6)	...	1,897 (6)	5,540 (9)	45,418 (122)
TOTALS	9,491 (40)	13,521 (42)	21,899 (82)	8,591 (27)	6,345 (11)	132,747 (419)
Av. slaves per ship	237	322	267	318	577	317
St. Dev.	133	131	134	125	183	158
Total of all ships landed including those unknown as to slaves	(114)	(81)	(109)	(51)	(18)	(1068)[b]

[a]This total includes all ships whose number of slaves carried was known, and thus includes a large portion unknown as to region of origin. This total, in turn, is only a small part of the 1,068 slave ships known to have landed in Cuba. This total includes 649 ships unknown as to the number of slaves they carried.

[b]This total includes 695 ships unknown as to region of origin.

Source: Great Britain, Parliamentary Papers, XLIX (1845), 74, "Slave Trade-Slave Vessels," report printed 25 Feb. 1845. I am indebted to Philip Curtin and David Eltis for providing me with their punched cards on this data. The original published list used by Curtin was modified by my own researches in the Brazilian newspapers, and by Eltis's re-analysis of the original PRO, Foreign Office files.

information on individual vessel arrivals go only to 1843. There-after reports by local British commissioners in Havana and Santiago seem to support the idea of a fluctuating trade that reached unprecedented lows in the late 1840s, only to revive again in the 1850s and 1860s to some 11,000 slaves per annum. It would appear that the trends established prior to 1843 continued, with probably a more important turn toward slaves in the Congo-Angola region, and even the use of a few steamships in 1859 and 1860.[15] It was only the outbreak of the Civil War in the United States that finally brought an effective end to the Cuban slave trade. But, even before its termination, planters had begun to shift into the importation of alternative sources of labor. In the 1830s there was the beginning of the indentured migration of Yucatan Indians and that of the Chinese coolies which began in the 1840s. By the 1870s some 124,000 Chinese had been brought to the island to cut cane along with free and slave blacks.[16] In turn, both the great social and political revolution that was known as the First Ten Years War (1868-1878), and the rise of the new sugar *centrales*, fostered the decline of slavery on the island itself. Thus when abolition finally occurred in the 1880s, there was only a small slave population on the island that made up a minority of the over half million Cubans who were blacks or mulattoes.

[15] D. R. Murray, "Statistics of the Slave Trade to Cuba, 1790-1867," *Journal of Latin American Studies*, vol. 3, no. 2 (1971), tables 4-7 and p. 148.
[16] Guerra y Sanchez, *Historia de la nación*, iv, pp. 189-195.

Chapter Ten

Conclusion

Having analyzed the movement of slaves in the trans-Atlantic crossing from the perspective of several centuries and many countries, I would like to conclude by detailing the major findings obtained from a study of the individual trades, and, secondarily, viewing the trade in its broader social and demographic influences upon the development of Atlantic society.

The first general conclusion to emerge from a study of all the individual trades is their surprising similarity. Despite the statements of some contemporaries and later historians, the manner of carrying slaves across the Atlantic seems to have been fairly similar across all European trades by the middle decades of the 18th century. All Europeans carried approximately the same number of slaves, in the same types of ships, and crossed the Atlantic in approximately the same amount of time. They also housed and fed their slave passengers in approximately the same way. Thus the many European Atlantic slave trades can be considered as one general European slave trade.

The cause for this uniformity has to do with the nature of the trade itself. The very ships that the Europeans used seem to have been very much determined by African needs and an optimal way of carrying slaves. The tonnage of English, French, and Portuguese slave ships that had been diverse in the period to 1700 became more uniform and approximated an optimal size in the 18th and 19th centuries. The norm in all trades was for ships in the middle-tonnage ranges. These ships were far from the largest in the world's commercial trades at the time, being far surpassed by both East and West Indian general cargo vessels. On average, most European slave ships were manned, by the standards of the other commercial trades, by unusually large crews. In all cases, this was related to the needs to control the slaves being transported, rather than to the size of the ships. While crew per ton and crew per slave ratios differed somewhat from trade to trade, the overall trends were the same in all trade routes.

All European traders also seem to have relied on the same African staples, above all rice and yams, to supply the basic diet for the slaves in the trans-Atlantic crossing. While the British may have introduced surgeons more rapidly than the other nations, there seems to be little to suggest that this had any measurable effect on mortality or the incidence of disease aboard ship. The general improvement in knowledge about diets and the use of crude vaccination seem to have pervaded all trades by the second half of the 18th century, a fact that may account for the uniform drop in mortality figures in the period from 1700 to 1830.

In looking more closely at the mortality data, there are several key developments which characterized this almost century and a half of trade activity (see graphs 1-4). The first is that throughout the entire period the majority of the ships were arriving with mortality below the mean mortality of the given period. At the same time, the frequency of high mortality on a minority of ships explains the high average mortality rates. This explains the large variance in the mortality figures. But if the 18th-century Nantes data are compared to the late-18th-century British and Portuguese and 19th-century Brazilian data, it is easy to see why the general mortality rates were coming down. First of all, far fewer ships were experiencing the high rates. Secondly, most ships were arriving with death rates among their slaves lower than the previous modal death rates. This combination of factors was systematically pushing down the mortality in all trades. The cause for this decline might be related to generally improved knowledge of health conditions, the general decline of epidemic diseases, or, conversely, the increasing immunity of African populations or improved economic conditions within Africa itself. At this point, it is still difficult to determine the answer.

What a study of slave mortality in all trades revealed is that, whatever the variations in mortality among slave ships, its cause was not directly related to the manner of carrying, or crowding, the slaves. Slaves clearly were tightly "packed" in the Middle Passage voyage. They had on average under half the amount of room afforded convicts, emigrants, or soldiers in the same period and they obviously had the most rudimentary sanitary facilities. That they were often subject to the worst of conditions during poor weather is obvious. Yet the number of slaves carried per ship and the mortality rates do not correlate in any significant

229

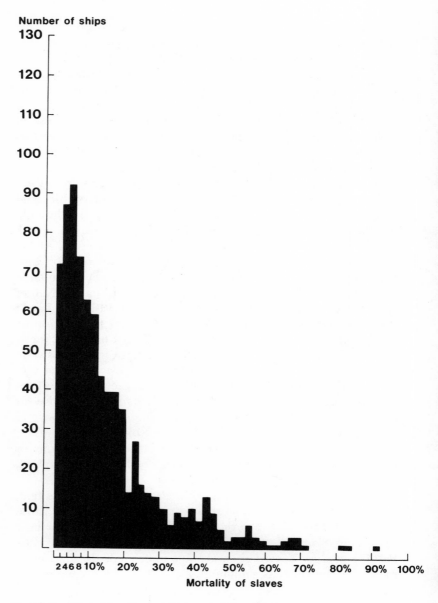

Graph 1. Slave Mortality on Nantes Slave Ships, 1711-1777.

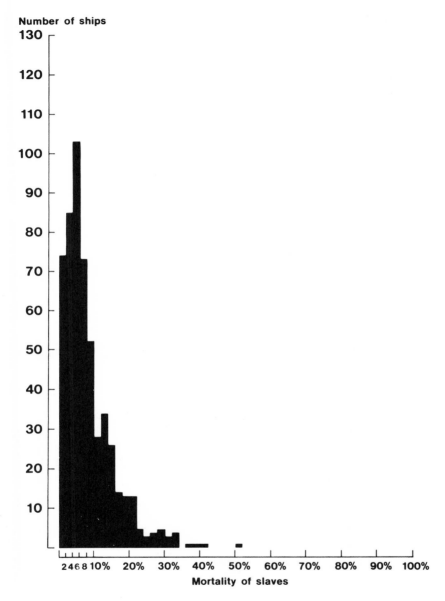

Graph 2. Slave Mortality on Ships Arriving in Rio de Janeiro, 1795-1819.

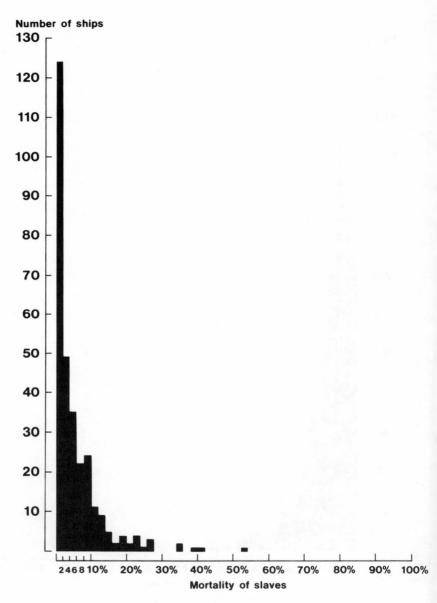

Graph 3. Slave Mortality on English Slave Ships, 1791-1799.

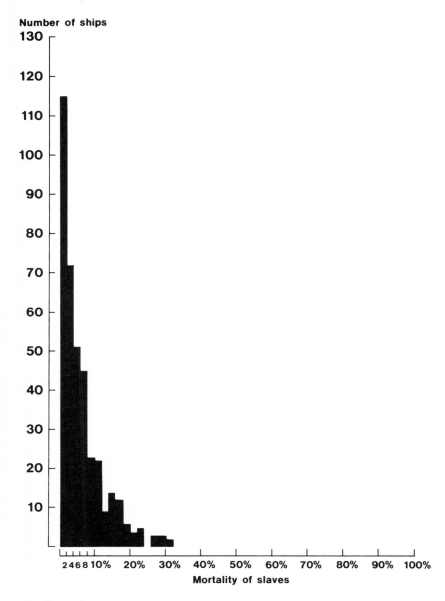

Graph 4. Slave Mortality on Ships Arriving in Rio de Janeiro, 1825-1830.

manner in any trade. Equally, in all trades, the larger the size of the ship as measured by its tonnage, the fewer slaves per ton were carried. Why this inverse relationship existed between tonnage and slaves and crew per ton can be related to any number of conditions. The most obvious explanation is that there were inherent space limitations due to the needs to carry adequate food and water supplies in order to achieve even minimal standards of safety for the length of the voyage. Or it might simply be that fear of higher mortality among the very-high-cost slaves prevented captains from fully carrying out a policy of crowding to the point of total disregard for life. The few data that are available on several trades suggest that slavers, especially on larger vessels, did not on average fill their ships to the capacity permitted them by a very generous law (at least prior to the British reforms of the 1780s).

But if it was not "tight-packing" that caused mortality to occur, then what factors did influence the incidence of slave deaths in the Middle Passage? In several trades there seems to be some positive correlation between time at sea and the number of slave deaths reported. This is most dramatically evident in the consistently higher death rates reported for East African shipping. It is also apparent when ships from West Africa tend to exceed their normal sailing times to the American coast.

Since dysentery was the major systematic killer that seemed to have affected almost all voyages, then it would appear that the average mortality experience was based on contamination of food and water supplies by infected persons and the spread of the infection to others using the same food and water. Captains' and surgeons' reports imply that these attacks of the "bloody flux," as contemporary British writers described the ameobic dysentery, seemed to come in cycles, with a number of slaves usually dying with each attack. Thus increasing exposure of the slaves to dysentery increased both the rates of contamination of supplies and the incidence of death. The really astronomic rates of mortality reached on the occasional voyage seem, however, to be related to outbreaks of smallpox, measles, or other highly communicable diseases that were not particularly related either to time at sea or to the conditions of food and water supply or to hygiene and sanitation practices.

Aside from the factor of time at sea, which seems to be related in important ways to both dysentery and the quality of food and supplies of water, the findings in the various trades also showed some important regional differences in mortality along the Western African coast. They suggest that local African disease and food-supply conditions also affected mortality on the outgoing slave-trade vessels. In the late 18th and early 19th centuries, for example, the ports of Luanda and Ambriz consistently had double the mortality rates of ports only a few hundred miles to the north (Malembo, Cabinda, and Rio Zaire) of them. Yet sailing times for all these ports were virtually identical, with the average sailings to Brazil from all ports being between 31 and 34 days. Within the context of the late-18th-century British trade, there is also the unusually higher mortality shown by slave ships leaving the Biafran coast, as opposed to the mortality experienced by other nearby regions. Was this regional mortality due to local disease or to food crises or to the impact of the wars and political collapse that might have led to such diseases or crises? Or was it related to such factors in the interior from which the specific group of slaves originated? It has been claimed that harvest failures in given years might have influenced the sharp year-to-year fluctuations in Angolan mortality rates, and this would seem to be a plausible line of reasoning.[1] Unfortunately, the detailed records needed to analyze such subsistence crises, or even such epidemic crises, are presently unavailable, and one can only conjecture why local regions showed marked differences in mortality.

While various local factors and general trade patterns can be discerned in the mortality experience of the Middle Passage, it should be stressed that a great deal of random influence seems to have been present at all times. Thus, while captains might expect a minimum or average mortality experience on an individual crossing, they also had the possibility of incurring a major mortality crisis. Aside from taking normal precautions of isolating the diseased and guaranteeing the hygiene and food consumption of all slaves, there was little that they seem to have been able to accomplish in keeping mortality low. That individual slave captains' trading experience or "humanity" was not a determining factor in affecting mortality was seen in the diverse mortality

[1] Joseph C. Miller, "Legal Portuguese Slaving from Angola, Some Preliminary Indications of Volume and Direction," *Revue française d'Histoire d'Outre-Mer*, LXII, nos. 226-227 (1975), pp. 156ff.

experience of the multiple-voyage captains in the 18th-century trade from Nantes.

Finally, there is the question of the comparative mortality experience of slaves and other seaborne migrating populations of the 18th and 19th centuries. Though immigrants, convicts, and soldiers were far less crowded aboard ship than slaves, they all experienced approximately the same rates of mortality in the 18th century. Yet in the 19th century it seems that the rates for all the non-slave migrating groups declined faster and reached much lower levels than those experienced by the slaves. Why this should be the case remains a puzzle, especially given the nature of the non-slave groups, most of whom had populations more at risk to death than did the slaves. Does this mean that there was a basic minimum mortality which could not be reduced in the slave trade even despite the introduction of steamships in the last years of the Cuban and Brazilian trades? Did Africans in general have poorer health than European peasants or convicts? Were they more disoriented and more subject to shipboard diseases? Or did the continued crowding of slaves aboard ships create a minimum environment for disease which no amount of speed or better foods could overcome? These are just a few of the intriguing questions raised by the findings from a comparative study of the Atlantic migrations, which can be resolved only by more detailed research into all of these movements.

In this entire discussion of slave mortality, it should be stressed that I have been concerned only with the trans-Atlantic mortality encountered in the normal operations of the shipping. I have not dealt with the high mortality caused by shipwrecks, sinkings, the suppression of numerous slave revolts, or the killing of slaves caused by pirating attacks of Europeans intent on stealing the slaves and ships of other Europeans.[2] All of these developments,

[2] That these factors could dramatically increase overall mortality in the Middle Passage is quite evident from the Dutch and French trades. Thus, Johannes Postma ("Mortality in the Dutch Slave Trade, 1675-1795," paper presented at the MSSB Conference on the Atlantic Slave Trade, Waterville, Maine, 1975) found numerous instances of slave rebellions and shipwrecks in which all slaves were lost. In the French slave trade from Nantes in the 18th century in the periods 1749 to 1755, 1763 to 1766, 10 slave ships were taken by slaves who revolted and seized the ships—the loss of life being unknown. There were also several sinkings of ships in bad weather in which slaves died. (Jean Meyer, *L'armement nantais dans la deuxième moitié du XVIIIe siècle* [Paris, 1969], p. 116.) Slaves also lost their lives in numerous small unsuccessful shipboard revolts.

as well as 19th-century attempts to avoid capture by British naval vessels, added to the overall Middle Passage mortality.

Another question is raised by the mortality experience of the slaves after landing, which includes deaths prior to sale that has been rather crudely described in the contemporary literature as "seasoning." Both in Africa and America, captured Africans experienced constant exposure to new disease environments that led to increased mortality. For example, the forced migration to coastal areas was often a severe shock to interior or highland peoples. Equally, the rather long cruising times along the West African coasts of the English and French traders created difficult health conditions, and, finally, the exposure of Africans to new American diseases after their landing in America created new mortality patterns. Here, as in the earlier arguments, we are faced by a host of conflicting estimates of total mortality, with traditional authorities estimating a loss of 50 percent for the entire movement of Africans from Africa to the plantations of America.[3] Recently, Curtin has speculated that Africans probably suffered higher mortality rates within Africa as they moved from one disease environment to another, than they did once they reached the coast itself.[4] This speculation is based on the experience of African troops serving in Africa and America in the 18th and 19th centuries. However, the sources on the trade itself have not been sufficiently analyzed with these problems in mind. Studies of ships' logs for the experience of the traders as they sailed along the African coast, of Monopoly Company records of local African health conditions and mortality experiences, and, finally, systematic exploitation of the parish birth, marriage, and death registers of the plantation regimes can still yield valuable quantitative data by which to determine the various disease environments and their impact on the migrating African slaves.

As should be obvious to the reader by now, the question of the mortality in the Atlantic slave trade has only just begun to

[3] The 50 percent estimate comes from Daniel P. Mannix and Malcolm Cowley, *Black Cargoes. A History of the Atlantic Slave Trade, 1518-1865* (New York, 1962), p. 123. While Walter Rodney offers no concrete estimates of his own, he argues that the overall mortality for the entire trade makes Curtin's estimate of 9-10 million persons far too small. (Walter Rodney, *How Europe Underdeveloped Africa* [London and Dar es Salaam, 1972], pp. 104-105.)

[4] Philip D. Curtin, "Epidemiology and the Slave Trade," *Political Science Quarterly*, Vol. 83 (1968), pp. 201-211.

be systematically analyzed. Determining the incidence of the Middle Passage mortality still leaves unanswered the actual causal factors that most influenced that mortality, especially as the traditional uni-causal "tight-packing" argument is held to be invalid. Equally, the Middle Passage death rates, and their relationship to the mortality experience of the Africans in the pre- and post-passage period of the trade, are still not understood or even systematically evaluated. It will require coordinated research efforts of African and American historians to link the three major sectors of the mortality experience together in order to explain the impact of the forced migration on the African populations and their Afro-American descendents.

Along with the Middle Passage mortality experience, the study of the naval registers and port listings in America and Africa record in graphic detail the variations in the volume of the African migration in terms of both space and time. Certain basic trends are apparent in the trade (as Curtin indicated in his pioneering study) that are reinforced from my analysis of alternative data. In the 17th and 18th centuries, the Upper Guinea and Gold Coast were the primary African slave-trade regions, soon followed in the 18th century by a heavy movement east and southward toward the Benin and Biafra areas as well as toward the Loango and Angolan coasts. Only in the late 18th century does the Southeast African coast become a major trans-Atlantic source of slaves.

One curious feature that appears in the French, Portuguese, and English trades in relation to regional variations in African supplies of slaves is the consistently higher number of slaves per ship carried off the Loango and Angolan coast. Along these coasts the French and others sent slightly higher tonnage ships that carried slightly higher numbers of slaves per ton, which led to a combined higher average number of slaves per ship being taken off these coasts. Also, once the East African coastal ports were brought fully into operation very late in the 18th century, then the tonnage, slave-per-ton ratios, and average number of slaves carried per ship were also significantly higher than in all the previous trades. Why these differences in volume and average numbers carried occurred in Angola and Mozambique is difficult to explain. However, it seems most probably related to the ability of captains to get larger numbers of slaves in the more controlled Southern African situation, than in the regions of West Africa.

Along with regional variations in the mortality and volume of the slaves forced to migrate from Africa, there is also discernible in the Atlantic slave trade a seasonal variation in the transportation of slaves from almost all the major African regions. This appears to be related to American crop conditions. The variations of the harvesting cycles from Brazil to the United States, are thus reflected in differing seasonal migrations from different regions. For the West Indies, the key importing season was January through June, while in Brazil the seasonal harvesting period was more extensive because of favorable soil and climate conditions. The temperate climates of North America presented a third harvesting season differing from the other two. This close association between American harvesting and African arrivals was based mostly on increased volume of shipping, for no trade showed any serious seasonal variation in slaves-per-ton ratios or the average number of slaves carried per ship. Nor did most trades show a significant correlation between mortality and seasonality, which might have explained the reluctance of captains to move their slaves during certain periods of time. While wind and current conditions did make for sailing-time modifications, there was no significant correlation, where the data were available, between seasonality and time in the trades indicating that this was not a consistent and major factor over most trades during long periods of time. But the availability of funds, the desire for immediate use of African labor, and the desire for return colonial produce cargoes seem to have been the dominating consideration that made slave deliveries more desirable during given time periods.

This general picture of how American demand factors influenced seasonal migrations should be modified somewhat for some of the African trades. There were obviously severe sailing restrictions imposed on ships sailing from East Africa that were highly correlated with season and were more influential than American requirements. The fact that slaves arrived during all months also strongly suggests that there were supply constraints on the slave traders that forced them to transport slaves even in periods when planter demand might be low. Finally, while in most trades no significant correlation could be discerned between mortality and season, this was not the case for the slave recordings for Rio de Janeiro in the 1795-1811 period. That higher mortality occurred in the low-volume periods may be coincidental, but it does suggest that sailing conditions and African climate and economic conditions may also have been influential in sailing patterns. Thus, while the main thrust of the documentary material seems to suggest the primacy of the American demand factors, the complexities of the trade also mean that other factors played their part in determining the movement of people from Africa.

Among the most important characteristics of the slave trade determined by African conditions were the sexual and age composition of the migrating slaves, as well as their ultimate origin. As we have noted in all the trades, there was a consistent predominance of males and adults over women and children. This confirms long-held beliefs by contemporaries and later historians, though the particular ratios of adults and males seems to have changed both over time and between various regions along the African coast. Initially, it was assumed that planters preferred working adult males for immediate field-hand labor, and thus it was demand factors that determined the preponderant role of males. But in analyzing both work practices and relative prices, it appears that this was not the case. Female Africans were used in the same manual and field occupations as males. Only excluded from skilled occupations, they formed a group co-equal to the men in all the basic agricultural field activities such as sowing, weeding, cultivating, and harvesting. This was reflected in quite similar price patterns for both sexes. If the skilled artisans are excluded, it appears that the price differentials between the sexes was of a relatively smaller magnitude than previously believed, thus suggesting that the relative demand for male as opposed to female slaves was not as sharply drawn as frequently implied.[5] Moreover, while European prices offered for slaves on the African coast may have differed somewhat, here

[5] Fogel and Engerman have estimated that up to the age of 18, female slaves in the U.S. earned more than males, after which their earning capacity fell by 20 percent to eventually 40 percent at the end of their working careers. Sale prices closely paralleled this earnings picture, with females matching slave males in price until 18 years of age, and costing around 20 percent less than males in the 18 to 35 age period. This relative price differential is not sufficient to explain the dominance of around 70 percent to 75 percent males in most of the Atlantic slave trades. (See Robert Fogel and Stanley Engerman, *Time on the Cross, The Economics of American Negro Slavery* [Boston, 1974], I, 75-77). If anything, this price differential is even less in the British West Indies, where 18th-century slave prices showed even higher relative prices for women. (Stanley L. Engerman, "Some Economic and Demographic Comparisons of the U.S. and British West Indian Slavery," *Economic History Review*, XXXIX, no. 2 [1976], pp. 258-275).

again the differences were insufficient to explain the flow of females. Moreover, in his recent study of the Senegambia trade, Curtin found that, on the coast, a standard price was being applied equally to males and females under the age of 30 by the 17th century, while interior African prices differed markedly by sex, with females being much more highly valued.[6]

Thus, American planter prices and European slave trader prices do not indicate any significantly discriminatory attitudes regarding the use of women slaves. If this was the case, then it is important to take into account fully the supply factors that influenced the differential entrance of sexes into the Atlantic slave trade.

° Here we are forced to return to an analysis of the impact of the African slave trade on African society, an extremely debated subject. If it is true, as Curtin and others have claimed, that there was also a market for slave labor within Africa itself, then it might be argued that only the least indispensable slaves were forced to migrate to the New World.[7] Since African slavery was quite dissimilar from the American chattel plantation variety, its demands for slaves were quite distinct as well. In some African societies, women were highly valued as slaves because they were the cheapest way to acquire status, kinship, and family. One of the distinguishing characteristics of Western African societies within the context of world cultures was their heavy concentration on matrilineal and matrilocal kinship systems. Since females were thus significant links in the kinship networks, their importance in the social system might have been enhanced. But even more important was the widespread Western African practice of using women exclusively for agricultural labor. Even slave captains, when asked the reason for the failure of women to appear in the slave markets as frequently as men, pointed to their vital

[6] Philip D. Curtin, *Economic Change in Pre-Colonial Africa: Senegambia in the Era of the Slave Trade* (2 vols.; Madison, 1974), I, 175-176.

[7] There is a considerable debate on the origins and development of internal African slavery at the time of the Atlantic slave trade. It has been argued that the intensity, if not the existence itself, of African slavery was intimately related to the growth of the Atlantic slave trade. Since slavery seems to have been closely related to highly stratified societies, and since these societies received their impetus for growth from the trade, then, it is argued, it was the Atlantic trade that fostered African slavery. (See Kwame Yeboa Daaku, *Trade and Politics on the Gold Coast, 1600 to 1720* [Oxford, 1970], pp. 28-32.) It has also been proposed that slavery was economically rational within the African context because of the existence of a labor shortage throughout West Africa even in the period prior to the Atlantic trade. (A. G. Hopkins, *An Economic History of West Africa* [London, 1973], pp. 23-27.)

role in local African agriculture as the primary cause. Thus, for both economic and cultural reasons, it would appear that there was a strong incentive in a large number of the Western African societies to stress the retention of women.[8] This meant not only in raiding, but also in those situations where local communities were forced to tax themselves in slaves for overlord groups. Whatever the specific causes, however, the systematic bias against removing women is clearly evident and the basic similarity in price and earning structure of New World male and female slaves is suggestive evidence for the view that African societies themselves did have significant control over who entered the slave trade, and that this control was not desired or particularly appreciated by the white American planters.

Whereas there is a disproportionate number of females in the 18th- and early-19th-century slave shipping lists, so too the number of children is quite small. In the Dutch, Portuguese, British, and Spanish trades, for which the records are most complete, the number of children is usually less than 10 percent of the total shipped.[9] Why this was the case also leads to numerous hypotheses that need to be tested. I myself had first assumed that this low incidence of children under 10 was due to their greater susceptibility to death in the Middle Passage. But it became evident that in most trades there was no significant difference between adult and child mortality. Given this, I would presume that the costs of transporting children were as high as adults, and since

[8] Simon and Phoebe Ottenberg, *Cultures and Societies of Africa* (New York, 1960), p. 30.

[9] In slave ships sailing from Benguela between 1738 and 1784, children under 10 years of age accounted for only 3 percent of the slaves shipped, while the figure from Luanda in 1734 to 1769 was 6 percent. For the Dutch slave trade in the 1681-1751 period the percentage of children under 15 was only 8 percent (Johannes Postma, "The Dutch Participation in the African Slave Trade: Slaving on the Guinea Coast, 1675-1795" [Ph.D. dissertation, Department of History, Michigan State University, 1970], pp. 177-178); while in the Danish slave trade in the late 18th century, adolescents together with children averaged 21 percent. (Sv. E. Green-Pedersen, "The Scope and Structure of the Danish Negro Slave Trade," *Scandinavian Economic History Review*, XIX, no. 2 [1971], p. 178.) By the end of the 18th and the beginning of the 19th century, the figures for the number of children in the trade seemed to be on the increase. In the Cuban trade, children under around 10 years of age represented 24 percent in the late 18th century, but increased their total to 30 percent in the period from 1815 to 1818. The corresponding figures for adolescents together with children was 30 percent in the 1790s and up to 50 percent in the 1815-1818 period.

their sale prices were markedly different, they rendered their transportation less advantageous an economic undertaking. Also, their use within Africa may have led to higher internal prices than the Europeans were willing to offer. Only new studies on the costs of transportation and provisioning in the trade can begin to answer this question seriously. Equally, one small piece of disturbing evidence is the increase in the number of children in the longest running of the Atlantic slave trades, the Cuban trade. By the 1820s, the Cubans were increasing their intake of both women and children, though both groups were still less than the number of adult males. Why children were so rapidly increasing in numbers is difficult to assess. One could speculate, however, that if the entrance of women into the trade was related to conditions in Africa, then loss of control by African middlemen may have resulted in the opening up of more women to the trade. This in turn might be related to changing political and economic conditions in the given zones of supply. Equally, it could be related to the shift of supply sources themselves in the later trade, with the Spanish and Portuguese traders after 1808 turning much more to sub-equatorial sources in the Congo and Angola, where such preferences and inhibitions in the trade might not have existed. Finally, the increasing number of less-desired children, as well as women, might be related to increasing demands for male labor within Africa as Western Africa itself shifted toward commercial agricultural exports to Europe.

Just as determining the cause for the lessened participation of women and children in the forced African slave migrations across the Atlantic raises important questions about the nature of African society, the arrival of the heavily adult and male migrants to the New World had important consequences for the development of American society. The most significant fact that Curtin uncovered in his recent study of the overall trends and the volume of the Atlantic slave trade was the great disparity among regions between the number of Africans who were received in the Western Hemisphere and the number of their descendents who ultimately made up the populations of the American republics. If the approximately 10 million figure of Africans who arrived as slaves between 1444 and 1869 is accepted—and with some upward revisions this seems to be the case—then what was its impact on American demographic growth?

As Curtin has shown, the three largest zones of contemporary African settlement in the New World—Brazil, the West Indies, and the United States—did not receive an equal number of Africans. While Brazil and the West Indies each got a third of the Africans arriving in the New World, the United States received less than 5 percent of the total number. If this is the case, then how can one explain the impressive growth of the black population of the United States? Recent commentators on this subject initially assumed that better physical treatment of blacks in the United States was the prime cause of this difference.[10] But as demographers began to analyze the problem, they immediately realized that they were dealing with two essentially different population structures. The United States slave population was more or less a closed population by 1808, whereas both Cuba and even more so Brazil were to receive massive imports of African slaves well into the second half of the 19th century. Thus the Brazilian and Cuban populations were constantly facing the impact of migrant populations that were heavily adult and male. As well as migrant populations carrying different diseases, the fact that fewer women than men arrived, and that most of the women had already entered into their reproductive years prior to their arrival in America, seriously limited the number of children to total adults who would finally be born in the New World. Thus the crude growth rates of the slave populations recently signalled by Curtin prove, on further reflection, not only to have been due to conditions within the host countries but also to such factors as the relative length of time and intensity that the African slave trade operated in a given region.

That the heavy migration of Africans into a relatively small resident black population can have a negative impact on growth rates is becoming clear even from the example of the United States. Recent detailed studies of the Maryland black population have shown that the constant arrival of Africans in the 17th century kept slave populations of the region from maintaining themselves until after the first decade of the 18th century. Not until a major native-born black population had achieved enough of a density to compensate for the biased age and sex characteristics

[10] See, e.g., C. Vann Woodward, *American Counterpoint* (Boston, 1971), pp. 78-106.

of the incoming African slaves, could the black population of Maryland begin to show signs of natural growth.[11] This same early period of negative growth was also quite evident in the first decades of massive African migrations into South Carolina.[12] Thus even in the early development of the slave system of the United States, there is evident the same response to massive African migrations as would be experienced by Brazil and Cuba in the late 18th and 19th centuries.

But even when one can discount for the impact of the African immigrants, there is still the question of the comparative rates of differential growth of the native-born slave population. The growth of such a population is, by definition, the difference between the rate of fertility plus the rate of immigration, less the rates of mortality and migration (or in this case, emancipation). In the cases of Cuba and Brazil, the few commentators who have dealt with these issues of growth have virtually ignored the out-migration from the slave status, that is, the manumission of the slaves. Without dealing with this issue, no true rates of black population growth can be developed.[13] Taking both these factors into consideration considerably modifies estimates made of natural population decline among the Afro-American slave population in the New World. While recent studies have also raised issues about the relative impact of diet upon fecundability and the importance of rates of child spacing among the various creole slave

[11] See Russell R. Menard, "The Maryland Slave Populations, 1658 to 1730: A Demographic Profile of Blacks in Four Counties," *William & Mary Quarterly*, 3d. Series, xxxii, no. 1 (January, 1975), pp. 29-54; and Allan Kulikoff, "Tobacco and Slaves: Population, Economy and Society in Eighteenth Century Prince George's County Maryland" (Ph.D. dissertation, 1975), chapter iv.

[12] Peter H. Wood, *Black Majority: Negroes in Colonial South Carolina from 1670 through the Stono Rebellion* (New York, 1975), pp. 153ff.

[13] Both I and D. R. Murray independently commented on this failure to account for emancipation, invalidating Curtin's entire analysis of the decline of slave population in Cuba. See D. R. Murray, "Statistics of the Slave Trade to Cuba, 1790-1867," *Journal of Latin American Studies*, iii, no. 2 (1971), p. 137, and Herbert S. Klein, "North American Competition and the Characteristics of the African Slave Trade to Cuba, 1790 to 1794," *William & Mary Quarterly*, 3d. Series, xxviii, no. 1 (January, 1971), pp. 98ff. Curtin's analysis of the Cuban population model is contained in Philip D. Curtin, *The Atlantic Slave Trade, A Census* (Madison, 1969), p. 32. I have also tried systematically to estimate this out-migration for the Brazilian population in the 19th century, in "The Colored Freedmen in Brazilian Slave Society," *Journal of Social History*, iii, no. 1 (fall, 1969).

populations as still retaining an influence on fertility, and of work routines and climate affecting mortality, these issues in no way invalidate the impact of the demographic imbalance caused by the slave trade.[14]

But whatever the outcome of the various current analyses of natural growth rates of the native and African-born slave populations in America, it is evident that a careful consideration of both the in-and-out migration of these populations, as well as the age and sex of the incoming and outgoing populations, are of fundamental consideration. Moreover, even the most preliminary studies of all American plantation societies unqualifiedly show that traditional beliefs about the average life expectancy of arriving African slaves are simply incorrect. While the exposure to new diseases took a serious toll among the new arrivals, the notion that the average life expectancy of a newly arrived African slave was only seven years has been disproved. This traditional assumption, often repeated in the general histories of slavery in America, is inconsistent with the data available on African arrivals and resident slave populations. Slave populations in all the major plantation areas consistently exceed the total African arrivals in the preceding seven years, even discounting for native births.

Within Africa, the migration of the American-bound slaves also had an important impact on the demographic development of the continent. As some scholars have noted, the 10 to 20 million Africans forced to leave their homes probably kept the overall rates of continental population growth low, if it did not cause actual declines in the period of most active trade.[15] But considerations of global rates of growth leave aside very important questions as to the nature of local and regional rates of development, and the influence of new disease environments as a result

[14] See, e.g., Engerman, "Some Economic and Demographic Comparisons," *loc.cit.*; and Jack Eblen, "On the Natural Increase of Slave Populations: the Example of the Cuban Black Population, 1775-1900," in Stanley L. Engerman and Eugene Genovese, eds., *Race and Slavery in the Western Hemisphere, Quantitative Studies* (Princeton, 1975), pp. 211-248. A more detailed survey of many of these issues was presented in Herbert S. Klein and Stanley L. Engerman, "The Demographic Study of the American Slave Populations" (paper presented at the Third International Colloquium on Demographic History, Montreal, 1975).

[15] J. D. Fage, "Slavery and the Slave Trade in the Context of West African History," *Journal of African History* x, 3 (1969), pp. 398-400.

of the major migrations of populations. As many commentators have pointed out, it was Western Africa that suffered most heavily from the European slaving activities, while most of Eastern Africa was largely untouched by these activities. Certainly, the constant migrations of groups between different ecological and disease zones introduced local diseases over far wider areas than would have been the case without the Atlantic slave trade.[16]

These general considerations, however, still do not account for the unique developments in local regions. But here the current state of the material renders more detailed analysis extremely difficult. For, despite all the efforts to date, determining the specific origins of the African slave migrants to America is still a difficult task.[17] The naval lists and port registers on which this study is based are deficient in identifying the socio-cultural, political, and linguistic origins of the African slaves. European knowledge of the interior, except in the unique Portuguese case, was limited to a few hundred miles from the coast. Except when major wars disrupted traditional supplies and brought in very large numbers of individuals from a single known defeated military power, Europeans had only the roughest idea of the origins of the slaves they bought. Using general names to designate areas consisting of often quite different language and cultural groups, routinely giving African port designations to all slaves being shipped, and finally confusing the African names they did use, European and American records offer only very crude and very approximate ideas as to which people were subjected to forced migration to America. It was, in fact, only in the 19th century, when the British were trying to return illegally taken Africans to their original homelands or registering slaves for emancipation or apprenticeship reasons, that a systematic attempt was made by Europeans

[16] Curtin describes the tremendous decline of the once populous group of Tanda in the region of Senegambia, which seemed to have lost its relative isolation from most diseases, due to the passage of slave traders through their region. Thus, while few Tanda actually entered the Atlantic slave trade, the group as a whole was severely depopulated in the period of the trade. (Curtin, *Economic Change in Pre-Colonial Africa*, ɪ, 178.)

[17] Recently, in an innovative alliance of linguistic reconstruction and historical analysis, Philip D. Curtin and Jan Vansina ("Sources of the 19th Century Atlantic Slave Trade," *Journal of African History*, v [1969]) were able to survey the languages of Africans liberated from slave ships by the British and settled in Sierra Leone, and thus to determine the history of African participation in the mid-19th-century trade.

to identify the exact political and linguistic groups to which the Africans belonged.[18]

This search for origins, of course, is not only illuminating for African history, but is directly relevant to the cultural history of the Americas. Ever since the pioneering reconstruction efforts of Herskovits,[19] scholars have attempted to assess the originating culture of the African slaves and its impact in the host cultures in America.[20] But, aside from the very unique and intimate pattern of relationships developed between the Brazilian region of Bahia and the Bight of Benin in the 19th century, the diversity of ports and regions contributing to the African migration has obscured the participation of individual nations and made it extremely difficult to judge the weight of individual groups and cultures. Even when such origins can be determined, there still remains the problem of defining the final Afro-American creole culture that emerges. As Orlando Patterson noted in his study of Jamaican black culture, the earliest Akan-speaking immigrants

[18] A major unexploited source for 19th-century African identifications is the detailed slaves lists with their attendant African group identifications in the captured slave manifestos of slavers taken by the British Navy. (See, e.g., the lists of those ships brought to Brazil for confiscation and housed in the ANRJ, Codice 181, vol. 3.) Similar information can be found in the 19th-century slave registrations in the British West Indies. (See, e.g., PRO, C.O., T-71, for the Trinidad lists, which are extremely detailed on this account.)

[19] Melville J. Herskovits, *The Myth of The Negro Past* (New York, 1941).

[20] Linguistic insights have been used from the American perspective to determine the movements of populations and the preservation of cultures in the New World. An early attempt in this respect was the study of Lorenzo D. Turner, *Africanisms in the Gullah Dialect* (Chicago, 1949), which suffers somewhat from the imprecision of its historical reconstruction of the slave trade. One of the more innovative recent studies was done on Twi naming patterns among Jamaican slave children (see David de Camp, "African Day-Names in Jamaica," *Language*, Vol. 43, no. 1 [1967]). In a somewhat more speculative vein, it has been suggested that a more intensive study of Afro-American pidgin or creole languages, though probably derivative of a Portuguese pidgin that was the lingua franca on the African coast (see Frederic C. Cassidy, "Tracing the Pidgin element in Jamaican creole," in Dell Hymes, ed., *Pidginization and Creolization of Languages* [Cambridge, 1971], pp. 203-222; and J. L. Dillard, *Black English, its History and Usage in the United States* [New York, 1972], chapter iii), might yield insights into African origins. It is proposed that the "deep structure" of creole is African derived and that even the vocabulary can yield African origins, by stressing private vs. public vocabulary, the former being more African related. (See Mervyn C. Alleyene, "Acculturation and Cultural Matrix of Creolization," in D. Hymes, *Pidginization and Creolization*, p. 176.)

created the basic cultural norms to which all later non-Akan speaking peoples had to adjust, even though later migrants overwhelmingly outnumbered early arrivals.[21]

Along with the demographic and cultural impact of the trade on America and Africa, there has emerged considerable debate on the economic and political influence of the slave trade, especially for Africa and Europe. Since the days of the trade, for example, the relative importance of small-scale raiding, state-level warfare, taxation or judicial punishment as the primary source for slaves has been a much debated issue. How much of the warfare endemic to a rapidly changing political system was directly related to the need for slaves, and how much was due to internal African considerations? Even if most wars concerned only African interests, as seems to be the current consensus, there still remains the possibility that European slave demands fostered the development of distorted class and state structures that encouraged long-term political instability.[22]

The question of the relative terms of trade in the commercial relations between the Europeans and the Africans engaged in the Atlantic slave trade has also recently raised substantial debate. While it is becoming increasingly clear that this was a highly complex trade in which the African sellers were far from the stereotype of helpless peasants bought off with baubles and beads, there still remains the question about ultimate benefits and social costs.[23] If Africans successfully defended their immedi-

[21] H.O.L. Patterson, "Slavery, Acculturation and Social Change: The Jamaican Case," *British Journal of Sociology,* vol. 17 (1966), pp. 156-157.

[22] Among recent commentators on these questions are: Walter Rodney, *A History of the Upper Guinea Coast, 1545 to 1800* (Oxford, 1970), pp. 102ff; I. A. Akinjogbin, *Dahomey and Its Neighbors, 1708-1818* (Cambridge, 1970), pp. 202ff; and Marion D. de B. Kilson, "West African Society and the Atlantic Slave Trade, 1441-1865" and Basil Davison, "Slaves or Captives? Some Notes on Fantasy and Fact," in Nathan J. Huggins et al., eds., *Key Issues in the Afro-American Experience* (2 vols.; New York, 1971), I, pp. 39ff. Also see Curtin, *Economic Change in Pre-Colonial Africa,* chapter iv; and Hopkins, *An Economic History,* pp. 117ff.

[23] There have been a large number of recent studies attempting to determine the relative economic benefits of the trade. Aside from Curtin's work on Senegambia and the general survey of Hopkins, there are the studies by Henry A. Gemery and Jan S. Hogendorn, "The Atlantic Slave Trade: A Tentative Economic Model," *Journal of African History,* ix, no. 2 (1974), pp. 223-246; Robert Paul Thomas and Richard Nelson Bean, "The Fishers of Men: The Profits of the Slave Trade," *Journal of Economic History,*

ate economic interests in the trade, did the middlemen African states, elites, or merchants take disproportionate shares of the wealth, thereby further distorting the region's economic as well as political instability? Thus, while recent research has stressed the autonomy and power of Africans to control their own polities, societies, and economies despite the importance of the European slave trade, the long-term impact of the trade on African development in the pre-colonial era is still to be fully assessed.[24]

As for Europe itself, the relative influence of the slave trade remains as much debated today as when Eric Williams offered his controversial thesis three decades ago about the immediate interdependence of the African slave trade, West Indian plantation slavery, and the Industrial Revolution in England.[25] The extent of the wealth generated by the slaves in the West Indian sugar islands, and the amount of slave-trade capital available for reinvestment in British manufacturing, are some of the topics that have begun to be evaluated only recently. Nor will gross measures be sufficient to resolve some of these issues of influence. For example, the fact that European mass-scale manufactured products were often developed for the African trade, and that much of the East Asian textile trade was closely tied to the slave trade, must also be weighed in the complex calculations of social costs and benefits of the trade in terms of Europe's own development.[26]

---

xxxiv, no. 4 (December, 1974), pp. 885-914; and E. Philip LeVeen, "The African Supply Response" (unpublished paper).

[24] Rodney has also raised the issue, common in dependency theory, about the influence of cheap European manufactured imports negatively affecting the development of Africa's own industrial potential. Rodney, *How Europe Underdeveloped Africa*, chapter iv.

[25] Eric Williams, *Capitalism and Slavery* (Chapel Hill, 1944).

[26] On these various debates, see Richard B. Sheridan, "The Wealth of Jamaica in the Eighteenth Century," *Economic History Review*, 2d. Series, xviii, no. 2 (August, 1965), pp. 292-311; and R. P. Thomas, "The Sugar Colonies of the Old Empire: Profit or Loss for Great Britain," *ibid.*, xxi, no. 1 (April, 1968), pp. 30-45, and Sheridan's rejoinder in *ibid.* For a recent analysis of the state of the Williams thesis, see Stanley Engerman, "The Slave Trade and British Capital Formation in the Eighteenth Century: A Comment on the Williams Thesis," *Business History Review*, xlvi, no. 4 (1972), pp. 430-443; and Pierre Boulle, "Slave Trade, Commercial Organization and Industrial Growth in Eighteenth Century Nantes," *Revue française d'histoire d'outre-mer*, lix, no. 214 (1972), pp. 70-112, and his "Marchandise de traite et développement industriel dans la France et l'Angleterre du xviiie siecle," *ibid.*, lxii, nos. 226-227 (1975), pp. 309-330; and Engerman's comments on Boulle in *ibid.*

But, whatever the final outcome is in determining the ultimate social, economic, and political influences of the trade on African, American, and European societies, the whole effort of reconstruction of the Atlantic slave trade experience provides the basis for a history of a people's migration that many had thought was impossible. Though the individual African experience of surviving the forced migration and becoming a slave in America cannot be recaptured, the quantitative reconstruction of the mass migration of Africans to the shores of the New World helps to define the limits within which that experience took place.

Appendix Tables

Table A.1
Number and Origin of Slaves Entering Rio de Janeiro, 1731-1735

Origin	1731	1732	1733	1734	1735
Angola	3,250	2,493	3,720	6,023	4,909
Bahia	1,702	1,730	957	1,347	939
Benguela		446	665		
Biafra				92	86
Cabo Verde		16	227	69	70
Cacheu			76	57	128
Ilha do Principe			115		
Mozambique					120
Mina			229		
Pernambuco	887	1,046	1,041	2,283	1,189
São Thome		148	314	665	75
TOTALS	5,839	5,879	7,344	10,536	7,516

Source: ANTT, Manuscritos da Livraria, Brasil, Livro 2, f. 240.

Table A.2
Slave Migrations from Luanda in the 18th Century
(exclusive of complete year returns)

Year	Adults	Children	Infants	Total Slaves	Total Ships
1710	3,549	n.a.	n.a.	n.a.	n.a.
1711	4,158	n.a.	n.a.	n.a.	n.a.
1712	4,188	n.a.	n.a.	n.a.	n.a.
1713	5,617	n.a.	n.a.	n.a.	n.a.
1714	5,581	n.a.	n.a.	n.a.	n.a.
1718	6,747	n.a.	n.a.	n.a.	16
1719	6,868	n.a.	n.a.	n.a.	17
1720	7,213	n.a.	n.a.	n.a.	16
1721	5,378	n.a.	n.a.	n.a.	16
1722	5,062	n.a.	n.a.	n.a.	12
1723	6,744	n.a.	n.a.	n.a.	18
1734	8,720	1,242	...[a]	9,962	n.a.
1735	8,059	1,198	...	9,257	n.a.
1736	10,961	1,290	...	12,251	n.a.
1737	8,946	967	...	9,913	n.a.
1738	6,780	1,023	...	7,803	19
1739	8,169	1,329	...	9,498	n.a.
1740	7,523	264	...	7,787	21
1741	8,321	796	...	9,117	23
1742	10,182	302	...	10,484	n.a.
1743	12,130	355	...	12,485	n.a.
1744	8,156	460	...	8,616	17
1745	11,122	824	...	11,946	n.a.
1746	9,397	1,147	...	10,544	n.a.
1747	8,366	1,438	...	9,804	27
1748	10,374	880	...	11,254	30
1749	8,901	774	...	9,675	24
1750	10,253	1,149	146	11,548	27
1751	8,323	476	70	8,869	23
1752	9,196	878	112	10,186	27
1753	9,043	973	136	10,152	25
1754	7,820	860	127	8,807	20
1755	9,077	35	108	9,220	22
1756	9,988	36	127	10,151	26
1757	10,653	31	80	10,764	27
1758	9,886	49	...	9,935	n.a.
1759	9,242	116	...	9,358	n.a.
1760	8,211	n.a.	n.a.	n.a.	n.a.
1761	7,911	n.a.	n.a.	n.a.	n.a.
1762	8,284	n.a.	n.a.	n.a.	n.a.
1763	7,525	n.a.	n.a.	n.a.	n.a.
1764	7,554	n.a.	n.a.	n.a.	n.a.
1765	10,764	n.a.	n.a.	n.a.	n.a.
1766	9,158	n.a.	n.a.	n.a.	n.a.
1767	8,928	n.a.	n.a.	n.a.	n.a.
1768	7,214	n.a.	n.a.	n.a.	n.a.
1769	5,651	n.a.	n.a.	n.a.	n.a.
1776	10,194	n.a.	n.a.	n.a.	n.a.
1784	8,974	n.a.	n.a.	n.a.	20

Table A.2 (Continued)

Year	Adults	Children	Infants	Total Slaves	Total Ships
1785	8,614	38	287	8,939	n.a.
1786	9,677	29	305	10,011	n.a.
1787	9,919	18	376	10,313	n.a.
1788	11,291	17	343	11,651	n.a.
1789	8,547	12	215	8,774	n.a.
1790	9,964	23	289	10,276	n.a.
1791	9,072	11	245	9,328	n.a.
1792	11,569	9	288	11,866	n.a.
1793	10,094	6	143	10,243	n.a.
1794	11,915	7	190	12,112	n.a.
1795	10,286	9	220	10,515	n.a.
1796	9,971	8	215	10,194	n.a.
1797	8,635	12	206	8,853	n.a.
1798	10,271	1	. . .	10,272	16
1799	7,661 [b]	n.a.	n.a.	n.a.	17

[a]Dots indicate that the children total of the previous column does not distinguish between crias de pe (children standing) and crias de peito (infants at the breast).

[b]This is an estimated total which I obtained by dividing the total royal export tax by 8$700 reis per adult.

Source: For 1710 to 1714, see Birmingham, Trade and Conflict, p. 137; 1718-1723 in AHU, Angola, cx. 16; 1734-1769, ibid., cx. 32 (with ships totals for 1738, 1740-1741, 1744, 1747-1749 from ibid., cx. 27) with the exception of 1750-1753 in cx. 26 and 1758-1759 in IHGB, Lata 96, no. 1, folio 34; 1776 in AHU. Codice 409, folio 111v; 1784 in AHU, Angola, maço 13; 1795-1797 in BNRJ, Seção de Manuscritos, 15, 3, 33; 1798 in AHU, Angola, cx. 46 and 1799 in cx. 47; 1785-1794 in IHGB, Lata 77, no. 1.

Table A.3
Slave Migrations from Benguela in the 18th Century

Year	Adults	Children	Infants	Total Slaves	Total Ships
1738	1,515	206	72	1,793	5
1740	834	64	. . .[a]	898	3
1741	593	176	5	774	2
1744	1,212	80	3	1,295	4
1747	856	99	8	963	3
1748	328	. . .	. . .	328	1
1749	807	99	10	916	3
1750	1,687	. . .	17	1,704	5
1751	1,371	. . .	7	1,378	6
1752	1,897	. . .	24	1,921	7
1753	2,495	297	27	2,819	9
1754	2,787	n.a.	n.a.	n.a.	9
1755	2,173	n.a.	n.a.	n.a.	8
1756	2,541	n.a.	n.a.	n.a.	8
1757	1,461	n.a.	n.a.	n.a.	5

Year	Adults	Children	Infants	Total Slaves	Total Ships
1758	2,419	n.a.	n.a.	n.a.	7
1759	3,192	n.a.	n.a.	n.a.	n.a.
1760	2,506	n.a.	n.a.	n.a.	n.a.
1761	3,889	n.a.	n.a.	n.a.	n.a.
1762	4,124	20	36	4,180	12
1763	3,423	5	17	3,445	10
1764	3,821	8	38	3,867	11
1765	6,081	22	80	6,183	18
1766	5,084	11	65	5,160	14
1767	6,583	12	40	6,635	18
1768	5,643	15	...	5,658	n.a.
1769	5,531	15	52	5,598	15
1770	4,726	7	...	4,733	n.a.
1771	5,276	17	...	5,293	13
1772	5,009	12	...	5,021	n.a.
1773	5,363	14	...	5,367	n.a.
1774	4,327	1	...	4,328	n.a.
1775	5,730	9	...	5,739	n.a.
1776	5,972	11	...	5,983	n.a.
1777	3,963	4	...	3,967	n.a.
1778	5,504	6	...	5,510	n.a.
1779	7,062	7	...	7,069	n.a.
1780	6,442	13	...	6,455	n.a.
1781	6,477	11	...	6,488	n.a.
1782	6,420	17	...	6,437	n.a.
1783	6,286	16	...	6,302	n.a.
1784	7,608	42	182	7,832	n.a.
1785	6,162	30	...	6,192	n.a.
1786	5,490	18	...	5,508	n.a.
1787	7,012	14	...	7,026	n.a.
1788	6,126	5	...	6,131	n.a.
1789	6,032	8	...	6,040	n.a.
1790	6,135	15	...	6,150	n.a.
1791	6,329	10	...	6,339	n.a.
1792	8,910	5	...	8,915	n.a.
1793	11,171	8	...	11,179	n.a.
1794	9,481	12	...	9,493	n.a.
1795	8,579	15	...	8,594	n.a.
1796	7,885	14	...	7,899	n.a.
1797	6,062	...	...	6,062	n.a.
1798	5,419	9	...	5,428	12
1799	3,941	1	...	3,942	n.a.
1800	7,057	8	...	7,065	n.a.

[a]This indicates a zero sum.

Source: 1738 was taken from AHU, Angola, cx. 21; 1740, 1744 in cx. 23; 1741 in cx. 22; 1747 in cx. 24; 1748-1753 in cx. 26; 1754-1758 in cx. 27; 1760-1761, 1768-1769 in cx. 32; 1762 in cx. 29; 1763-1764 in cx. 30; 1765-1766 in cx. 31; 1767 in AHU. Angola, maço 9; 1771 in cx. 33;1776 in AHU, Codice 409, folio 112; 1784 in AHU, Angola, maço 13; for ships in 1798 in cx. 47; 1759, 1770-1783, 1785-1800 from IHGB, Lata 106, doc. 8.

Bibliography

I. MANUSCRIPT MATERIALS

Archives Départemental de La Loire Atlantique, Nantes, France. Series B, 4577-78, 4583-84.

Archivo General de Indias, Sevilla, Spain. Audiencia de Santo Domingo, legajos 1835, 2207.

Arquivo Geral da Marinha, Lisbon, Portugal. Caixa "Entradas e saidas de Navios, Registro do Porto de Lisboa, 1741-1800."

Archivo Historico Nacional, Madrid, Spain. Sección de Ultramar, legajo 3533.

Archivo Historico Nacional, Madrid, Spain. Sección de Ultramar, lega- 16-27, 29-33, 36-38, 46, 47, 51, 53, 62-66. Angola, maços 9, 13, 14. Pará, Papeis Avulsos, caixa 35. Codice 409.

Arquivo Nacional, Rio de Janeiro, Brazil. Policia, Codices 242, 397. Codice 184.

Arquivo Nacional, Torre de Tombo, Lisbon, Portugal. Manuscritos Miscellaneos, no. 926. Manuscritos da Livraria, Brasil, Libro 2.

Biblioteca Nacional, Lisbon, Portugal. Colecção Pombalina, Codice 617.

Biblioteca Nacional, Rio de Janeiro, Brazil. Seção dos Livros Raros, L, 6, 8; Seção de Manuscritos, 15, 3.

British Museum (British Library), London, Great Britain. Additional Ms. 38345.

Centre de Recherches sur l'Histoire de la France Atlantique, Nantes, France. Fonds Rinchon, Boîtes, 10-12.

House of Lords, Record Office, London, Great Britain. Papers, 28 July 1800 (5/J/11/2); 19 June 1799; 25 June 1799 and 9 July 1799.

Instituto de Historia e Geografia Brasileira, Rio de Janeiro, Brazil. Latas, 77, 96, 106.

Public Record Office, London, Great Britain. Colonial Office 142/19-25.

II. NEWSPAPERS

Jornal do Comercio, Rio de Janeiro, 1825-1830.
Diario do Rio de Janeiro, Rio de Janeiro, 1825-1830.

III. UNPUBLISHED WORKS

Anstey, Roger, "The Slave Trade of the Continental Powers, 1760-1810," *Economic History Review*, forthcoming.

257

Bibliography

Austen, Ralph, "A Census of the Transsaharen Slave Trade, or Approximating the Uncountable." Paper presented at the MSSB Conference, Waterville, Maine, 1975. (This and all subsequent papers of the Conference will be published by H. A. Gemery and J. S. Hogendorn, eds. *The Uncommon Market: Essays in the Economic History of the Atlantic Slave Trade* [New York, forthcoming]).

Chandler, David L., "Health and Slavery: A Study of Health Conditions among Negro Slaves in the Viceroyalty of New Granada and its associated Slave Trade, 1600-1810." Ph.D. dissertation, Department of History, Tulane University, 1972.

Daget, Serge, "Catalogue des navires . . . de participation au trafic négrier atlantique entre 1814 et 1833," Abidjan, December 1973. Mimeo.

Eisenberg, Peter, "From Slave to Free Labor on Sugar Plantations: The Process in Pernambuco." Paper read at the 1970 meetings of the American Historical Association.

Eltis, D., "The Direction and Fluctuation of the Transatlantic Slave Trade 1821-43: A Revision of the 1845 Parliamentary Paper." MSSB Conference on the Atlantic Slave Trade, Waterville, Maine, 1975.

————, "The Export of Slaves from Africa 1821-43." Unpublished ms.

Hamm, Tommy Todd, "The American Slave Trade with Africa, 1620-1807." Ph.D. dissertation, Department of History, Indiana University, 1975.

Jobson de Andrade Arruba, José, "O Brasil no comércio colonial (1796-1808." Ph.D. dissertation, Departmento de Historia, Facultad de Filosofia, Letras e Ciencias Humanas, Universidade de São Paulo, 1972.

Karasch, Mary, "Manumission in the City of Rio de Janeiro, 1807-1851." Paper presented to the American Historical Association, San Francisco, December, 1973.

Kessler, Arnold, "Bahian Manumission Practices in the Early Nineteenth Century." Paper presented to the American Historical Association, San Francisco, December 1973.

Kiernan, James Patrick, "The Manumission of Slaves in Colonial Brazil. Paraty, 1789-1822." Ph.D. dissertation, Department of History, New York University, 1976.

Klein, Herbert S. and Stanley L. Engerman, "The Demographic Study of the American Slave Populations." Paper presented at the IIIrd International Colloquium on Demographic History, Montreal, 1975.

————, and Charles Garland, "The Allotment of Space Aboard 18th Century Slave Ships." Unpublished ms.

Kotlikoff, Lawrence J., "Towards a Quantitative Description of the

New Orleans Slave Market." University of Chicago, Workshop in Economic History, Report #7475-21, 1975.

Kulikoff, Allan, "Tobacco and Slaves: Population, Economy and Society in Eighteenth Century Prince George's County, Maryland." Ph.D. dissertation, Department of History, Brandeis University, 1975.

LeVeen, E. Phillip, "British Slave Trade Suppression Policies, 1820-1865: Impact and Implications." Unpublished Ph.D. dissertation, Department of Economics, University of Chicago, 1971.

————, "The African Supply Response." Unpublished paper.

Lima Martins, Ismalia, "Os problemas de mão de obra da grande lavoura Fluminense. O tráfico intra-provincial (1850-1878)." M.A. thesis, Universidade Federal Fluminense, 1974.

McCusker, Jr., John James, "The Rum Trade and the Balance of Payments of the Thirteen Continental Colonies, 1650-1775." Ph.D. dissertation, Department of History, University of Pittsburgh, 1970.

Mello, Pedro Carvalho de, "The Economics of Slavery on Brazilian Coffee Plantations, 1850-1888." Ph.D. dissertation, Department of Economics, University of Chicago, 1976.

————, "The Economics of Labor in Brazilian Coffee Plantations, 1850-1888," Workshop in Economic History, University of Chicago, 1974, Report #7475-8.

Mettas, Jean, *Répertoire des expéditions négriers français au XVIIIe siècle*, Paris, forthcoming.

Miller, Joseph C., "Some Aspects of the Commercial Organization of Slaving at Luanda, Angola: 1760-1830." Paper presented at the MSSB Conference on Trans-Atlantic Slave trade, Waterville, Maine, August, 1975.

————, "Sources and Knowledge of the Slave Trade in the Southern Atlantic." Unpublished paper.

Minchinton, Walter E. "The Triangular Trade Revisited." Paper presented at the MSSB Conference on the Trans-Atlantic Slave Trade, Waterville, Maine, August, 1975.

Peralta Rivera, Germán, "Les mécanismes du commerce esclavagiste (1595-1640)." Paris: tesis du 3° cycle E.P.H.E., 1976.

Postma, Johannes, "The Dutch Participation in the African Slave Trade: Slaving on the Guinea Coast, 1675-1795." Ph.D. dissertation, Department of History, Michigan State University, 1970.

————, "Mortality in the Dutch Slave Trade, 1675-1795." Paper presented at the MSSB Conference on the Trans-Atlantic Slave Trade, Waterville, Maine, August 1975.

Slenes, Robert W. "The Demography and Economics of Brazilian Slavery: 1850-1888." Ph.D. dissertation, Department of History, Stanford University, 1976.

Bibliography

Wax, Darold D. "Colonial Maryland and the Slave Trade." Unpublished ms.

IV. PRINTED MATERIALS

Acosta Saignes, Miguel, *La vida de los esclavos negros en Venezuela*, Caracas, 1967.

Aguirre Beltran, Gonzalo, *La población negra de Mexico, 1519-1810*, Mexico, 1946.

Aimes, Hubert H. S., *A History of Slavery in Cuba, 1511-1868*, New York, 1907.

Akinjogbin, I. A., *Dahomey and Its Neighbors*. Cambridge, 1970.

Almanak imperial do comércio e das corporações civis e militares do imperio do Brasil, Rio de Janeiro, 1829.

Alpers, Edward A., *The East African Slave Trade*, Nairobi, 1967.

———, "The French Slave Trade in East Africa (1721-1810)," *Cahiers d'études africaines*, x (1970).

Alves, Marieta, "O comércio maritimo e alguns armadores do seculo xviii na Bahia," *Revista de Historia* (São Paulo), xxxiv, 69 (1967).

Anstry, Roger, *The Atlantic Slave Trade and British Abolition, 1760-1810*, London, 1975.

———, "The Volume and Profitability of the Atlantic Slave Trade, 1761-1810," in Stanley L. Engerman and Eugene D. Genovese (eds.), *Race and Slavery in the Western Hemisphere: Quantitative Studies*, Princeton, 1975.

———, "The Volume of the North American Slave-Carrying Trade from Africa, 1761-1810," *Revue française d'Histoire d'Outre-Mer*, LXI, nos. 226-227 (1975).

Bancroft, Frederic, *Slave Trading in the Old South*, New York, 1931.

Bean, Richard, "A Note on the Relative Importance of Slaves and Gold in West Africa Exports," *Journal of African History*, xv, No. 3, (1974).

Berbain, Simone, *Études sur la traite des noirs au golfe de Guinée, Le comptoir française de Juda au xviiie siècle*, Paris, Mémoires de IFAN, No. 3, 1942.

Bethel, Leslie, *The Abolition of the Brazilian Slave Trade*, Cambridge, 1970.

Birmingham, David, *Trade and Conflict in Angola: The Mbundu and their Neighbors under the Influence of the Portuguese, 1483-1790*, Oxford, 1966.

Boulle, Pierre, "Slave Trade, Commercial Organization and Industrial Growth in Eighteenth Century Nantes," *Revue française d'Histoire d'Outre-Mer*, LIX, No. 214 (1972).

————, "Marchandises de traite et développement industriel dans la France et l'Angleterre du xviiie siècle." *Revue française d'Histoire d'Outre-Mer*, LXII, nos. 226-227 (1975).

Bourgeois-Pichat, "The General Development of Population in France since the Eighteenth Century," in D. V. Glass and D.E.C. Eversley, eds., *Population in History, Essays in Historical Demography*. London, 1965.

Bowser, Frederick P., *The African Slave in Colonial Peru, 1524-1650*, Stanford, 1974.

Boxer, C. R., *The Golden Age of Brazil, 1695-1750: Growing Pains of a Colonial Society*, Berkeley, 1969.

————, *The Dutch Seaborne Empire, 1600-1800*, New York, 1965.

Brásio, Padre António, *Monumenta Missionaria Africana*, 9 vols., Lisbon, 1952–.

Brathwaite, Edward, *The Development of Creole Society in Jamaica, 1770-1820*, Oxford, 1971.

Brazil, Directoria Geral de Estatística, *Recenseamento geral da população do Brazil a que se procedeu no dia 1º de agosto de 1872*, 21 Vols., Rio de Janeiro, 1872-1876.

————, *Relatório annexo ao do Ministerio dos Negocios do Imperio de 1878*, Rio de Janeiro, n.d.

Brazil, Ministerio do Imperio, *Relatório dos Negocios do Imperio, 1858*, Rio de Janeiro, 1858.

Brazil, Ministerio do Planejamento e Coordenação Econômica, Escritorio de Pesquisa Econômica Aplicada, *Plano decenal de desenvolvimento econômico e social: Demografía, diagnóstico*, Rio de Janeiro, 1966.

Brito Figueroa, Federico, *Ensayos de historia social Venezolana*, Caracas, 1960.

————, *La estructura economica de Venezuela colonial*, Caracas, 1963.

————, *La estructura social y demográfica de Venezuela colonial*, Caracas, 1961.

Buarque de Holanda, Sergio, ed., *Historia geral da civilização brasileira*, 8 vols., São Paulo, 1963.

Buxton, Thomas Fowell, *The African Slave Trade and its Remedy*, London, 1840.

Camp, David de, "African Day—Names in Jamaica," *Language* 43, No. 1 (1967).

Cardoso, Fernando Henrique, *Capitalismo e escravidão no Brasil meridional. . .* , São Paulo, 1962.

Carreira, António, *As companhias pombalinas de navegação comércio e tráfico de escravos entre a costa africana e o nordeste brasileiro*, Porto, 1969.

Chailley, Marcel, *Histoire de l'Afrique Occidentale Française, 1638-1959*, Paris, 1968.

Chambon, M., *Traite général du commerce de l'Amerique pour Marseilles*, 2 vols., Amsterdam and Marseilles, 1783.

Chandler, David L., "Health Conditions in the Slave Trade of Colonial New Granada," in Robert B. Toplin, ed., *Slavery and Race Relations in Latin America*, Westport, Connecticut, 1974, 51-88.

Christie, W. D., *Notes on Brazilian Questions*, London, 1965.

Claypole, W. A. and D. J. Buisseret, "Trade Patterns in Early English Jamaica," *Journal of Caribbean History*, v (November, 1976).

Colmenares, German, *Historia economica y social de Colombia, 1537-1719*, 2nd ed., Medellin, 1975.

Conrad, Robert, *The Destruction of Brazilian Slavery, 1850-1888*, Berkeley, 1972.

Correia Lopes, Edmundo, *A escravatura (subsidios para a sua historia)*, Lisbon, 1944.

Cortes, Vicenta, *La esclavitud en Valencia durante el reinado de los reyes católicos (1479-1516)*, Valencia, 1965.

Craton, Michael, *Sinews of Empire, A Short History of British Slavery*, New York, 1974.

Craven, Wesley Frank, *White, Red and Black*, Charlottesville, 1971.

Curtin, Philip, *The Atlantic Slave Trade, A Census*, Madison, Wisconsin, 1969.

————, *Economic Change in Pre-Colonial Africa: Senegambia in the Era of the Slave Trade*, 2 vols., Madison, 1974.

————, "Epidemiology and the slave trade," *Political Science Quarterly*, LXXXIII, No. 2 (June, 1968).

————, "Measuring the Atlantic Slave Trade," in Stanley L. Engerman and Eugene D. Genovese, eds., *Race and Slavery in the Western Hemisphere: Quantitative Studies*, Princeton, 1975.

————, "Measuring the Atlantic Slave Trade Once Again: a Comment," *Journal of African History*, XVII, no. 4 (1976).

————, and Jan Vansina, "Sources of the 19th Century Atlantic Slave Trade," *Journal of African History*, v (1969).

Daaku, Kwame Yeboa, *Trade and Politics on the Gold Coast 1600 to 1720*, Oxford, 1970.

Daget, Serge, "L'abolition de la traite des noires en France de 1814 à 1831," *Cahiers d'études africaines* 11 (1971).

Dardel, Pierre, *Navires et marchandises dans les ports de Rouen et du Havre au xviiie siècle*, Paris, 1963.

David, Paul A. et al., *Reckoning with Slavery, A Critical Study in the Quantitative History of American Negro Slavery*, New York, 1976.

Davidson, Basil, "Slaves or Captives. Some Notes on Fantasy and Fact," in Nathan J. Huggins et al., eds., *Key Issues in the Afro-American Experience*, New York, 1971, vol. i.

Davies, K. G., *The Royal African Company*, London, 1951.

————, "The Living and the Dead: White Mortality in West Africa, 1684-1732" in Stanley L. Engerman and Eugene D. Genovese, eds., *Race and Slavery in the Western Hemisphere: Quantitative Studies* (Princeton, 1975).

Davis, Ralph, *The Rise of the English Shipping Industry in the Seventeenth and Eighteenth Centuries*, London, 1962.

Dean, Warren, *Rio Claro, A Brazilian Plantation System, 1820-1920*, Stanford, 1976.

Debien, Gabriel, *Les esclaves aux antilles françaises (xviie-xviiie siècles)*, Basse-Terre and Fort-de-France, 1974.

Deerr, Noel, *A History of Sugar*, 2 vols., London, 1949-1950.

Deschamps, Hubert, *Histoire de la traite des noirs de l'antiquité à nos jours*, Paris, 1971.

Diaz Solar, Louiz M., *Historia de la esclavitud negra en Puerto Rico, 1493-1890*, Madrid, 1953.

Diffenderfer, Frank, *German Immigration into Pennsylvania*, Lancaster, Pennsylvania, 1900.

Dillard, J. L., *Black English, its History and Usage in the United States*, New York, 1972.

Dobyns, Henry F., "Estimating Aboriginal American Population. . . ," *Current Anthropology* 7 (October, 1966).

Donadíu y Puignau, Delfin, *Diccionario de la lengua castellana. . .* , 4 vols., Barcelona, 1890-1895.

Donnan, Elizabeth, *Documents Illustrative of the History of the Slave Trade to America*, 4 vols., Washington, D.C., 1930.

DuBois, W.E.B., *The Suppression of the African Slave Trade to the United States of America, 1638-1870*, Cambridge, Massachusetts, 1896.

Dupaquier, Jacques, "Sur la population française au xviie et xviiie siècle," *Revue historique*, 92° année, ccxxxix (Janvier-Mars, 1968).

Eblen, Jack E., "Growth of the Black Population in Antebellum America, 1820-1860," *Population Studies*, 26 (July 1972).

————, "New Estimates of the Vital Rates of the United States Black Population During the Nineteenth Century," *Demography*, 11 (May 1974).

Bibliography

Eblen, Jack E., "On the Natural Increase of Slave Populations. The Example of the Cuban Black Population, 1775-1900," in Stanley L. Engerman and Eugene D. Genovese, eds., *Race and Slavery in the Western Hemisphere: Quantitative Studies* (Princeton, 1975).

Edel, Matthew, "The Brazilian Sugar Cycle of the Seventeenth Century and the Rise of West Indian Competition," *Caribbean Studies*, IX, No. 1 (April 1969).

Eisenberg, Peter L., *The Sugar Industry in Pernambuco, 1840-1910*, Berkeley, 1974.

Eltis, D., "The Traffic in Slaves between the British West Indian Colonies, 1807-1833," *Economic History Review*, Second Series, XXV, No. 1 (February 1972).

Ely, Roland T., *Cuando reinaba su majestad el azucar*, Buenos Aires, 1963.

Emmer, Pieter C., "The History of the Dutch Slave Trade: A Bibliographical Survey," *Journal of Economic History*, XXXII, No. 3 (1972).

Engerman, Stanley L., "The Slave Trade and British Capital Formation in the Eighteenth Century: A Comment on the Williams Thesis," *Business History Review*, XLVI, No. 4 (Winter, 1972).

―――, "Some Economic and Demographic Comparisons of U.S. and British West Indian Slavery," *Economic History Review*, XXIX, No. 2 (1976).

――― and Eugene Genovese, eds., *Race and Slavery in the Western Hemisphere: Quantitative Studies*, Princeton, 1975.

Escalante, Aquiles, *El negro en Colombia*, Bogotá, 1964.

Everaert, J., "Les fluctuations du trafic négrier nantais (1753-1792)," *Les Cahiers de Tunisie*, XI, No. 43 (1963).

Fage, J. D., "Slavery and the Slave Trade in the Context of West African History," *Journal of African History*, X, No. 3 (1969).

Falconbridge, Alexander, *An Account of the Slave Trade on the Coast of Africa*, London, 1788.

Falla recitada na abertura da assemblea legislativa da Bahia, Bahia, 1855-1857.

Feinberg, H. M., "New Data on European Mortality in West Africa: The Dutch on the Gold Coast, 1719-1760," *Journal of African History*, XV, No. 3 (1974).

Ferreira Soares, Sebastião, *Notas estatísticas sobre a produção agricola e carestea dos gêneros alimentícios no Imperio do Brasil*, Rio de Janeiro, 1860.

Fogel, Robert and Stanley L. Engerman, *Time on the Cross, The Economics of American Negro Slavery*, 2 vols., Boston, 1974.

French, Christopher J., "Eighteenth-Century Shipping Tonnage Measurements," *Journal of Economic History*, XXXIII (1973).

Furtado, Celso, *Formação economica do Brasil*, São Paulo, 1975 edition.

Galloway, J. H., "The Last Years of Slavery on the Sugar Plantations of Northeastern Brazil," *Hispanic American Historical Review*, LI, No. 4 (November, 1971).

Gaston-Martin, *Histoire de l'esclavage dans les colonies françaises*, Paris, 1948.

——, *Nantes au xviiie siècle. L'ère des négriers (1714-1774)*, Paris, 1931.

——, *Négriers et bois d'ébène*, Grenoble, 1934.

Geiser, Frederick, *Redemptioners and Indentured Servants in the Colony and Commonwealth of Pennsylvania*, New Haven, Conn., 1901.

Gemery, H. A. and J. S. Hogenborn, "The Atlantic Slave Trade: a tentative economic model," *Journal of African History*, xv, No. 2 (1974).

Gibson, Charles, *Spain in America*, New York, 1966.

Glass, D. V. and D.E.C. Eversley, eds., *Population in History*, London, 1965.

Gonsalves de Mello, José Antonio, *Henrique Dias, governador dos pretos, crioulos e mulatos do estado do Brasil*, Recife, 1954.

Goulart, Mauricio, *Escravidão africana no Brasil (das origenes a extinção)*, São Paulo, 1949.

Granada, German de, "Testimonios documentales sobre la preservación del sistema antroponimico twi entre los esclavos negros de la Nueva Granada," *Revista Española de Linguistica*, I, No. 2 (1971).

Granpré, Louis O'Hier, *Voyage à la côte occidentale d'Afrique fait dans les années 1786 et 1787*, 2 vols., Paris, 1801.

Gray, Lewis Cecil, *History of Agriculture in the Southern United States to 1860*, 2 vols., 2nd ed., Gloucester, Massachusetts, 1958.

Gray, Richard and David Birmingham, eds., *Pre-Colonial African Trade*, London, 1970.

Great Britain, House of Commons, Parliamentary Papers, *Accounts & Papers*, 1788, xxii (565); 1789, xxiv (622, 633) and xxv (635) and xxvi (646); 1790, xxix (698) and xxxi (705, 705b). Also 1801-1802, iv; and 1802, viii, and xlix (1845), 73.

——, Select Committee on Slave Trade, *Second Report*, 30 May, 1848.

——, Select Committee on Emigrant Ships, *Second Report*, xiii (1854), 349.

Green-Pedersen, Sv. E., "The Scope and Structure of the Danish Negro Slave Trade," *Scandinavian Economic History Review*, xix, No. 2 (1971).

Bibliography

Green-Pedersen, Sv. E., *Om forholdene på danske slaveskibe med soer-lig henblik på dødeligheden 1777-89*, Elsinore, 1973.

————, "The History of the Danish Negro Slave Trade, 1733-1807," *Revue française d'Histoire d'Outre-Mer*, LXII, Nos. 227-227 (1975).

Guerra y Sanchez, Ramiro et al., *Historia de la nación cubana*, 10 vols., Havana, 1952.

Haring, C. H., *The Spanish Empire in America*, New York, 1947.

Herskovits, Melville, J., *The Myth of the Negro Past*, Boston, 1958.

Higgins, W. Robert, "The Geographical Origins of Negro Slaves in Colonial South Carolina," *South Atlantic Quarterly*, LXX (1971).

Higham, C.S.S., *The Development of the Leeward Islands Under the Restoration, 1660-1668*, Cambridge, 1921.

Hogg, Peter C., *The African Slave Trade and its Suppression, A Classi-fied and Annotated Bibliography. . .* , London, 1973.

Hopkins, A. G., *An Economic History of West Africa*, London, 1973.

Hoppe, Fritz, *A Africa Oriental Portuguesa no tempo de Pombal, 1750-1777*, Lisbon, 1970.

Hymes, Dell, ed., *Pidginization and Creolization of Languages*, Cambridge, 1971.

Henry, Louis, *Manuel de demographie historique*, Geneve-Paris, 1967.

Humboldt, Alexander von, *Ensayo político sobre la isla de Cuba*, Havana, 1960 edition.

————, *Political Essay on the Kingdom of New Spain*, 4 vols., London, 1811.

Iglesias, Francisco, *Politica econômica do govêrno provincial minero (1835-1889)*, Rio de Janeiro, 1958.

Inikori, J. E., "Measuring the Atlantic Slave Trade: an Assessment of Curtin and Anstey," *Journal of African History*, XVII, no. 2 (1976).

Jaramillo Uribe, Jaime, "Esclavos y señores en la sociedad colombiana del siglo xviii," *Anuario Colombiano de Historia Social y de la Cultura*, Vol. I (1963).

The Journal of A Slave Trader (John Newton), 1750-1754, eds., B. Martin and M. Spurrell, London, 1962.

Kapp, Friedrick, *Immigration and the Commissioners of Emigration*, New York, 1870.

Kilson, Marion D., "West African Society and the Atlantic Slave Trade, 1441-1865," in Nathan J. Huggins et al., eds., *Key Issues in the Afro-American Experience*, New York, 1971, Vol. I.

King, James F., "Evolution of the Free Slave Trade Principle in Span-ish Colonial Administration," *Hispanic American Historical Review*, XXII (1942).

Kiple, Kenneth F., *Blacks in Colonial Cuba, 1774-1889*, Gainesville, 1976.

Klein, Herbert S., "The Colored Freedmen in Brazilian Slave Society," *Journal of Social History*, III, No. 1 (Fall, 1969).

———, "The Cuban Slave Trade in a Period of Transition, 1790-1843," *Revue française d'Histoire d'Outre-Mer*, LXII, Nos. 226-227 (1975).

———, "North American Competition and the Characteristics of the African Slave Trade to Cuba, 1790 to 1794," *William & Mary Quarterly*, 3rd Series, XXVIII, No. 1 (January, 1971).

———, "The Portuguese Slave Trade from Angola in the Eighteenth Century," *Journal of Economic History*, XXXII (1972).

———, *Slavery in the Americas: A Comparative Study of Cuba and Virginia*, Chicago, 1967.

———, "Slaves and Shipping in Eighteenth Century Virginia," *Journal of Interdisciplinary History*, V (Winter, 1975).

———, "The Trade in African Slaves to Rio de Janeiro, 1795-1811; estimates of mortality and patterns of voyages," *Journal of African History*, X, No. 4 (1969).

———, "O trafico de escravos africanos para o porto de Rio de Janeiro, 1825-1830," *Anais de Historia*, V (1973).

——— and Stanley L. Engerman, "Facteurs de mortalité dans le trafic français d'esclaves au xviiie siècle," *Annales, economies, sociétés, civilisations*, XXXI, No. 6 (1976).

———, "Shipping Patterns and Mortality in the African Slave Trade to Rio de Janeiro, 1825-1830," *Cahiers d'études africaines*, XV, No. 59 (1975).

———, "Slave Mortality on British Ships, 1791-1797," in *Liverpool, The African Slave Trade and Abolition*, Roger Anstey and P.E.H. Hair, eds., Liverpool, 1976. (Lancashire and Cheshire Historic Society Transactions.)

Klingaman, David C., "The Development of the Coastwise Trade of Virginia in the Late Colonial Period," *Virginia Magazine of History and Biography*, LXXVII (1969).

Knight, Franklin, *Slave Society in Cuba During the Nineteenth Century*, Madison, 1970.

Konetzke, Richard, ed., *Colección de documentos para la historia de la formación social de Hispano-américa, 1493-1810*, 5 vols., Madrid, 1953-1962.

Laemmert, Eduardo von, *Almanak administrativo, mercantil e industrial da Côrte e Provincia do Rio de Janeiro para o anno de 1861*, Rio de Janeiro, 1861.

Lamb, D. P., "Volume and Tonnage of the Liverpool Slave Trade, 1772-1807" in Roger Anstey and P.E.H. Hair, eds., *Liverpool, The African Slave Trade and Abolition*, Liverpool, 1976.

Bibliography

Lane, Frederic C., "Tonnages, Medieval and Modern," *Economic History Review*, xvii (1964).

Lathan, A.J.H., *Old Calabar, 1600-1891. The Impact of the International Economy Upon a Traditional Society*, Oxford, 1973.

Lisanti, Luis, ed., *Negoçios colonais (uma correspondencia commercial do seculo xviii)*, 5 vols., Brasilia, 1973.

Liverpool and Slavery: An Historical Account of the Liverpool-African Slave Trade, by a Genuine "Dicky-Sam," Liverpool, 1884.

Lockhart, James, *Spanish Peru, 1532-1560: A Colonial Society*, Madison, Wisconsin, 1968.

Lombardi, John V., *The Decline and Abolition of Negro Slavery in Venezuela, 1820-1854*, Westport, Conn., 1971.

————, *People and Places in Colonial Venezuela*, Bloomington, 1976.

Ly, Abdoulaye, *La Compagnie du Senégal*, Paris, 1958.

Mac Donagh, Oliver, *A Pattern of Government Growth, 1800-1860. The Passenger Acts and their Enforcement*, London, 1961.

Magalhaes Godinho, Vitorino, *A econômia dos descobrimentos henriquinos*, Lisbon, 1962.

Mannix, Daniel P. and Malcolm Cowley, *Black Cargoes. A History of the Atlantic Slave Trade, 1518-1865*, New York, 1962.

Marcilio, Maria Luiza, *La ville de São Paulo, peuplement et population, 1750-1850*, Rouen, 1968.

———— et al., "Considerações sobre o preço do escravo no periodo imperial: Uma análise quantitativo," *Anais de Historia*, vol. 5 (1973), pp. 179-194.

Martin, Phyllis M., *The External Trade of the Loango Coast, 1576-1870*, Oxford, 1972.

Mattoso, Kátia M. Queirós, "A proposito de cartas de alforia na Bahia, 1779-1850," *Anais de Historia*, iv (1972).

Mauro, Frederick, *Le Portugal et l'atlantique au xviie siècle*, Paris, 1960.

————, *Le xvie siècle européen: aspects économiques*, Paris, 1966.

Medeiros dos Santos, Corcino, "Relações de Angola com o Rio de Janeiro (1736-1808)," *Estudos Historícos*, xii (1973).

Mellafe, Rolando, *La esclavitud en Hispanoamérica*, Buenos Aires, 1964.

Menard, Russell R., "The Maryland Slave Population, 1658-1730: A Demographic Profile of Blacks in Four Counties," *William & Mary Quarterly*, 3d Series, xxxii, No. 1 (1975).

Merritt, J. E., "The Triangular Trade," *Business History*, iii, No. 1 (December, 1960).

Mettas, Jean, "Honfleur et la traite des noirs au xviiie siècle," *Revue française d'Histoire d'Outre-Mer*, lx, No. 218 (1973).

————, "La traite portugaise en Haute Guinée, 1758-1799: Problèmes et methodes," *Journal of African History*, XVI, No. 3 (1975).

Meuvret, J., "Demographic Crisis in France from the Sixteenth to the Eighteenth Century" in D. V. Glass and D.E.C. Eversley, eds., *Population in History. Essays in Historical Demography* (London, 1968).

Meyer, Jean, *L'armement nantais dans le deuxième moitié du xviiie siècle*, Paris, 1969.

————, "Le commerce négrier nantais (1774-1792)," *Annales: economies, sociétés, civilisations*, XV (1960).

Middleton, Arthur Pierce, *Tobacco Coast: A Maritime History of Chesapeake Bay in the Colonial Era*, Newport News, Virginia, 1953.

Miller, Joseph C., "Legal Portuguese Slaving from Angola, Some Preliminary Indications of Volume and Direction, 1760-1830," *Revue française d'Histoire d'Outre-Mer*, LXII, Nos. 226-227 (1975).

————, "The Slave Trade in Congo and Angola," in Martin L. Kilson and Robert I. Rotberg, eds., *The African Diaspora. Interpretive Essays* (Cambridge, Mass., 1976).

Minchinton, W. E., "The Slave Trade of Bristol with the British Mainland Colonies in North America, 1699-1770," in Roger Anstey and P.E.H. Hair, eds., *Liverpool, the African Slave Trade, and Abolition*, Liverpool, 1976.

Murray, D. R., "Statistics of the Slave Trade to Cuba, 1790-1867," *Journal of Latin American Studies*, III, No. 2 (1971).

Nardin, Jean-Claude, "Encore des chiffres: La Traite négriere française pendant la première moitié du xviiie siècle," *Revue française d'Histoire d'Outre-Mer*, LVII, No. 209 (1970).

Newton, Arthur Percival, *The European Nations in the West Indies, 1493-1688*, London, 1933.

North, Douglass C., "Sources of Productivity Change in Ocean Shipping, 1600-1850," *The Journal of Political Economy*, LXXVI, 5 (September/October, 1968).

Nunes Dias, Manuel, *Fomento e mercantilismo: A Companhia geral do Grão Pará e Maranhão (1755-1778)*, 2 vols., Belem, 1970.

————, "Le mouvement des 'navires de registre' entre La Havana et les ports d'Espagne à l'époque du 'commerce libre' (1787-1789)," *Revue d'histoire economique et sociale*, XLV (1967).

Ostrander, Gilman, "The Making of the Triangular Trade Myth," *William & Mary Quarterly*, 3d. Series, XXX (1973).

Ottenberg, Simon and Phoebe Ottenberg, *Cultures and Societies of Africa*, New York, 1960.

Palacios Preciado, Jorge, *La trata de negros por Cartagena de Indias*, Tunja, Colombia, 1973.

Bibliography

Palmer, Colin A., *Slaves of the White God, Blacks in Mexico, 1570-1650*, Cambridge, Mass., 1976.

Pares, Richard, *Yankees and Creoles: The Trade Between North America and the West Indies before the American Revolution.* New York, 1968.

Parkinson, C. Northcote, ed., *The Trade Winds*, London, 1948.

Patterson, H.O.L., "Slavery, Acculturation and Social Change: The Jamaican Case," *British Journal of Sociology*, Vol. 17 (1966).

Patterson, K. David, *The Northern Gabon Coast to 1865*, Oxford, 1975.

Pereda Valdes, Ildefonso, *El negro en el Uruguay, pasado y presente*, Montevideo, 1965.

Peytrand, Lucien, *L'esclavage aux antilles françaises avant 1789*, Paris, 1897.

Pezuela, Jacobo de la, *Diccionario geográfico, estadístico, histórico de la isla de Cuba*, 4 vols., Madrid, 1863-1866.

Phillips, U. B., *American Negro Slavery*, New York, 1940.

Pitman, Frank W., *The Development of the British West Indies, 1700-1763*, New Haven, 1917.

Postma, Johannes, "The Dutch Slave Trade. A Quantitative Assessment," *Revue française d'Histoire d'Outre-Mer*, LXII, Nos. 226-227 (1975).

———, "The Dimensions of the Dutch Slave Trade from West Africa," *Journal of African History*, XIII, No. 2 (1972).

———, "The Origin of African Slaves: the Dutch Activities on the Guinea Coast, 1675-1795," in Stanley L. Engerman and Eugene D. Genovese, eds., *Race and Slavery in the Western Hemisphere: Quantitative Studies* (Princeton, 1975).

Ramos, Arthur, *Introdução a antropologia brasileira*, Rio de Janeiro, 1943.

Rau, Virginia, ed., *O "Livro de Rezão" de António Coelho Guerreiro.* Lisbon, 1956; DIAMANG, Publiçaôes Culturais, No. 30.

Rees, Gareth, "Copper Sheathing, An Example of Technological Diffusion in the English Merchant Fleet," *Journal of Transportation History*, New Series, I, No. 2 (September, 1971).

Reinhard, Marcel R. and Andre Armengaud, *Histoire generale de la population Mondiale*, Paris, 1961.

Relatório apresentado á assemblea legislative provincial de São Paulo, São Paulo, 1968-1970.

Relatório com que sua exe. Barão de Itauna Passou a administração da provincia. . . . , São Paulo, 1869.

Richardson, David, "Profitability in the Bristol-Liverpool Slave Trade," *Revue française d'Histoire d'Outre-Mer*, LXII, Nos. 226-227 (1975).

Rinchon, Dieudonné, *Les armements négriers au xviiie siècle*, Bruxelles: Mémoire de la Académie des Sciences Colonials, 1955.

———, *Pierre Ignace Liévin van Alstein, Captaine négrier* (Dakar: Mémoires de IFAN, No. 71, 1965).

———, *La traite et l'esclavage des Congolais par les européens*, Bruxelles, 1929.

———, *Le trafic négrier, l'organisation comerciale de la traite des noirs*, Bruxelles, Nantes, Paris, 1938.

Riverend Brusone, Julio Le, *Historia económica de Cuba*, 2nd ed., Havana, 1965.

———, *Los origenes de la económia cubana (1510-1600)*, Mexico, 1945.

Roberts, G. W., "A Life Table for a West Indian Slave Population," *Population Studies*, V (1951).

———, *The Population of Jamaica*, Cambridge, 1957.

Rodney, Walter, *A History of the Upper Guinea Coast, 1545 to 1800*, Oxford, 1970.

———, *How Europe Underdeveloped Africa*, London and Dar es Salaam, 1972.

———, *West Africa and the Atlantic Slave Trade*, Nairobi: Historical Association of Tanzania, Paper No. 2, 1967.

Rosenblat, Angel, *La población indigena y el mestizaje en America*, 2 vols., Buenos Aires, 1954.

Saco, José Antonio, *História de la esclavitud de la raza Africana en el nuevo mundo. . .* , Barcelona, 1879.

Sanderson, F. E., "The Liverpool Delegates and Sir William Dolben's Bill," *Transactions of the Historical Society of Lancashire and Cheshire*, cxxiv (1972).

Scelle, George, *Histoire politique de la traite négrier aux Indes de Castille*, 2 vols., Paris, 1906.

Schwartz, Stuart B., "The Manumission of Slaves in Colonial Brazil: Bahia 1648-1745," *Hispanic American Historical Review*, liv, No. 4 (November, 1974).

Sharp, William F., "The Profitability of Slavery in the Colombian Choco, 1680-1810," *Hispanic American Historical Review*, Vol. 55, No. 3 (August, 1975).

Shaw, A.G.L., *Convicts and the Colonies. A Study of Penal Transportation from Great Britain and Ireland to Australia and Other Parts of the British Empire*, London, 1966.

Shepherd, James F. and Gary M. Walton, *Shipping, Maritime Trade and the Economic Development of Colonial North America*, Cambridge, 1972.

Sheridan, R. B., "The Wealth of Jamaica in the Eighteenth Century," *Economic History Review*, 2d. Series, xviii, No. 2 (1965).

Bibliography

Sheridan, R. B., *Sugar and Slavery. An Economic History of the British West Indies 1623-1775*, Baltimore, 1973.

———, "The Commercial and Financial Organization of the British Slave Trade, 1750-1807," *Economic History Review*, 2d. Series, xi, No. 2 (1958).

Silva Rebelo, Manuel dos Anjos da, *Relações entre Angola e Brasil, 1808-1830*, Lisbon, 1970.

Souza e Silva, Joaquim Norberto de, *Investigações sôbre os recenseamentos da população geral do Império*, Rio de Janeiro, 1870 [reprinted, Rio de Janeiro, 1951].

Stein, Robert, "The Profitability of the Nantes Slave Trade, 1783-1792," *Journal of Economic History*, xxxv, No. 4 (December, 1975).

Stein, Stanley J., *Vassouras: A Brazilian Coffee County*, Cambridge, Mass., 1957.

Suarez, Constantino, *Vocabulario cubano*, Havana, 1921.

Sutch, Richard, "The Breeding of Slaves for Sale and the Westward Expansion of Slavery, 1850-1860," in Stanley L. Engerman and Eugene D. Genovese, eds., *Race and Slavery in the Western Hemisphere: Quantitative Studies*, Princeton, 1975.

Syrett, David, *Shipping and the American War, 1775-83*, London, 1970.

Taunay, Affonso de E., *História do café no Brasil*, 15 vols., Rio de Janeiro, 1939-1943.

———, "Subsidios para a história do tráfico africano no Brasil," *Anais do Museu Paulista*, X (1941).

Taylor, Philip, *The Distant Magnet*, New York, 1971.

Teixeira Botelho, José Justino, *História militar e politica dos portugueses em Moçambique*, 2 vols., Lisbon, 1934.

Thomas, R. P., "The Sugar Colonies of the Old Empire: Profit or Loss for Great Britain?" *Economic History Review*, 2d. Series, xxi (1968).

——— and Richard N. Bean, "The Fishers of Men: The Profits of the Slave Trade," *Journal of Economic History*, xxxiv, No. 4 (December, 1974).

Toplin, Robert Brent, *The Abolition of Slavery in Brazil*, New York, 1972.

Torres Ramirez, Bibano, *La compañia gaditana de negros*, Sevilla, 1973.

Turner, Lorenzo D., *Africanisms in the Gullah Dialect*, Chicago, 1949.

Unger, W. S., "Bijdragen tot de geschiedenis van de Nederlandse slavenhandel. . . ." [Part ii] *Economisch-Historish Jarrboek*, xxviii (1961).

United Nations, Department of Social Affairs, Population Division, *Sex and Age of International Migrants: Statistics for 1918-1947*. Population Studies, No. 11, New York, 1953.

272

U.S. Bureau of the Census, *Historical Statistics of the United States, Colonial Times to 1970*, 2 vols., Washington, D.C., 1975.

————, *Negro Population, 1790-1915*, Washington, D.C., 1918.

U.S. Congress, Senate, *Report of the Select Committee on the Sickness and Mortality on Board Emigration Ships*, Washington, D.C., 1854.

Van Woodward, C., *American Counterpoint*, Boston, 1971.

Verger, Pierre, *Flux et reflux de la traite des nègres entre le golfe de Bénin et Bahia de Todos os Santos, du dix-septième au dix-neuvieme siècle*, Paris, 1968.

————, "Mouvements des navires entre Bahia et le Golfe du Bénin (xviie-xixe siècle)," *Revue française d'Histoire d'Outre-Mer*, 56 année, LV, No. 198 (1968).

Verlinden, Charles, *Les origines de la civilisation atlantique*, Paris, 1966.

————, *Precedents médiévaux de la colonie en Amerique*, Mexico, 1954.

Vila Vilar, Enriqueta, "Los aseintos portugueses y el contrabando de negros," *Anuario de Estudios Americanos*, XXX (1973).

Viles, Perry, "The Slaving Interest in the Atlantic Ports, 1763-1792," *French Historical Studies* (Fall, 1972).

Viotti da Costa, Emilia, *De Senzala a colonia*, São Paulo, 1966.

Wax, Darold D., "Preferences for Slaves in Colonial America," *Journal of Negro History*, LVIII, No. 4 (October, 1973).

Westergaard, Weldemar, *The Danish West Indies Under Company Rule (1671-1754)*, New York, 1971.

Williams, D. M., "Abolition and the Re-Deployment of the Slave Fleet, 1807-11," *Journal of Transport History*, New Series, Vol. II, No. 2 (September, 1973).

Williams, Eric, *Capitalism and Slavery*, Chapel Hill, 1944.

Williams, Gomer, *History of the Liverpool Privateers and . . . the Liverpool Slave Trade*, London and Liverpool, 1897.

Wood, Peter H., *Black Majority. Negroes in Colonial South Carolina*, New York, 1974.

Young, William, *The West-India Common-Place Book*, London, 1807.

Zavala, Silvio, "Relaciones históricas entre indios y negros in Ibero-américa," *Revista da las Indias*, Vol. 28 (1946).

Index

Africa: age and sex composition of slaves leaving, 243-47; British exports to, 168-69; changing sources of slaves, 75-79; East, *see* East Africa; French sailing times to, 189-90, 192-93; French slave trade in, 75-76, 78, 177, 187-88; Portuguese slave-trading methods in, 37-45. *See also* Portuguese slave trade; seasonal variations in slave trade from, 33-35, 56-57, 67-68, 79-80, 242-43; slave migrations from, analysis of, 241-44; slave migrations to U.S., 249-50; slavery in, 244-46; slave trade to Jamaica, 141-52, 156-58; slave trade to Virginia, 122-23, 125-29, 139-40; slave traders, African, 37-38, 82, 252-53; women in social structure, 244-45
agriculture: slave labor in, 7, 9, 17; slave labor in Brazil, 105, 112-15, 117. *See also* plantation agriculture
Alabama, 18
alcoholic drinks in slave trade, 42, 207
Ambriz, 75, 235
America, *see* United States
American colonies, *see* North American colonies; Portuguese colonies; Spanish America
American Revolution, 180; troop mortality rates, 71
Amerindians, *see* Indians, American
Angola, 11, 12, 241; British slave trade from, 128, 147, 148, 150, 156, 173; Cuban slave trade from, 150, 225, 227; French slave trade from, 187, 189, 192; Portuguese slave trade from, 23-50, 54, 55, 60, 75, 78, 79, 82-83, 87, 106, 128, 235, 246
Anstey, Roger, 47, 127
Area, calculations of slaves per area, 195n
Arkansas, 18
arqueação, 29, 35

Asia: Dutch and Portuguese in, 11-12; laborers from, in Cuba, 20
asientos, 10, 210, 211
Australia, convicts transported to, 90

Bahia: in internal slave trade, 97n, 109, 114; in slave trade, 32, 38, 40, 54, 65, 251
Barbados, 141; slavery, 12; in slave trade, 129, 136, 173
Benguela, 24, 26, 27, 35, 37, 46, 60, 67, 75, 106. *See also* Angola
Bermuda, 135
Bight of Benin, 187n, 225, 241, 251
Bight of Biafra, 147, 148, 150, 152, 161, 162, 173-74, 187n, 225, 235, 241
Birmingham, David, 23
Bissau, 44, 46
blacks: after emancipation, 21-22; in population of U.S., 246-52. *See also* freedmen
Brazil: age structure of slaves, 102-04; Anglo-Brazilian anti-slave-trade treaty, 75n; coffee production, 16-17, 21, 95-96, 102, 113-15, 117-18; creole slaves, 106, 107, 112, 120; decline of slavery in, 20-21, 95-96, 115, 120; Dutch expelled from, 12, 16; Dutch trade with, 11-12; emancipation of slaves, 21, 115, 116; end of trans-Atlantic slave trade, 73, 75; freedmen in, 20-21, 115-16; gold mining, 14-17, 25; internal slave trade, 95-120; male/female ratio of slaves, 100-02; native-born and African-born slaves, 105-07; occupations of slaves, 103-07; registration of slaves, 100, 103; seasonal harvesting period, 242; slave labor, 11, 14-15; slave population, 17, 96, 100-07, 115-17, 247, 248; slave trade to, *see* Portuguese slave trade; sugar production, 9-12, 16, 95; time of voyages from Africa, 40-41n

275

LIBRARY OF CONGRESS CATALOGING
IN PUBLICATION DATA

Klein, Herbert S.
  The middle passage.

  Bibliography: p.
  Includes index.
  1. Slave-trade—History.   I. Title.
HT975.K55   380.1'44   77-85545
ISBN 0-691-03119-3
ISBN 0-691-10064-0 pbk.

DATE DUE			
AP 19 '84	APR 19 '84		
AP 26 05	APR 30 '85		
FEB. 13 1992	FEB. 17 1992		

DEMCO 38-297